THE TRUTH
RELIGION
OBSCURES

Jim Fielder

Investigating 24 questions
through the One Truth

*Scriptural support for those
in a high-control religion*

"Everyone on the side of truth listens to me," said Jesus.

"What is truth?" asked Pilate.

(John 18:37-38)

2023

CONTENTS

Preface 5

Introduction 7

Q1. Is Religion the Way to God? 19

Q2. What is Grace? 30

Q3. What is the Purpose of Life? 37

Q4. What is the Bible All About? 44

Q5. Is the Bible True? 51

Q6. How do you Study the Bible? 58

Q7. Does God Exist? 66

Q8. One or Many? 73

Q9. What is His Name and Nature? 82

Q10. Who is Jesus? 89

Q11. What do You Love about Jesus? 96

Q12. Jesus' Death, Resurrection, and Kingdom? 104

Q13. Is the Holy Spirit a Person? 115

Q14. Does the Spirit Affect You 122

Q15. What are the Angels and Demons up to? 128

Q16. How do we Defeat Sin? 134

Q17. Why do we Suffer? 144

Q18. What Happens at Death? 154

Q19. What Does it Mean to be Born Again? 162

Q20. Is Our Salvation Secure? 172

Q21. How Can We Share the Gospel of Grace? 182

Q22. How do We Grow in Prayer? 193

Q23. How do We Grow in Love? 200

Q24. How Can We Grow in Christ? 210

Conclusion 219

Suggested Answers 224

Picture Credits 261

Indexes 262

PREFACE

For over 60 years, I allowed a highly controlling religious group to monitor every aspect of my life. Since childhood, I had blindly accepted and publicly defended all the pre-packaged information instilled in me. Yet, occasionally, I found myself privately at variance with a number of the teachings, not to mention specific policies, which were loosely based on their ideologically driven choice of Bible references used as 'proof texts'. Scriptures were used prolifically but rarely explained from their contextual and historical settings. So, you are justified in asking why. Why did you live with unvoiced cognitive dissonance for so long if you were troubled by various issues?

A short and simplified answer. From an early age, I had swallowed the core concept that the leadership was God's officially chosen mouthpiece. Those following such indoctrinating groups are instructed to study, yes, but solely the information dispensed through their official channel. Suppress any doubts, along with the urge to investigate outside their 'authorized' material. Any whiff of deviation from their strict norm could lead to being ousted and shunned. Fear restrains. However, from 2012, Jesus got His grip on me. I couldn't help but speak out about Him. The leaders (pastors/elders) accused me of "speaking too much about Jesus!" In 2017 I was evicted from their movement (or some religions would say excluded, excommunicated or disfellowshipped) as an apostate, tantamount to enforced separation from family and friends - religious apartheid.

While recognizing people's right to choose their religion, it is with a sense of deep regret that I not only raised my own family to believe and rigidly follow my sectarian path but drew others down the same twisted road. Although I did this out of sincerity, I nevertheless would wish to apologize to each one, as I have already done so personally to a number. I have had some opportunities to redress the balance a little by dialogue with numerous new friends, a few interviews on YouTube and radio, and hopefully further assist those in any high-control religion by providing a framework for their further thought and study into these essential fundamental questions.

First and foremost, I give thanks to our Lord for his love and great patience in bringing me to an increasing awareness of Him until I came to the point of repentance and faith in Jesus as Lord, dying to self, and raised to a new life (Rom 6:1-7). I was, and continue to be, bowled over by his grace in all its undeservedness and meritlessness.

I needed to learn the priceless lesson that the TRUTH was not a set of doctrines or a particular religious denomination but Jesus himself, the reality of life. Only through a relationship with him can we experience the real life. The relevance of this TRUTH to the 24 Questions will be explained in the following introduction. We shall then consider some alternative answers while avoiding dogmatism.

May these mini-essays stir you to reassess how you respond to certain questions from a former fixed one-track sectarian mold (or perhaps, that should be (fungal) 'mould'!) to a broader perspective. I hope this proves to be more than an academic exercise, but may our time together in the Word engender a living, thriving, fruitful, and deepening relationship with our Saviour (John 15:5; Rev 3:20). We can rightly call Him our brother, Lord, Saviour, and King. All praise to the Father in his name!

Jim Fielder

INTRODUCTION

Cover-ups! Misinformation. Manipulation of facts. Such smoke and mirror tactics have left a sad trail throughout man's history, the truth only coming to light often decades later. Consider the following assorted short list of 10 one-sentence summaries of famous cover-ups. They touch on key obfuscations and scandals from different fields in the 20th and into the 21st century:

- Watergate Scandal (1972-1974): A break-in at the Democratic National Committee headquarters was covered up by the Nixon administration, leading to the eventual resignation of President Richard Nixon.

- Tobacco Industry (20th century): The industry obscured the truth about smoking's dangers, funded research to discredit the scientific consensus, and manipulated public opinion through advertising campaigns and lobbying efforts.

- Iran-Contra Affair (1985-1987): The Reagan administration secretly sold arms to Iran to fund Contra rebels in Nicaragua, but when the scandal broke, officials tried to conceal their involvement and misled Congress.

- Enron Scandal (2001-2002): Enron Corporation executives used accounting tricks and false financial statements to hide billions of dollars in debt and inflate the company's stock price.

- Soviet Union (1922-1991): During the Soviet era, the Communist Party leadership maintained their power and control over the population by suppressing and distorting information, censoring the media, banning books, and rewriting history to fit their ideological agenda.

- Catholic Church (c. 1980–2000s): The Catholic Church and other religious communities have been covering up sexual abuse by minimizing the victims' accounts, often transferring abusers to other parishes, and hiding the evidence from law enforcement and the public.

- Thalidomide (1950s-1960s): This drug, prescribed to pregnant women for morning sickness, caused severe congenital disabilities in thousands of children worldwide, with its manufacturer Grünenthal obfuscating the truth about its safety and refusing to take responsibility for the harm caused.

- Jonestown Massacre (1978): Jim Jones, the leader of the Peoples Temple, led over 900 of his followers to commit mass suicide in Jonestown, Guyana, using his charisma and psychological manipulation to control, isolate, and deceive them.

- Tuskegee Syphilis Study (1932-1972): The U.S. Public Health Service studied the progression of untreated syphilis in African American men but misled participants about the nature of the study and withheld treatment, even after penicillin became widely available.

- Volkswagen Emissions Scandal (2015): Volkswagen admitted to installing software in their diesel engines to cheat emissions tests, deliberately misleading regulators and consumers about the true levels of pollutants emitted by their vehicles, which led to significant environmental damage and legal penalties.

The list of disinformation and propaganda is endless. You can likely add more to this woeful catalogue. It is evident that many governments, business corporations, and powerful religious institutions have engaged in illegal or unethical behaviour and, in some cases, have prioritised profit over public health while attempting to cover up their actions when facing exposure.

But before we move on, you will have noted that this reference book, which focuses particularly on the role of religion, is entitled "THE TRUTH Religion Obscures". Question: Is there a difference between to obscure and to obfuscate? Yes, there is a difference. "To obscure" means to make something unclear, usually - though not exclusively - unintentionally. For example, a person's true intentions, motives, or identity can be obscure; a landmark can become obscured by fog or smoke, as can a message by language barriers or difficult-to-understand language. "To obfuscate," on the other hand, means to deliberately make it more confusing or difficult to understand, typically to mislead or deceive someone, using language or other tactics to *hide* the truth or confuse the issue. So, although it is true that religion has been culpable of both obscuring and, at times, deliberately obfuscating a central TRUTH, this writing generally leans towards adopting the term "obscures" in seeking to give the benefit of the doubt to some groups, who with genuine sincerity, appear to be Christ-focused.

In our investigation together, we hope to uncover and unpack several Bible truths, but all through the filter of the ONE central, most precious TRUTH that religion, primarily highly controlled groups, seeks to obscure, hide, or even in some cases, deliberately obfuscate. We will state this one TRUTH shortly.

This collection of short articles, or essays, provides several alternative answers to each of 24 frequently asked questions. Although a verse-by-verse analysis (exegesis) of scripture is favoured by many, on this particular occasion due to the study habits of those in many high control religions, it was deemed more suitable to adopt a thematic, topic-by-topic approach. Some views may appear controversial, even objectionable to you, yet hopefully plausible and nondogmatic. These pieces, although varying in length, are on average each six pages (15 minutes readings). They are not intended to provide detailed and definitive analyses; they are designed to provide foundational material and further questions to stimulate your own self-study of certain Bible teachings.

"Does doctrinal TRUTH matter - so long as we LOVE one another?"

Does it matter what you believe? Isn't Christianity first and foremost about showing love to others, and doing good to those in need? After all, don't doctrines divide?

It is undeniable that the Bible places great importance on demonstrating love. We only have to reflect on Jesus reciting the two greatest commandments and his relating the parable of the Good Samaritan.

Moreover, and primarily, God's love acted to meet the deepest needs of men in the atoning sacrifice of His Son (Rom 5:8). So, Christians are called to fulfil their obligation to love others by actively tending to their current needs whenever it is within their capacity to do so.

At this point, we should also ask, is it possible for someone without a belief in God or Christ to demonstrate love for others? Don't we see some outstanding, even heroic, self-sacrificing acts of human kindness and generosity from unbelievers? Jesus himself said to his disciples, "If you then, though you are evil, know how to give good gifts to your children, how much more will your Father in heaven give the Holy Spirit to those who ask him" (Luke 11:13). So it is possible to do good and to be kind to your children, and yet be certified by Jesus himself as 'evil'. One Bible scholar, I H Marshall, commenting on 1 John 4:7-10, claims that it is because all men are created in the image of God that they have the capacity to love, and it is the result of "common grace" that even nonbelievers can demonstrate even an incomplete kind of love. He continues, "Human love however highly motivated, falls short if it refuses to include the Father and Son as the supreme objects of its affection." (Marshall, Epistles of John, 212).

Therefore, while it is undeniable that the Bible places great importance on demonstrating love, it's essential to understand that Christianity's foundation is not solely based on the command to love others. Instead, it commences with the profound biblical doctrines concerning God, Christ, the gospel and man. God's saving love for his people in the gospel of Jesus Christ is the essence, the heartbeat of Christianity, which, then by the Holy Spirit, provides the driving force for us to love others. God commands us to love because he first loved us by sending Jesus to die for our sins. So, Is Christianity a religion of doctrine or of love? The answer is both.

Consider, for example, how the Bible affirms the central teachings of Christ's resurrection, repentance, justification, eternal salvation, etc. When grasped, believed and clarified these foundational scriptural doctrines serve as the catalyst for expressing love.

Notably, the majority of references to doctrine in the New Testament underscore the importance of safeguarding against unsound doctrine and challenging teachings that deviate from the faithful transmission of biblical truth. Recall how Jesus condemned the Jewish scribes and Pharisees for elevating the commandments of men over divine doctrines, accusing them of "teaching as doctrines the commandments of men" (Matt 15:9; Mark 7:7). Was the Lord Jesus tolerant towards the Sadducees who differed from Him doctrinally concerning the resurrection (Matt 22:23-33)?

Then remember how Paul, in Gal 1:6-9, condemned those who preach a different gospel, even if they were very rigorous about the law of love. This is because, without the doctrine of the gospel, there can be no authentic Christianity. So, when Paul lists the qualifications for an elder, he tells Titus that they, "must hold firmly to the trustworthy word [of God] as it was taught to him, so that he will be able both to give accurate instruction in sound [reliable, error-free] doctrine and to refute those who contradict [it by explaining their error]." (Titus 1:1,9,16, Amplified) It is the job of church leaders to know and teach sound doctrine, for the health of the church. Furthermore, the Roman Christians were told to "watch out for those who cause divisions and create obstacles contrary to the doctrine that you have been taught" (Rom 16:17; cf Acts 20:26-31; 2 Tim 4:2-4; 1 Thess 2:13). And the Ephesians were warned not to be carried about by "every wind of doctrine," - false teaching that mature believers must reject (Eph 4:14; 1 Tim 6:3-5; 2 Tim 2:16-18).

It's essential to recognize that one's doctrine profoundly influences how one leads their life. God's people need to grow in accurate doctrine, with a focal point on Jesus Christ, as the fertile ground from which love flourishes. While theological disagreements may persist among fellow Christians, our shared foundation is unequivocally our Lord Jesus Christ (Eph 4:14-16; 2 Pet 3:17-18).

Who may benefit from "THE TRUTH" book?

- Anyone who has a sincere interest in the Bible should find this series beneficial. Do you identify with any of the following descriptions?
- You have been reading the Bible for years but still don't feel that you grasp its main message or teachings. So, when a friend raises some challenging religious *questions*, you are unsure how to respond.
- Your religion is causing you to perpetually feel *guilty*, as if you're never measuring up or doing enough. This constant state of self-doubt leaves you drained and exhausted.

- Despite your commitment to your religion, you find yourself wrestling with *doubts*. What exacerbates the situation is the fear of losing not only friends but also family, should you choose to walk away or fade into the background.
- You are wanting to *leave* a high control group but are unsure how to proceed. Will you be able to cope with any repercussions? (See Q23 – "What's My Next Step?" in the Additional Information)
- You have left a denomination or are in the process of doing so but feel lost. What next?

Could an explanation based on scripture provided here serve as a catalyst for re-evaluating your deeply ingrained religious beliefs, whether from the past or present?

These articles aspire to especially aid those in any of the numerous high-control religions. You will discover that the information could equally be helpful to those caught in the net of groups like LDS (Mormonism), Scientology, SDA (Seventh-day Adventists), Jehovah's Witnesses, Exclusive Brethren, Unification Church (Moonies), Christadelphianism, Christian Science, Iglesia in Cristo, and others. Here in the UK, the above groups form merely 0.6% of the total population or 1.5% of those describing themselves as "Christian". But each individual is so very precious to our God. You are valuable to Him! (Isa 43:4-6). And you, dear reader, may be sincerely embedded in such a denomination, and others could be fading escapees.

What is written in the following articles is not trying to assume the role of some 'heresy hunter', itching for a theological fight, or to engage in some rant involving name-calling and condemnation. However, we endanger our life if we ignore Jesus' clear warnings: "If anyone tries to flag you down, calling out, 'Here's the Messiah!' or points, 'There he is!' don't fall for it. Fake Messiahs and lying preachers are going to pop up everywhere. Their impressive credentials and bewitching performances will pull the wool over the eyes of even those who ought to know better. But I've given you fair warning". Jesus later commended one congregation of Christians for their discernment of untruth: "'I know your deeds and your labor and perseverance, and that you cannot tolerate evil people, and you have put those who call themselves apostles to the test, and they are not, and you found them to be false". (Matt 24:23-25, Message; Rev 2:2).

Increasingly, people are awakening to the falsity of numerous religious groups which exercise a stranglehold of authoritarian control over their supporters, not only in matters of doctrine but also in the minutiae of their followers' everyday lives, even subtly governing every decision of their personal consciences. This control is accomplished mainly by directly asserting that believers are obliged to implicitly obey all the wise instructions and policies from their chosen leaders, who are the channel exclusively chosen by God. "Obey!" - even if such directions appear unsound from a human standpoint. However, such control is often maintained indirectly by adopting not only a scripture-hopping selection of Bible verses but carefully packaged wording, such as, only 'spiritually weak ones' will fail to follow the lead of the decisions and lifestyle of the mature Christians in the group.

Feeling Lost?

Perhaps you currently feel lost in a fog of dissonance and doubts. You are not alone! You may be among tens of thousands facing a profound dilemma. In what way? Several such strict groups shun doubters and dissenters to some degree, but in some cases, it sadly leads to extreme exclusionism. Scientology has a practice known as "disconnection". This is tantamount to ostracism - a wall of silence - imposed by those you viewed as lifelong 'friends' and, yes, even your family. Their hierarchy tells them that this unloving practice of shunning actually demonstrates love! Simply put, this amounts to emotional blackmail laid on you as a wayward 'lost sheep', a 'black sheep', a 'goatlike one' - now publicly labelled as an 'apostate' - to pressurise you to return to the fold. In their eyes, the very fact of you ever raising doubts and questions signals a challenge to the authority of their 'one true' religion, which they view as tantamount to turning away from God, Jehovah!

This non-Christlike threat of being shunned as a 'living ghost' into an abyss of isolation can create a deep sense of foreboding. When faced with this intimidation, many choose to try and fade away or remain, as a Mormon may express it - "actively non-believing", or, as some JWs term their stance - PIMO ('publicly-in-mentally-out' of the religion). This course is very understandable and entirely a personal decision. There are many factors to take into consideration. You will likely be aware that the majority, in time, drift into unbelief. But, again, this is a very personal matter. It's important to respect others and not add to their stress by forcefully imposing our Christian beliefs on them. We also hope they will show us the same respect and not insist that we agree with their opposing views.

Yet other individuals make the hard choice to stay inside the confines of such religious groups because they don't know where else to go. There are relatively few, though, who remain because they have at some point turned to Christ as their personal saviour through repentance and faith and wish to help others in the 'prison' to find real freedom in Christ. This stance brings to mind Jesus' parable of wheat growing alongside weeds. I personally experienced that latter stressful state for over five years, carefully watching my words and actions as I was monitored by other leaders (pastors/elders). But it became increasingly difficult to suppress my heartfelt expressions and conscience without negatively impacting my relationship with the Lord. Eventually, I was 'disciplined' and formally evicted (excommunicated/disfellowshipped) in 2017 after being warned for "talking too much about Jesus Christ". As a result, I was severed from that religious group, yet to this day remain a non-denominational Christian.

Through this journey, I have come to value my relationship with Jesus Christ above any loyalty to a particular organisation or a work. At long last, I came to accept His gift of grace rather than trying to earn my salvation through my own efforts.

What questions will we consider?

- Which *Religion* is closest to the truth?
- Why do we *Suffer* if a God of love exists?
- What happens at *Death*?
- How can you be *Born Again*?
- Is God a *Trinity*?

Questions, and more questions! We will work our way through 24 such questions in an attempt to help individuals readdress, re-evaluate, fundamental questions. In most cases several alternative answers will be proposed while avoiding opinionated dogmatism. I would not presume to be your teacher but merely present diverse options. However, I may humbly state my personal take on certain points here and there. In effect, this topically arranged series (or 'course') is intended as a self-study aid. Naturally everyone, including you and me, is entitled to hold to a preferred explanation on certain issues without constantly being criticized or attacked by those arriving at different conclusions.

But tell me, what was your initial reaction when reading the above questions? Was it with an open mind or did you immediately want to fervently jump in to defend your viewpoint, perhaps even with mockery or underlying hostility?

Do you have an open mind?
In the past, I used to feel and even protest that I had an 'open mind' but then sometimes betrayed the very opposite. I am fully aware that this attitude, this dissonant mindset instilled into me by my former religion, can linger even now. You will understand better if I pose several personal questions to you:

- Are you sometimes willing to admit "I don't know the answer"?
- While appearing to listen to a churchgoer's comments, are you judgmentally shredding their views in your mind because they belong to

false religion? Have you become accustomed to linking any other belief system, apart from your own (the "Truth'), as part of "Babylon the Great"?

- Have you experienced a fear of opening up material that may run contrary to your preconceptions? Has curiosity and critical thinking overcome such fear?

- Are you missing the sense of security provided by a particular religion which claims to have all the answers to life's big questions?

Keeping an open mind, however, does not mean accepting all crazy, illogical extremist theories, which are often fueled by an organisation's or individual's ego. Nor does it mean succumbing to plausible-sounding arguments that tend to devalue Christ while stressing works-salvation. Having said that, reading the Bible with an open mind is essential, always letting context be king. A veil of preconceptions or biases can hinder a reader from critical thinking and a greater understanding of Bible truth. Certain Jews, mentioned in Acts 17:11, are praised who "warmly and enthusiastically welcomed the message and then, day by day, would check for themselves to see if what they heard from Paul and Silas was truly in harmony with the Hebrew Scriptures" ("The Voice").

A breath of fresh AIR

After open-minded personal research, many people decide to, or at least wish to, leave high-control religions. Most of these 'escapees' experience a profound sense of relief and freedom, as if they have come up for air after being claustrophobically confined inside a hamster wheel of repetitive, time-consuming routines.

Sadly, though, at the same time, they may be suffering the deep emotional torment of being shunned, either partially or entirely, by those who stay inside "God's one channel". Naturally, many feel angry and lost. As a result, more than a few of these escapees abandon all formal religion, though perhaps still professing to be 'spiritual'. This disconnection can sadly lead to a casual indifference in matters of faith, even to hedonistic behaviour to compensate for 'lost time' as they engage in their new life. Hence, it is no surprise that a great number drift into non-committal agnosticism or militant atheism. There is no desire here to be overcritical or judgmental of people who make such a free choice. Nevertheless, it is hoped that they will consider what the message of grace is really about because it concerns their life, now and eternally. For too long, many of us lived in a **FOG**, that is, an atmosphere of being,

Fearful, **O**bligated, and **G**uilty.

Now, instead, we want to help others to come up for **AIR**, which is an atmosphere of being,

Assured, **I**nvigorated, and **R**ested.

This is the fresh AIR of Grace! We mention the word grace frequently because it is central to our message. We will discuss the meaning and vital importance of grace in our very first article.

So, what TRUTH is religion obscuring?

Religion obscures or hides the one essential TRUTH that you *only need Jesus for your salvation*. He is the TRUTH! He is not merely the truth that leads to eternal life; He IS eternal life!

"Jesus said to him, "I am the way, and the truth, and the life; no one comes to the Father except through Me" (John 14:6). "And we know that the Son of God has come, and has given us understanding so that we may know Him who is true; and we are in Him who is true, in His Son Jesus Christ. This is the true God and eternal life" (1 John 5:20).

To express this another way: what are religions, particularly highly controlling religions, obscuring from you? This: that you don't need them! Jesus is all you need. Please permit me to explain.

Thankfully, a Christian's salvation does not depend on loyalty to a religious channel, a leadership, or endless convoluted rules, but only upon living faith in Jesus as saviour. God does not want us enslaved to the building up of an account of good works to qualify for His approval and merit salvation. He desires our direct focus on Him in love; however, religion is often fueled by fear, leading to the creation of counter-productive rules and hoops to jump through, akin to what the Pharisees did in Jesus' day (Matt 23:13-14). The basic error of the Pharisees was to externalize religion. But Jesus Christ did not come to promote religion or to flatter those who were religious by saying that He was glad to see their religious activities. Anyone or anything keeping you from having a free and open relationship with Jesus needs to go.

You may call to mind the Psalm, which says, "Don't put your trust in human leaders; no human being can save you" (Ps 146:3, GNT). Well known words, but often quoted by Jehovah's Witnesses to just apply to distrust of all religious and political leaders of this world – excluding, of course, their Governing Body leadership. Gill's Commentary corrects this view, "Put not your trust in princes.... not in foreign princes, in alliances and confederacies with them; nor in any at home. David did not desire his people to put their trust in him, nor in his nobles and courtiers; but in the Lord Christ, who, as he is the object of praise, is also the proper object of trust". (see also, Ps 62:9; Isa 2:17,22; Jer 7:13-14).

If we choose to simply have a religion rather than a relationship with Jesus, we will lose out on the abundant blessings of grace. Do you see how this simplifies things? Only by God's grace are we saved, not by our own tenuous works of righteousness (see 2 Cor 11:3-4; also Questions 1 and 2). Nor does receiving God's approval and eternal life depend upon successfully nailing down every question, becoming an expert in Greek, and resolving every doctrine, but upon our relationship with Jesus - who is the 'TRUTH". The Lord does, however, promise a gradual clearer understanding of truth through Holy Spirit, our true teacher (John 12:16; 16:12-13; 1 John 2:27). Theologian Don Carson makes a lot of sense in affirming that while it is true that we do not know things exhaustively, we may know them truly. We humans "may approach greater and more accurate knowledge," he writes in the NT Dictionary of Biblical Theology, "even though we can never gain absolute knowledge." A Christian will come to see that faith and reason are not necessarily in conflict or incompatible.

So, we will respond to the 24 questions through the lens of Jesus being the Truth. C H Spurgeon was renowned for his Christ-oriented sermons. He stated, "Preach Jesus Christ, brethren, always and everywhere; and every time you preach be sure to have much of Jesus Christ in the sermon".

There are many modern-day preachers who also focus on the Christ as the central truth. But more often than not, religions, primarily highly controlled sects, place their group's inner quorum between you and Christ to assume the role of being the way to the Way, Jesus Christ. In other words, religion, especially highly controlled religion, is structured for us to depend on them and their rules as the way of salvation – a pseudo mediator. Many adherents, in fact, call their religion, or more precisely their leadership, the TRUTH. This could be a one-person leadership: 'Acting Leader' (Moonies); 'Captain of the Sea' (Scientology). Or a body of men: 'Governing Body' (JWs); 'General Conference' (SDA); 'First Presidency' (LDS). Followers will likely ask newer members, "How long have you been in the Truth?"

Jesus said, "You will know the truth, and the truth will set you free" (John 8:32). This is far more than uncovering the truth about a mysterious or arcane organisation – its false teachings and egregious schemes. It is also far more than gaining a more profound academic knowledge of Bible truths. Just what were the truth and freedom to which Jesus alluded? The 'truth' certainly references the facts about Jesus and the teaching that he brought. We see more here, though, because Jesus, as we already referred to, later said that he was "the way, the truth, and the life" (John 1:14; 14:6). Jesus himself is THE TRUTH, the reality of life. Only through a connection with him can we experience the real life, without the bondage of sin. He further explained, in verses 34-37a of John 8,

"I tell you the truth, everyone who sins is a slave of sin. a slave is not a permanent member of the family, but **a son is part of the family forever**. So, if the **Son sets you free**, you are truly free. Yes, I realize that you are descendants of Abraham".

You see, the Jews, claimed to be free. What was really the case? They boasted of being part of a good family line back to Abraham, yet they were chained in bondage, both to their graceless legalistic religion, and in captivity to sin. Are you making a bid for your *double freedom* from religion and sin to become a son in this eternal family? This is only possible by the grace of God in accepting Jesus as your liberator.

What are some features of this series?

- For ease of **understanding**, we will generally avoid theological terminology. However, at the end of each article, you will find a few helpful, concise explanatory footnotes which are indexed at the end of the book, along with the key scripture passages.

- This series is designed for **self-study or group study**. The format lends itself to a workbook style or a book for reference.

- The series contains 24 questions, grouped under **eight subjects** (units), with each of the 24 articles eventually relating to a 15–20 minutes video. On average, each piece, including footnotes, is six pages long, excluding the Digging Deeper section.

- After reading or viewing each presentation, you will find the section **Digging Deeper** (into Bible TRUTH) which presents *5 questions* for personal study along with a link to *Suggested Answers*. These Digging Deeper pages also include an *Action Point* and *additional information* within a **QR** code that provides, on average, 15 links to video clips primarily found on 'YouTube' (YT), online articles, songs and various study tools. Busy readers will be pleased to note that the majority of the over 350 information links are under 10 minutes in length. For believers, the simple suggested *prayer* at the conclusion of the articles may be helpful. However, it is better to understand the sentiment behind the prayerful phrases rather than merely recite the wording.

- These articles provide summaries of Christian teachings as a springboard for your own deeper study. You may not necessarily agree with everything proposed herein, but as you open the Scriptures and **pray for the Spirit** to teach you, matters will undoubtedly become clearer over time. We need God's wisdom, not that of men or our own.

- Various **Bible translations** will be referred to, but unless otherwise stated, we will use the NASB 2020.

- The purpose of this collection is to make the simple **gospel of grace** clear, with the aim of drawing readers into an ever-deepening relationship with God as His sons or daughters through Jesus Christ, for God desires each of us to be part of his family, forever!

My earnest and prayerful wish is that this course, or rather, series of short articles, may be instrumental in your search for freedom and life – namely, the Truth, who is Jesus Christ.

"But be constantly growing in the sphere of grace and
an experiential knowledge of our Lord and Saviour Jesus Christ.
To him be glory both now and to the day of eternity".
2 Peter 3:18, An Expanded Translation (Wuest).

You may now wish to look over the contents. Although I would recommend following the numerical sequence, one or two random questions may jump out, and you could plunge right in.

THE TRUTH
Jesus is the door – enter life through Him - John 10:9-10

Q1. IS RELIGION THE WAY TO GOD?

Once, the Devil was walking along with one of his demons. They saw a man ahead of them pick up something shiny. "What did he find?" asked the demon.
"A piece of the truth," the Devil replied.

"Doesn't it bother you that he found a piece of the truth?" asked the demon.

"No," said the Devil, "I will see to it that he makes a religion out of it".

So many have become confused by the plethora of religious groups claiming to be unique, the only way to God, to have the 'truth.'[1]

Bahai	"The Bahá'í Faith is not just another religion. It is a way of life that offers practical solutions to the challenges facing humanity". - Bahá'í International Community, The Bahá'í Faith
Church of Jesus Christ of Latter-day Saints (LDS)	"The Lord restored His Church in these latter days for the salvation of souls, and it is the only true church upon the face of the earth". - Russell M. Nelson, President of the Church of Jesus Christ of Latter-day Saints (April 2021 General Conference)
Christian Science	"Christian Science is the only religion that reveals the healing power of God through prayer and spiritual understanding". - Mary Baker Eddy, Founder of Christian Science

---

[1] **Truth**. The basic understanding of the word 'aletheia is that it is the manifestation of a hidden reality. Alētheia not only stands for irrefutable facts - in opposition to pretence or appearance (Php 1:18) - but it also expresses the truth itself, that which is unattainable to the human mind, and which can only be perceived through revelation from God. God Himself the great reality. That which correctly sets forth His nature is pre-eminently the Truth of Creation (natural revelation), the Truth of Scripture (Spirit revelation), and the Truth of Christ (divine revelation). See John 14:6,17; 1 John 5:20.

The 'Gospel of Truth', a second-century gnostic writing, on the other hand, centres on the redemption of people not out of sin and its consequences, but from ignorance and error by giving them mystical knowledge that will benefit them in the afterlife. But Truth in the NT surpasses a mere collection of facts freeing us from misconceptions or ignorance; it calls for a new way of living – walking in the truth - in a present personal 'knowing' relationship with God and Jesus (John 17:3,17; 3 John 4). See Additional Information link below to the "Gospel of Truth".

Unit 1: Grace

Iglesia ni Cristo	"The Iglesia ni Cristo is the only Church that teaches the true doctrine of Christ, and it is the only way to have a relationship with God". - Iglesia ni Cristo website
Jehovah's Witnesses	"We must recognize that Jehovah's organization alone, in all the earth, is directed by God's holy spirit or active force. Only this organization functions for Jehovah's purpose and to his praise. To it alone God's Sacred Word, the Bible, is not a sealed book". - Watchtower, Feb 15, 1981, p. 17
Scientology	"It [Scientology] is the only road anyone can travel which offers any real hope of freedom. It is the only road which will take the being to higher states of ability and ethical behavior". - L. Ron Hubbard, "Scientology: 8-80"
Seventh-day Adventist Church (SDA)	"Seventh-day Adventists believe that their church is the remnant church of Bible prophecy". - Seventh-day Adventists Believe, A Biblical Exposition of 27 Fundamental Doctrines (2005)
Unification Church, (Moonies)	"The Divine Principle, which is the teaching of the Unification Church, is the only way to understand the Bible and God's will". - Unification Church website.

Increasingly here in the UK (as shown in the chart below) more and more are becoming disillusioned by everything labelled as 'religious'. This is evidenced by a 2021 census that, for the first time, fewer than half of people (46%, down from 59.3% in the last census in 2011) in England and Wales describe themselves as Christian. Please, do not be misled into thinking that Churchianity and Christianity are the same thing.

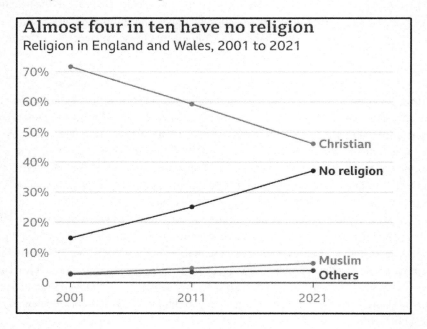

What has been your experience with RELIGION?

Permit me to make an assumption: that you likely had or currently have interactions at some level with the likes of Jehovah's Witnesses, Mormons, Seventh-Day Adventists, or some other religious denomination outside of mainstream Christianity. Have you ever listened to the similarity in the claims of these groups to possess the TRUTH? (See two examples in <u>Additional Information</u> below, on p18).

Would you say that there are a few relatively beneficial aspects in these movements? Some reflect on several great *people* they befriended at that time, others on the basic Bible *knowledge* they accrued, still others found some *events*, like large conventions, held a measure of excitement.

Conversely, there are certain negative aspects: a life *controlled* in every detail by a hierarchy; *fear of failing* to reach the standards and rules, with the consequence of facing the leaders (elders or priests); the *guilt* and sheer exhaustion from never doing, or giving, enough in studying, preaching, and donating; constantly having to keep updated with *changes* in teachings and policies; or experiencing the thin veneer of *hypocritical,* conditioned love. **This is man-made Religion** - a performance trap of fear. Not **Grace**[2] **but a Race** – a religious race.

All religions outside of genuine Christianity essentially become a list of dos and don'ts. Why is this the case? Because they aim to motivate a person to climb up to God. This, as we shall later discuss, is a grace reversal. They are all about what we must do to save our lives, or reach heaven, paradise, or its equivalent. True Christianity is different. Instead of us trying to reach up to God, Christianity is about Him coming down to us.

If you have mustered up the courage to escape this religious hamster wheel, how do you now feel? Many find themselves, in a word – **lost.** Yes, you may well feel a sense of being relatively free of an imposed monotonous routine, which, sadly, often comes with the price of also being 'relatives-free' as family members now choose to avoid you. 'In a no man's land' – as some describe it. This is frequently the time when an escapee starts to drift into unbelief, or jump into a different controlling religion with their own authoritative hierarchy and set of rules and routines. Of course, we should respect everyone's freedom to choose their own path. However, before jumping from the frying pan of a high-control group (e.g.

---

[2] **Grace**. See Q2.

a sect or cult[3]) and into the fire of a similar religion, we need to define what we mean by the word religion.

How would you define the word 'religion'?

The Oxford English Dictionary says the word originally meant "**to bind** to religious vows, practices, or traditions". Another source comments that the word's etymology is confusing, some linking it the sense of 're-reading aloud' and others asserting it was clearly derived from the Latin 're-legare', meaning "to bind" - see the link 'additional information' in the question sheet. If this is the case, then by this definition, religion could be viewed as a kind of **bondage.** This is reminiscent of Jesus observation about the scribes and Pharisees, "they *bind* (desmios, a bound one, a prisoner) *together* burdens heavy and grievous to be borne, and lay upon the shoulders of men, but with their finger they will not move them" (Matt 23:4). Please note, this is not an attempt to label all things done in the name of religion as false, for Jesus said of the Pharisees, who were 24/7 devoted

---

[3] **Sect / Cult.** Although these two words can carry negative connotations outside a religious setting, in the realm of religion, some, but not all, would define them as follows. a) A sect is a breakaway group of dissenters from an established religion. Often a non-mainstream religious group will claim that they are not an offshoot of any other church system, but research into their early history may well uncover a different story. b) Members of a cult usually follow and fully obey one human figure, or a central group of leaders, as the only way of salvation. Some groups will claim that they do not follow any human, but only look to Jesus Christ, however, their subservience to the authority of their central human leader, or leaders, betrays the opposite. c) Many cults live in isolated communities, or if not physically, certainly with the exclusive mindset of being different from the evil 'worldly' society, always thinking in terms of us vs them.

Michael Moore, a cult researcher, gives a better description of a cult: "A cult is an organisation that enslaves minds and destroys families using cult mind control. Cult mind control involves orchestrated deception, social pressure, psychological abuse, and repetitive indoctrination (brainwashing) centring around an unchallengeable ideology enforced in a totalitarian way in a closed socially separatist community setting. (Not all cults have live-in campuses, but all are socially separatist.) Each of these four tactics by themselves are ancient, but combined simultaneously, they cause the subject to throw up their hands and give up mentally resisting. That "secret sauce" uncovered by experimentation in the mid-1800s is what's new. That is mind control". Therefore, whether they perpetrate cult mind control is the only litmus test.

Author Steven Hassan, an international expert on cults, propounded the **BITE** acronym, which can help one understand what kind of control a leader has over the members of a cult (ie Control over Behavior, Information, Thought, and Emotion). Many cults live in isolated communities, or if not physically, certainly with the exclusive mindset of being different from the evil 'worldly' society, always thinking in terms of us vs them.

Unit 1: Grace

to God, "The Pharisees and the teachers of the Law are experts in the Law of Moses. So obey everything they teach you, but don't do as they do. After all, they say one thing and do something else". (Matt 23:2-3, CEV) That is, follow all that they read and properly explain from the Law of Moses. The word "all" could not be taken without restriction, for Christ himself accuses them of teaching many things contrary to that law, and of making it void by their traditions (Matt 15:1-6). So, likewise today, in so far as a religion or a Christian group seeks to follow Christ and explain scripture correctly then they should be respected. Now let's home in on two divergent pathways.

What are the two contrasting paths?

Let's examine some of Jesus' words earlier in the same gospel. **Matthew chapter 7** continues his "sermon on the mount". In this final section (vs 13-19), he contrasts two opposing paths: choosing the way of religious traditions or the way of Christ. First, we will consider verses 21-23.

"Not everyone who says to Me, 'Lord, Lord,' will enter the kingdom of heaven, but the one who does the will of My Father who is in heaven will enter. Many will say to Me on that day, 'Lord, Lord, did we not prophesy in Your name, and in Your name cast out demons, and in Your name perform many miracles?' And then I will declare to them, 'I never knew you; leave Me, you who practice lawlessness.'"

On three occasions, Jesus spoke about people who would cry "**Lord, Lord**" (Matt 7:21-22; 25:11; Luke 6:46). In each case, he is *not* talking about true believers, because these people, though very religiously busy, Jesus **never** knew. He did not say, "I knew you once (you were in my book) but now I'm writing you off". No, he clearly says, "I *never* knew you".

They may *know about* Jesus but have never *known Him*, in a relationship sense. Rather, they believe they will be accepted largely, if not exclusively, on account of their accomplishments. They are in effect saying, 'I did all these things for you. I stand on my own merits. Jesus, you died for nothing.' Yes, they appear to be zealous Christians, avowing their belief, but are self-righteous.[4] Instead of

---

[4] **Self-righteous**. A dictionary definition of self-righteousness is "confidence in one's own righteousness, especially when smugly moralistic and intolerant of the opinions and behavior of others". Biblically speaking, self-righteousness, which is related to legalism, is the idea that we can somehow generate within ourselves a righteousness that will be acceptable to God (Rom 3:10). In the New Testament, Jesus and the apostle Paul came down particularly hard on those who attempted to live in self-righteousness. Yet, because of past ingrained religious practices over the years, growing Christians, those in Christ, can easily fall into this temptation to try to do something to merit salvation (Rom 10:1-4; Gal 3:1-3).

resting in His work, they have wearied themselves with hard labour. Instead of putting their faith in Christ, they've backed themselves, constantly drawing attention to their personal achievements or an organisation's accomplishments (Rom 10:1-4, Message Bible). "I often wonder if religion is the enemy of God. It's almost like religion is what happens when the Spirit has left the building". (Paul Hewson -Bono). Personally speaking, as a former member of a high-control group, I felt like a guest in an important man's house, keeping to the house rules but having no direct relationship to him - nor part of his family.

Notice, Jesus says only those who do **the will** of the Father enter the kingdom of heaven. The question is, what is God's will? Here is Jesus' answer in John 6:28-29, "They said to Him, "What are we to do, so that we may accomplish the works of God?" Jesus answered and said to them, "This is the *work* of God, that you *believe* in Him whom He has sent".

Is it really that simple? YES! Paul, in the words found at Romans 10:9, put it this way, "If you confess with your mouth Jesus as Lord and *believe* in your heart that God raised Him from the dead, you will be saved". When someone in total belief yields their life to Him and is thereby saved, their life will never be the same again. The persons thinking, desires, and actions will be altered. Are you willing to genuinely surrender your life to Him?

When we examine the concluding section of Matthew 7, we see Jesus illustrating just two contrasting paths by way of illustrations. This is not a matter of 'all religions being roads leading to God', because Jesus mentions only two *ways* (13-14), two *trees* (15-23), and two *builders* (24-27).

Take for example, Matthew 7:13-14, "Enter through the narrow gate; for the gate is wide and the way is broad that leads to destruction, and there are many who enter through it. For the **gate is narrow and the way is constricted** that leads to life, and there are few who find it".

Consider this perspective. What is the narrow gate? What did Jesus say? "I am the *door*" (John 10:9). The truth is that Jesus is the door – enter life through Him. Unfortunately, the religious Pharisees blocked access to Jesus with their many traditions. "But woe to you, scribes and Pharisees, hypocrites, because you shut the kingdom of heaven in front of people; for you do not enter it yourselves, nor do you allow those who are entering to go in" (Matt 23:14).

"I am the *way* and the truth and the life. No one comes to the Father except through me" (John 14:6; Acts 4:12)"Through *him* we, both peoples, have the *approach* to the Father by one spirit" (Eph 2:18).

The narrow gate is faith in Christ alone. The wide gate and road include all religions of high control, 'never-enough' works, and self-righteousness. At that time, the Jewish listeners were already on wide **LAW ROAD**, but were invited to repent and change road to "Come to **CHRIST**!" Why is the true gate so narrow? In that we have to enter Jesus individually, rather like a turnstile. We individually must jettison the bulky baggage of self-righteousness, self-achievement, and self-confidence. This is repentance that says "No" to self; not just getting rid of a few 'hand luggage' habits! No baggage at all is allowed to be taken through. **SELF** must go, merit and demerit must go. Only Christ matters any more. No wonder we are to 'sit down to count the cost' of becoming a disciple. By that once in our life acceptance, belief, and submission to Christ, we enter the door marked "CHRIST" not "RELIGION".

Now, there may be aspects to religious practice that can prove to be helpful in promoting personal growth and transformation. But let's get this right. We can pose the question again another way: Why is the gate so hard to enter? Is it because God has high standards? Of course, He does have impossibly high standards – perfection - but Jesus has met them all on our behalf! We might say, "I am a mess, a failure. How could I approach a Holy God in this sorry state?" So, instead of entering through the door of Jesus we choose the Law door of religion – religious legalism - by trying rather than trusting, by emphasising performance and achievement rather than the grace of God. Instead of coming to the throne of grace and receiving all that we need through Jesus, we find ourselves stuck outside trying to remove the stains of sin with the abrasive sandpaper of religious rules and regulations. Instead of looking at the perfect Lamb, we are constantly looking at our flawed imperfect selves and at boastful works-oriented organisations.

Outside the true door there stands a threatening bouncer named "Religion". Often, he lifts up a mirror to reflect our own reassuring, but distorted, appearance of goodness or righteousness. Then, inconsistently, this bully says, "keep out, you're not good enough yet!" You **don't qualify** for baptism because of less than 100% meeting attendance, a low number of hours spent preaching, a smoking habit, or dressing casually when meeting and preaching. After qualifying for baptism, some religions threaten to shun[5] anyone dissenting to their leadership or policies. They want you to rely on them – a religious institution expecting deeds and donations. Conversely, Grace replies, 'Christ has met all the high standards for you! Forgiven[6] you!'

He is the door and path of grace. Accept his divine righteousness[7], his accomplishment on the cross.[8] Have you entered this door? We must reach the

---

[5] **Shunning**. The practice of shunning is generally viewed as an unloving and unchristian practice - a form of emotional blackmail to keep control of members. For example, the Church of Scientology has a practice known as "disconnection," which involves shunning or cutting off contact with individuals who are deemed to be "suppressive" or who have left the church. How this judgmental behaviour contrasts with the Father's love in the parable of the prodigal. When the wayward son returned, was he given a probation period of silent treatment in isolation to test his resolve? Certainly not! It was the older brother, like the Pharisees, who shunned. These self-righteous leaders saw themselves as God's true people - morally and spiritually superior to rebellious deviators. In his own estimation, he was the more faithful, respectable, reputable, and worthy son, who had slogged his guts out for years! He sees himself as in a "master-slave" transactional relationship with his father, needing to work hard to merit approval and reward. What honours God is not cold slave labour but childlike faith in his all-sufficient grace (Acts 17:25, 28). The words "my brother" stuck in his throat, so he said, "this son of yours". He would likely pass by his brother in the street without any acknowledgement, not even a "hello". He certainly did not want to demean himself by attending any banquet in his honour; he would prefer it was his brother's funeral! Surely instead of the 'fattened calf' being killed, it was this rebellious younger son who should be killed for immorality (Deut 21:18-21). Jesus did not finish the prodigal illustration, but we know how it played out. The religious leaders refused to come to Jesus and were the ones who instigated his murder. In effect, the older son beat up and killed the father, represented on earth by Jesus. They felt they were serving God in their cruelty and were desperate to protect the status quo and their impeccable public image (John 16:2). By God's grace, each of us must tackle insidious prideful tendencies. Leave your case with our Father; pray for anyone shunning you (Luke 6:27-33; also, Psalm 31 from The Message Bible).

[6] **Forgiven**. See footnote 82 on page 108.

[7] **Righteousness**. See footnote 57 on page 84.

[8] **Cross.** JWs object to using the word cross, preferring "torture stake" instead. Perhaps they insist on this view to emphasise their uniqueness. Their three main objections: linguistics, pagan origin, and historical evidence, can be considered in the Additional Information link.

point of admitting, "Lord, I don't have this – I can't do it! I need your help". This is FAITH! As we receive his grace and are persuaded that Jesus has 'got this', the result is rest and life. Does this mean becoming a passive, lazy Christian after entering the Jesus door? No, just the opposite! Ephesians 2:8-10 clearly tells us that we have been saved *by* grace alone, then adds, *for* good works. When saved you will be filled with a burning new desire, implanted, and empowered by God, to obediently walk in the ways of your Lord, bearing His fruit in every good work (Col 1:10; Phil 2:23).

What can we conclude?

Jesus in Matthew chapter 7 is not describing a process of sorting through the thousands of Christian denominations to choose one that sounds closer to the truth than others. But what is the choice? It is between the path of **external religion**, based on works of self-righteous *performance*, and the **Christ-path,** the *grace route* of accepting the gift of forgiveness, righteousness, and life, by what Jesus has done.

It is true that the narrow road travellers never feel good enough in themselves, but they do possess the confident assurance of having passed through the gate, of being precious to God, that Jesus constantly carries them, and have at last found true rest!

One final question to ponder: Where does the broad road intersect the narrow road? Just one place: Calvary. At the cross one can leave the broad road, accept Christ as Saviour, and start along the narrow way. Today, will you stop and think, *what am I looking at?* Am I looking at myself, a religion, or at the resurrected Jesus who hung on the cross for me?

So, what do you think, is religion the way to God? The TRUTH is that Jesus alone is the way to God; he is the door, the entrance into life. Finally, notice these warm, inviting words of Jesus in Matthew 11:27-30 from the Message Bible,

"No one knows the Son the way the Father does, nor the Father the way the Son does. But I'm not keeping it to myself; I'm ready to go over it line by line with anyone willing to listen. "Are you tired? Worn out? Burned out on religion? Come to me. Get away with me and you'll recover your life. I'll show you how to take a real rest. Walk with me and work with me—watch how I do it. Learn the unforced

---

The atonement that Jesus provided does not depend on the number of pieces of wood or where they were placed. We should focus on the fact that Jesus paid for our sins and not get distracted by less important topics like the specific shape of the instrument of execution. If kidnappers demanded a ransom price to be paid over for the release of a member of your family, would the currency presently in your personal bank account, whether GBP, USD, or EUR, be the main issue, when it can be transferred into the amount required?

rhythms of grace. I won't lay anything heavy or ill-fitting on you. Keep company with me and you'll learn to live freely and lightly".

Later, we will consider how the Lord has kindly provided us with others, genuine believers in Christ, His body members, with whom we can feed and associate in love.

Now, please consider the following five questions in this section. And, yes, you can sneak peek at a page of suggested 'Answers'. Next time we will discuss part b in this unit: "What is Grace?"

"Christianity: God coming toward man through Christ."
- Tozer

DIGGING DEEPER – IS RELIGION THE WAY TO GOD?

Scan the QR code for informative links to each of these questions.

1. Has God always had an **organisation** on earth? How would you reason on this question?

2. From your experience, can you list a few man-made 'religious' **rules** that you now see as adding to the Bible and being overly restrictive? Why do you think that religion often imposes so many rules? What are some consequences?

3. Read **Matthew 12:1-8**. Before finding link via the QR code, what do you think is the main point?

4. How could you explain **Luke 13:24**, "strive to enter through the narrow gate" – if we are not saved by our works?

5. Read **Philippians 3:8**. From the context, what was the "rubbish" that Paul threw out?
   Read Philippians 3:1-11 from the Message Bible.

See Suggested Answers at the end of this book.

Action Point

Starting from Ephesians 2:8-9, and by using cross references in your Bible, list at least three other scriptures that say we are NOT SAVED BY WORKS. If your Bible doesn't have cross references, check this handy link inside the QR.

Prayer

If you are unsure or confused about salvation presently, ask yourself, 'Do I want to know Christ better? If so, why not directly tell him about your desire? If you are saved already, pray through Ephesians 2:1-10 thanking our Father afresh for salvation through His manifold grace and not by your works.

Q2. WHAT IS GRACE?

Author and theologian C. S. Lewis arrived late to a debate. The subject? 'What makes Christianity unique?' What teachings especially demark Christianity? Who Christ is, or perhaps the resurrection, or the kingdom? "Oh, that's easy," said Lewis, "It's **grace**".

All other world religions are *performance-based*, constantly working for God's approval and salvation. But grace means that God accepts you with *no conditions* when you put your full trust in His Son. You see, grace is not merely divine assistance for the process of moral transformation, but a one-sided divine rescue.

Imagine you are travelling on a TRAIN

You are convalescing from a serious illness. A generous travelling companion has paid your fare and even boarded the carriage to accompany you. You can relax as the powerful engine up front draws your carriage along. Similarly, Jesus invites the weary to get on board with him for the grace journey. He will lovingly draw us along in the power of His Spirit. He warmly invited his listeners, "Get away with me and you'll recover your life. I'll show you how to take a real rest ... Learn the unforced rhythms of GRACE. I won't lay anything heavy or ill-fitting on you. Keep company with me and you'll learn to live freely and lightly". (Matt 11:28-30, Message)

Legalistic[9] religion, though, wrenches grace from the free flow of God's Spirit. Religion raises the grace track into a vertical ladder of exacting rules requiring moral fitness and strenuous good works to climb into heaven one exhausting rung at a time. False teachers uproot (grace) scriptures from their context to

---

[9] **Legalism.** Legalism is the belief that we can earn favour with God by keeping the law. Living under law is one of three ways we can relate to God. The other two are living wholly under grace, alternatively, living under a mixture of grace with law. The scriptures state that we are to live solely under grace while warning about the dangers of living under law (Rom 6:14-15; 7:8–9). What is our proper relationship with the law? We are to have no relationship with the law at all. It is not that we have been made lawless. Rather, we have been given something better - we are to walk in the new way of the Spirit (Rom 7:6, 8:4, Gal 5:18).

make Christian life a punishing guilt trip instead of a restful journey by Spirit. Are you a Christian POW ... a joyless 'Performance Oriented Worker'?

From start to finish, scripture is permeated with God's grace because it is the very expression of God's love to men. The very first usage of the word is found in Genesis 6:8, "Noah found grace (chen) in the eyes of Jehovah". (Youngs). But perhaps you are more familiar with Exodus 34:6, where we read of this principal attribute of God, "Then the Lord passed in front of him and proclaimed: "Yahweh—Yahweh is a compassionate and **gracious God**, slow to anger and rich in faithful love and truth" (HCSB).

Turning to the NT, the basic Greek word for grace is **'charis'**. We can see this is the basis for other words like charisma, eucharist, charity, and the girl's name Carissa. The Greek verb 'chairo', means to rejoice, and was sometimes used as a one-word greeting. Seeing the link between grace and joy in the original NT language is interesting. But we need to define the word grace. For simplicity we can adopt the acronym FACE to help us consider four aspects.

The FACE of GRACE

1. FREE (gift or favour)

The NT writers used grace in this sense when sending "thanks" or a kind "gift" to someone. For example, 1 Corinthians 16:3 says, "When I arrive, whomever you approve, I will send them with letters to take your *gift* (charis) to Jerusalem". On a side note, this is the only place where the JW's Kingdom Interlinear Translation uses 'grace' - but only under the Greek left-hand column - whereas other Bibles liberally use the word grace over 120 times. Even from this example it becomes evident that charis means more than just "undeserved kindness" because Paul was hardly saying that this gift to the poor brothers was undeserved. No, it was simply a kind gift. Also, in 1 Corinthians 15:57, "But *thanks* (charis) be *to God*, who gives us the victory through our Lord Jesus Christ". Was God undeserving of thanks? Again, in Luke 2:40, "Now the Child continued to grow and to become strong, increasing in wisdom; and the *favor* (charis) of God was upon *Him*". Did God's favour rest on an underserving Jesus? Helpful in this regard is the clarity in Romans 3:22-24, **"But by the** *free gift* of God's grace (charis) all are put right with him through Christ Jesus, who sets them free" (GNT).

It is true that the expression "undeserved kindness" is an essential aspect of grace when used in the narrower sense of 'God in relation to sinful mankind'. However, if this special *aspect* of undeservedness is constantly emphasised it would:

(a) Focus on a *man's status* of '*unworthiness*' than the *worthy God* – the source of grace. After all, God has always been from eternity, and will always be, the God of all grace. There is no ebb and flow with our God of grace. Grace is His love in action. God loves to give, as is most evident in redemption.

(b) If God shows grace only when we are undeserving, does that imply that God's grace to us lessens as we mature, and sin less, and then stop when we are glorified?

(c) The goal of God's grace is not just to be nice to us, to make us feel better when we receive some blessings. No, but it is to draw souls to Himself through Christ; to impart Himself to us and in us – all to His glory. The author Evelyn Waugh aptly wrote in his description of grace, "The unmerited, unilateral act of love by which God continually calls souls to himself".

Christians believe **all** is of His grace, whether election before the foundation of the world, salvation through the one time offering of Christ, faith, repentance or the new birth (John 5:24; Eph 1:3-4; 2:8-10; John 5:24, 1 John 5:1).

2. ACCEPTANCE

"To the praise of the glory of His grace, by which He made us *accepted in the Beloved*" (Eph 1:6 NKJV). Spurgeon wrote about this verse, "Are there grander words in any language than these four? There seems to be a sacred poem in these words. To my heart, there is more heavenly music in those four words than in any oratorio I ever heard".

Have you accepted your acceptance? When presented with the gospel message, one lady responded by saying she had tried her best to please God, but added "I'm afraid God will never accept me". The woman was astonished to hear the evangelist reply, "I agree with you. He never will". Then he went on to explain, "No, He never will. But God has accepted His Son, and if you accept Him by faith, you will find God's acceptance which you desire!" God accepts all who accept His Son by grace through faith!

Grace goes beyond an expression of acceptance - it is revealed in action. The Hebrew word "chen" (grace) or forms of it appear 78 times in the OT. It has the connotation of *stooping*. Bible scholar Donald Barnhouse perhaps said it best: "Love that goes upward is worship; love that goes outward is affection; love that stoops, is grace". We are accepted in Jesus, who is grace personified in that he reaches down to serve, and pick us up. We could say grace has gravity!

3. CHRIST

Therefore, grace is not a subject, a doctrine, or a mere theological term. It is a person. His name is Jesus. John 1:17 says, "The law was given [passed on] through Moses, grace and truth *came* [in person] through Jesus Christ" (Amplified). He is the embodiment of grace.

Unit 1: Grace

To simply illustrate: Dad could send you a present through the post, but how much better if he comes in person with hugs. Grace is not an 'at an arm's length' topic. It is a person who came to us – Jesus – the *personification of grace*. Saved by grace is to be saved by Jesus!

The gospel of grace, or the word of grace (Acts 20:32), is synonymous with the gospel of Jesus, for Jesus is the embodiment of the Father's grace (1 Cor 1:4). The grace of God comes to us through Jesus, and we grow in grace by growing in the grace and knowledge of Jesus Christ (2 Pet 3 :18). This may well call to mind another acronym for GRACE, namely, God's Riches At Christ's Expense. Sacrificial grace in the form of Jesus on the cross was not cheap. It cost him his life. Yet it is offered to you for free. Daily we should preach this grace to ourselves.

Typically, it's not that Christians seek to blatantly replace the gospel. What we try to do is simply *add* on to it: "Christianity and self- improvement," Christianity and environmentalism," Christianity and social justice," "Christianity and political action," etc. However, in the words of Tullian Tchividjian, "Jesus plus nothing equals everything; everything minus Jesus equals nothing".

4. EMPOWERMENT

So, this brings us to the final piece - empowerment. "God is able to make every grace overflow to you, so that in every way, always having everything you need, you may *excel in every good work*" (2 Cor 9:8 CSB). And here is a clear statement in Titus, "For the grace of God has appeared, bringing salvation to all people. It trains us to reject godless ways and worldly desires and to live self-controlled, upright, and godly lives in the present age" (Titus 2:11-12, NET). It is not by a list of religious rules that we are trained and empowered to do good, to live righteously - it is only through the grace of God.

Romans 5 says that God makes His grace abound over sin. The gospel ignites the Christian life, but we often fail to see that it's also the *fuel* to keep us going and growing as Christians. The gospel doesn't just rescue us from the past and for the future; it also empowers us in the moment, at our point of need, whatever that may be (Rom 1:16). If we try to live the Christian life on our own, mustering up the willpower to fight sin and press on to perform – we will only crash and burn. "God's law was given so that all people could see how sinful they were. But as people sinned more and more, God's wonderful *grace became more abundant*. So just as sin ruled over all people and brought them to death, now God's wonderful grace rules instead, giving us right standing with God and resulting in eternal life through Jesus Christ our Lord" (Rom 5:20-21, NLT). Kenneth Wuest translates the expression "God's wonderful grace became more abundant" as, "grace superabounded with more added to that". God makes His grace superabound over abundant sin! It is impossible to out-sin the grace of God.

Summary. Have you seen the FACE of grace? It is **f**ree, **a**ccepts you, is **C**hrist, and **e**mpowers.

F	FREE	Gift or favour; God draws us to Himself through Christ.	Rom 6:23; Eph 2:8-10
A	ACCEPTANCE	Accepted because we accept the Son in faith.	Eph 1:5-6; Heb 10:18
C	CHRIST	Christ is the embodiment of grace.	John 1:14-17; 1 Cor 1:4
E	EMPOWERMENT	Grace empowers sanctification, restoration, evangelisation.	2 Cor 9:8; Titus 2:11-14

Simply put, Jesus is the face of grace. In contrast, religion offers a toxic mix of grace plus human achievement to be saved! Insisting on paying for a present would be an insult to a generous giver. Instead, please, simply accept His amazing grace. "Thank you, Lord!"

When an ungodly person hears the gospel, receives and responds to the gift of repentance[10] over his sinful, non-Christ-centred life, and believes in full acceptance of God's gift of grace, what follows? He will know that he has already been forgiven, saved, come to life, possesses Christ's righteousness, and has been adopted[11] as a son into God's family. Through the Spirit God dispenses Himself

---

[10] **Repent**. To repent (metanoia) means to change your mind. It is the mind saying it is wrong and I do not want to do it again. But, above all, it is the will saying: I turn away from it and I turn to God. Repentance may be accompanied by feelings, it will certainly involve thoughts, but if it is real it will issue in an act. In the context of the new covenant, it means changing your mind about the goodness of God as revealed in Jesus Christ. Initially, salvation repentance means switching from unbelief to faith and from darkness to light. It involves a turning from sin and a turning to God; to make a heart directed about-face away from self to God (Acts 20:21; 26:20). Repentance and faith are two sides of the same coin; both are a response to God's love and grace; both are *gifts from God* (Acts 5:31, 11:18, 2 Tim. 2:25). After salvation, we daily need to 'be transformed by the renewing of our mind' in repentance and turn away from sinning in thought, attitude, and action, because we are His forgiven sons with a new heart, walking in the light (Rom 12:2; Rev 2:5; 3:3). It is not the amount of our confession and repentance that forgives and saves a person - it is only the blood of Christ (Eph 1:7-8). Also, footnote Repentance on page 107.

[11] **Adoption**. Adoption as sons speaks of being placed, by legal declaration, in the position of a son or daughter who now possesses the same care and inheritance rights as the parent's

into him, and the Spirit will empower the saved believer to obey the Lord - to be and do all he is called for. Does this describe you yet? Then you will be empowered to reflect the FACE of grace to others. Just as God has poured his grace into you, you in turn can let his grace flow into the lives of others, to the glory of God. In the words of theologian John Stott, "Grace is love that cares and stoops and rescues".

"The grace of the Lord Jesus be with all" (Rev 22:21).

"Grace is not simply leniency when we have sinned.
Grace is the enabling gift of God not to sin.
Grace is power, not just pardon".
- John Piper

---

natural children. All debts were cancelled. This word (huiothesia) is used five times in the NT, all by Paul (Rom 8:15, 23; 9:4; Gal 4:5; Eph 1:5). This high position in the family of God gives us something in Jesus that Adam never had. "When people ask us the speculative question why God went ahead with the creation when he knew that it would be followed by the fall, one answer we can tentatively give is that he destined us for a higher dignity than even creation would bestow on us". (Stott)

Unit 1: Grace

DIGGING DEEPER - WHAT IS GRACE?

Scan the QR code for informative links to each of these questions.

1. What is the point of the **railway track** illustration? (2 Tim 1:9)

2. In its broad meaning, how does the word GRACE include more than "undeserved kindness"? What is your **definition of grace**?

3. Why can we say grace is a **person**?

4. What is the **purpose** of grace?

5. How is our God of grace the greatest **heart surgeon**? (Ezek 36:26)

See Suggested Answers at the end of this book.

Action Point

Be aware today of different opportunities for you to become a reflector (dispenser) of grace in practical ways. (Col 4:6; Acts 20:24)

Prayer

Gracious God, my creator, my Father, who has chosen me to be in a relationship with you. Through Jesus, you have extended grace to me and saved me. Day by day, help me to comprehend your grace more and more in my life. Flood me with your grace this day so that I can respond to your love in serving others. Thank you for your amazing grace. Amen.

THE TRUTH
Whatever you do, work heartily,
as for the Lord [Jesus] and not for men. - Col 3:23

Q3. WHAT IS THE PURPOSE OF LIFE?

How's life? Do you view life presently as pointless, or purposeful?

The search for the purpose of life has puzzled people for thousands of years. Just think of all the philosophers, theologians, scientists, and humanists who have debated this. The entire A to Z: from Aristotle to Zwingli. Consider some perspectives:

Philosophical: ideas ranging from finding personal happiness and fulfilment, to contributing to society, to seeking truth and knowledge.

Religious: belief in a specific purpose given by a deity, such as serving God or fulfilling a divine plan.

Scientific: often seen as a result of biological and evolutionary processes, such as the survival and reproduction of genes.

Humanistic: perceive it as individual self-actualization and the pursuit of happiness and well-being.

Ultimately, the purpose of life is a personal and individualized concept shaped by a person's beliefs, values, and experiences. Whatever the individual's perception, surely no one wants to live their entire life in meandering uncertainty, filled with fear and hopelessness. To get personal for a moment, what is *your* ultimate goal? Does it basically involve one of the following, or perhaps a combination of them?

To be happy? Pursuing interests like hobbies and travel? Ultimately, eternal life in a paradise?

To help others? After all, "there's more happiness in giving than receiving" – right?

To honour God? Shouldn't we be in fear and awe of the One who created us?

There we have it: happiness, helping, or honouring? All sound like good goals, most will agree. However, do we have the wrong starting point by asking ourselves, 'What do **I** want from life?' 'What is **my** dream for the future?' How so? Because **God** is the *source* of life. Not only the source but the *purpose* of life. To have a personal knowing acquaintance with Him, the glorious invisible reality, as His sons and daughters (Ps 42:1-2; Job 42:1-6). The Message Bible gives us a loose translation of Romans 8:8, where it says, "Focusing on the self is the opposite of focusing on God. Anyone completely absorbed in self ignores God, ends up thinking more about self than God".

In the middle of the Bible we find a concise statement in Isaiah explaining God's purpose in creating man, and man's purpose in life. "Everyone who is called by My name, and whom I have created for My glory, whom I have formed, even whom I have made". (Isaiah 43:7) We were created by God, to enjoy Him as his children, and to radiate and glorify Him.

As we find joy in Him, He unconditionally loves us and enjoys fellowship with his family.

Imagine a four-year-old boy 'helping' his daddy to wash the car. In one sense, the youngster is more of a hindrance than a help, slowing the father down. Yet, what is far more precious to the father is the joy-filled relationship as they have fun together in a soapy giggly mess! How he loves his daddy! Likewise, let's not conflate zealous religious activity with spirituality or 'busyness' with a relationship with God. Any works should be an outworking of our relationship with the Lord – the fruit of it, not the root of it. Don't put the cart before the horse.

But hold on a moment, didn't Jesus describe man's primary goal as work and behaviour in **Matthew 6:33**, when he declared, "Seek first the kingdom and his righteousness"? Furthermore, didn't he later give his disciples in **Acts 1:8** the instruction, "you will be my witnesses ... to the remotest part of the earth"? Surely then, doesn't this mean we must purposefully and continually preach the kingdom if we want God's approval and to live forever? We will use the above two verses as a springboard to make a few observations about glorifying God through seeking the kingdom, and giving a witness. Finally, we will focus our attention on practical ways that our life today can evidence His glory.

What about seeking first the kingdom?

When you read that expression," seek first the kingdom," does your mind immediately think 'preach, and preach more, about God's government'? The verses leading up to Matthew 6:33 do not mention any preaching campaign at all. The context discusses the materialistic treasure-seeking of unbelievers in contrast to Christ's followers. True disciples will not compromise their allegiance to God by anxiously fretting over money and things of this life. (This does not rule out higher education, which Jehovah's Witnesses counsel against[12]). Disciples of Christ prioritise God and His rule which leads them in His righteousness. Therefore, they seek, above all, a relationship with Him and his King, Jesus Christ, and thereby evidence the fruit of this relationship in their everyday life.

We willingly, by Spirit led repentance, submit obediently to Jesus' reign, for he was appointed King when he first returned to heaven in 33 AD. We keenly seek this Kingdom's complete revelation and restoration at the return of Christ. The good news of God's grace in Christ includes the message of this present and future glorious Kingdom.

But didn't Jesus say that our good works glorify God? (Matt 5:16). There again, the NT teaches that our salvation[13] precedes any works, such as giving practical help in the community or preaching. Going to work without knowing Jesus personally would be like failing to put batteries in a toy car and just pushing it along the floor. Titus 3:4-5 is just one of many scriptures showing salvation is not based on the

---

[12] **Higher Education**. "Let the honest-hearted person compare the kind of preaching of the gospel done by the religious systems of Christendom during all the centuries with that done by Jehovah's Witnesses since the end of World War I in 1918. They are not one and the same kind. That of Jehovah's Witnesses is really "gospel" or "good news," as of God's heavenly kingdom that was established by the enthronement of his Son Jesus Christ at the end of the Gentile Times in 1914". (Watchtower 1981 May 1, p. 17). Also, "Situations that may require a review of an appointed brother's qualifications [some questions raised] If an appointed brother, his wife, or his children pursue higher education, does his life pattern show that he puts Kingdom interests first in his life? (w05 10/1 p. 27 par. 6) Does he respect what has been published by the faithful slave on the dangers of higher education? Do they have theocratic goals? Does the pursuit of higher education interfere with regular meeting attendance, meaningful participation in field service, or other theocratic activities?" (Shepherd the Flock of God 8:30)

[13] **Salvation.** In a nutshell, salvation means being salvaged from sins (Matt 1:21). Another way that this is expressed, based on 1 Thessalonians 1:9-10, is we are saved from God, by God, for God. "You turned to God from idols to serve the living and true God, and to wait for his Son from heaven, whom he raised from the dead, Jesus who delivers us from the wrath to come". (also, Rom 5:9). See also footnote 100 on page 129.

works we perform but on the work Jesus has already done as our Saviour, "But when the kindness of God our Saviour and His love for mankind appeared, He saved us, *not on the basis of deeds* which we have done in righteousness, but according to His mercy, by the washing of regeneration and renewing by the Holy Spirit".

Ephesians 2:8-10 says similarly that we are saved not *by* works but *for* works that God will produce through us after salvation. A good tree, of necessity, must be planted, germinated, and have taken root before bearing any good fruit (Matt 7:17-18; John 15:4-5).

What about being his witnesses?

Have you thought about what Jesus meant by his post-resurrection words in Acts 1:8? "You will be my witnesses". The testimony of the early Christians centred on Jesus. We can clearly see this from such scriptures as Acts 8:35; 10:42-43, and 2 Corinthians 4:4-6. Yet was this merely preaching an objective impersonal doctrine; shouting out the message 'Christ is Saviour'? Please notice that the apostles couldn't embark on this post-resurrection witnessing until they were first "baptised with the Holy Spirit". Then having been born again, they were internally energised and had something to subjectively give personal testimony about - namely, what the Lord in his grace had done for them. So, this passage in Acts 1:4-8 doesn't strictly refer to a campaign of verbally "preaching" a detached message, but to delivering one's own conversion testimony, in the power of the Spirit, of how Jesus has completely changed your life. "Come and hear, all who fear God, and I will *tell of what He has done for my soul*" (Ps 66:16; Mark 5:20; John 4:39; Acts 9). Your changed life, backed up by words, will reveal how you have been redeemed, forgiven, justified[14], and sanctified – all because of His shed blood (Luke 24:46-48; Rev 1:9; 12:11).

---

[14] **Justification**. This is an act of God in His grace whereby he, once-for-all-time at salvation, declares a person righteous, acquitted from all sin, free of sins *penalty*, and therefore right with God. The 'Pidgin English' translation is compact, 'God 'e say 'im alright'! The only condition demanded of the sinner is (God-given) faith in the death, burial, and resurrection of God's Son. **Sanctification** is generally viewed as a growth process into deeper holiness of behaviour, a being set free of the *power* of sin after justification. Considering such scriptures as 1 Cor 1:2; 6:11 and Heb 10:10,14 - which talk of sanctification as having already taken place - some opine that our sanctification (our being set apart) is now complete because we are now in Christ by grace, therefore their remains, each day, certain lingering wrong thinking, attitudes, and actions to repent over and clean up; compare John 13:10; Rom 12:1-2. Finally, at glorification, the very *presence* of sin will be removed.

Unit 1: Grace

"The meaning of life is to know God, and to enjoy God,
and to reflect some of the beauty of God as we know him in Christ,
and one day to see him perfectly and unendingly enjoy him".
– John Piper

Piecing this together it becomes clear that our purpose in life is not merely to obey a set of religious rules and preach about survival into a new world order. Our purpose is to glorify God and enjoy Him as his children in Christ, resulting in a testimony of His saving grace. The Westminster Shorter Catechism posed the question, "What is the chief end of man?" Answer: "Man's chief end is to glorify God and to enjoy him forever". C S Lewis said succinctly, "In commanding us to glorify him, God is inviting us to enjoy him".

What does this mean for us today in practical terms? Here are three ways that evidence that we have received the glory of His grace in our lives.

Worship

"Honor the LORD for the glory of his name. Worship the LORD in the splendor of his holiness" (Ps 29:2, NLT).

John Piper explained, "Worship is the term we use to cover all the acts of the heart and mind and body that intentionally express the infinite worth of God. This is what we were created for". Many spend some alone time with God every morning, even if only for a few quiet moments. They view these times not as a repetitious routine but as a rewarding rest. Opportunities to praise and glorify Him as Abba Father. They will provide you with a fountain in your heart at which you can slake your thirst throughout the day. How about gathering with other Christians who love the Lord Jesus as they openly pray and discuss scripture by the Spirit? How this contrasts to attending dry scripted 'Bible educational meetings' which, although filling our mind with key scriptures, can be devoid of heartfelt expressions of devotion and worship!

Christlikeness

"Now all of us, with our faces unveiled, reflect the glory of the Lord as if we are mirrors; and so we are being transformed, metamorphosed, into His same image from one radiance of glory to another, just as the Spirit of the Lord accomplishes it" (2 Cor 3:18, Voice Bible).

Do you enjoy the sunshine, especially after a period of inclement weather? You likely feel uplifted as you receive the sun's rays, even get a tan. A friend passes the comment, "You've caught the sun today!" Does your radiant tan make the sun itself more radiant? Not at all. You cannot add to the sun's glory but merely draw attention to it. So, it is as we receive the Lord Jesus into our lives, we start to shine, drawing attention, not to ourselves, but to His radiant glory and beauty. We come to more and more mirror Christ when we, for example, love others, like the disadvantaged in the community or even our enemies.

We need to be clear about this. We don't give God glory and honour through *our* blood, sweat and tears. Rather we can only "give to God" what we first have received from Him. We give Him glory and honour by recognising *Jesus'* blood, sweat, and tears – thus by us responding to what God already has accomplished on our behalf, only by His grace. Ephesians 1:4-6 puts it this way, "In love, He predestined us to adoption as sons and daughters through Jesus Christ to Himself, according to the good pleasure of His will, to the praise of **the glory of His grace**..." If we realise what He's done for us and who we are, we cannot help but respond, "to God be all the glory, honor and praise". God will never be glorified by our behaviour for Him, only by His grace to us!

Witness

"You see, we don't go around preaching about ourselves. *We preach that Jesus Christ is Lord*, and we ourselves are your servants for Jesus' sake. ... But we continue to preach because we have the same kind of faith the psalmist had when he said, "I believed in God, so I spoke". ... All of this is for your benefit. And as God's grace reaches more and more people, there will be great thanksgiving, and God will receive more and **more glory**" (2 Cor 4:5,13,15, NLT).

As mentioned above, our personal testimony of what Jesus has done in our own life is a key and integral part of the message. This stands in sharp contrast to preaching a message primarily focused on surviving Armageddon by connection with a religious organisation for salvation.

What's the takeaway? "Whatever you do, work heartily, as for the Lord [Jesus] and not for men (Col 3:23). Our ultimate goal is Jesus - to know him, enjoy him now and eternally - to the glory of the grace of the Father. This is the real purpose of life!

"Let God have your life; He can do more with it than you can".
- Dwight L. Moody

Digging Deeper - What is the Purpose of Life?

Scan the QR code for informative links to each of these questions.

1. What should be our primary **purpose** in life?

2. How is **grace** involved in glorifying God? (Eph 1:6)

3. What does seeking first His **kingdom and righteousness** involve?

4. Meditate, then pray over just one verse every day over the coming seven days from **John 17:20-26.** How would you answer the following?

   Day 1 - **v20** How can you be involved in this verse today?

   Day 2 – **v21** Does being "one" mean organisational unity?

   Day 3 - **v22** Name 3 gifts from Jesus (vs 2, 14, 22).

   Day 4 - **v23** What does " as You have loved me" mean to you?

   Day 5 - **v24** What is Jesus' deep desire? (Song of Sol 6:5)

   Day 6 - **v25** How does Jesus refer to God six times?

   Day 7 - **v26** What does the "name" mean?

5. To complete our first 3-part section on the subject of GRACE, you may enjoy this music video **"grace upon grace".** Why not sing along!

See Suggested Answers at the end of this book.

Action Point

Here are two examples of short personal testimonies. Have you ever spoken out your testimony? Please read Mark 5:19; Acts 26:1-32; 1 John 5:9-12; Rev 12:11.

Prayer

We give you glory and honour Lord by receiving the gift of salvation through Jesus' blood, sweat and tears. I pray that I may willingly submit to the work of the Holy Spirit in my life, even on those occasions when I do not understand, and ask that all that is of me may decrease and all that is of Christ may increase, until He is all in all in my life, to Your praise and glory. This I ask in the name of Jesus. Amen.

Q4. WHAT IS THE BIBLE ALL ABOUT?

Mr Kambarami, the General Secretary of the Bible Society in Zimbabwe, tried to give a New Testament to a very belligerent man. The man insisted he would roll the pages and use them to make cigarettes. Mr Kambarami said, "I understand that, but at least promise to read the page of the New Testament before you smoke it". The man agreed, and the two went their separate ways. Then, 15 years later, the two men met at a convention in Zimbabwe. The Scripture-smoking pagan had been saved and was now a full-time evangelist. He told the audience, "I smoked Matthew, and I smoked Mark, and I smoked Luke. But when I got to John 3:16, I couldn't smoke anymore. My life was changed from that moment".

Considering the Bible's power to change lives, how fitting that over *100 million* copies of the Bible are sold each year.

- **Gideons** International distribute over 80 million annually – that's two copies per second!

- **Wycliffe** Global Alliance, by 2022, had translated the complete Bible in 724 languages and portions of it in 2865 languages. That's a total of *3589* – potentially reaching seven of the eight billion people on earth. They have the vision of translating a portion of the Bible into all of the over 7,100 languages of the world by 2033. For comparison, as of 2020, Jehovah's Witnesses published their own Bible, the New World Translation, in whole or in part in 200 languages.

- **China** is the largest producer of Bibles in the world. Just one factory in Nanjing (Amity Press) prints about 15 million copies a year in over 90 languages.

In this three-part section of our course, we will consider the questions:

a. What is the Bible all about?
b. Is it True?
c. What is the GRACE Method of Personal Study?

So let us consider the first part today, 'What is the Bible all about?'

1. THE WRITERS

The Bible was written by about 40 men, over a period of 1,600 years, on three continents: Israel (Asia); parts of Jeremiah from Egypt (Africa); several NT letters from European cities.

One-third of the Bible was written by murderers, namely Moses, David, and Paul. God, in his grace, can use people from all sorts of backgrounds to accomplish His will.

2. THE BOOKS

The term "the Bible" is from the Greek 'ta biblia', which means "the scrolls" or "the books".

In point of fact, it is a library of 66 books in two sections: the OT in Hebrew and Aramaic[15] - taking a thousand years to complete - and the NT in Greek – written over a period of 50-70 years.

The chart displays the typical sequential list of Bible books, each with its focus on Christ, organised under main headings:

Your copy of the Old Testament may include certain 'apocryphal'[16] books. The canonicity[17] of these additional writings is questioned by many. The Old Testament, the Hebrew Bible, is also known in Judaism as the Tanakh[18]. This

---

[15] **Aramaic**. Biblical Hebrew is the main language of the Hebrew Bible. Aramaic accounts for only about 250 verses out of a total of over 23,000. Biblical Aramaic is closely related to Hebrew, as both are in the Northwest Semitic language family.

[16] **Apocrypha.** The biblical apocrypha (Greek: apókruphos, lit.'hidden') denotes the collection of apocryphal ancient books thought to have been written sometime between 200 BC and AD 400.The Roman Catholic, Eastern Orthodox, and Oriental Orthodox churches include some or all of the same texts within the body of their version of the Old Testament, terming them deuterocanonical books. Traditional 80-book Protestant Bibles have fourteen books in an intertestamental section – the period of about 400 years from Malachi to John the Baptist.

[17] **Canonicity**. The word canon (kanon) originally meant measuring reed, but eventually developed the meaning of 'standard'. Pertaining to the New Testament, the term refers to those books accepted by the church as the standard that governs Christian belief and conduct. The basic criteria for inclusion were having Apostolic approval and acceptance by authoritative churches, such as those of Ephesus, Jerusalem, Antioch, Rome, Carthage, and so on.

[18] **Tanakh**. The traditional form of the modern Hebrew Bible used in Rabbinic Judaism is the Masoretic Text (7th to 10th century CE), which consists of 24 books. The contents of the

acronym adopts the letters T, N, and K of Tanakh to stand for the three-part collection: Torah (law), Nevi'im (prophets), Ketuvim (writings, poets, and wisdom).

These three sections originally were comprised of 22 parts or books. In this chart, however, you will find we have divided the now 39 books of the OT under three different headings as a memory aid: HISTORY + POETRY + PROPHECY. The New Testament of the Greek scriptures are comprised of 27 books. You will notice we have used similar headings of HISTORY + LETTERS + PROPHECY.

3. THE STORY

How could we summarize the central message of the Bible in just one sentence? Here is my attempt: 'Our Holy Father is glorified in his demonstration of love and grace in saving sinners through his Son's death and resurrection, so that they may become sons in his Kingdom family, enjoying intimacy with Him eternally.'

If you like alliteration, the storyline of the Bible could be expressed in these six words:

Eden →Exodus → Exile → Emancipator →Enlightener →Eternity!

The emancipator is Jesus through his shed blood. The enlightener is the Holy Spirit. In other words, the Bible is one big rescue story. God, in his love rescues us through Jesus to bring us back into a relationship with Him. The OT is the story of one man *Adam*, and one nation Israel - from the one man *Abraham* - leading to the NT, which focuses on the one man, our Saviour, *Jesus*.

But we should let the Bible itself describe its core message. Here in Revelation 1:4-6, we find such a description in John's concise, delightful statement of praise. First, he draws attention to *God's grace* and the role of the *Son* and the *Spirit*, then continues to reveal how God's grace saved sinners for a kingdom – all for *God's glory*. "John to the seven churches that are in Asia: *Grace* to you and peace from Him who is, and who was, and who is to come, and from the *seven spirits* who are before His throne, and from *Jesus* Christ, the faithful witness, the firstborn of the dead, and the ruler of the kings of the earth. To Him who loves us and *released us from our sins by His blood* - and He made us into a *kingdom, priests* to His God and Father—*to Him be the glory* and the dominion forever and ever. Amen".

Medieval Masoretic text are similar, but not identical, to those of the Protestant Old Testament, in which the material is divided into 39 books and arranged in a different order.

The Old Testament		
HISTORY	**POETRY**	**PROPHECY**
GEN (Seed)	**JOB** (Comforts, Redeems)	**ISA** (Suffering Servant)
EXOD (Passover Lamb)	**PS** (Shepherd)	**JER** (Potter, Branch)
LEV (High Priest)	**PROV** (Wisdom)	**LAM** (Weeping Prophet)
NUM (Cloud, Fire)	**ECCL** (Meaning of Life)	**EZEKI** (Son of Man)
DEUT (Gtr Moses)	**SONG** (Bridegroom)	**DAN** (4th man in Furnace)
JOSH (Commander)		**HOS** (Faithful Husband)
JUDG (Judge)		**JOEL** (Spirit Provider)
RUTH (Kinsman Redeems)		**AMOS** (Just)
1 SAM (Prophet Priest King)		**OBAD** (Triumph)
2 SAM (King of Grace)		**JONAH** (Missionary)
1 KGS (Gtr Solomon)		**MIC** (Messiah)
2 KGS (King of Kings)		**NAH** (Avenger)
1 CHR (Son of David)		**HAB** (Love's Embrace)
2 CHR (Kingdom Restorer)		**ZEPH** (Warrior Restorer)
EZRA (Temple Restorer)		**HAG** (Treasure)
NEH (Wall Rebuilder)		**ZECH** (Sprout, Stone)
EST (Protector)		**MAL** (Covenanter)

The New Testament		
HISTORY	**LETTERS**	**PROPHECY**
MATT (King)	ROM (Our Righteousness)	REV (Lamb Lion Lord)
MARK (Servant)	1 COR (Rock, Resurrector)	
LUKE (Son of Man)	2 COR (Reconciler)	
JOHN (Son of God)	GAL (Freedom, Life)	
ACTS (Resurrected Lord)	EPH (Head of Church)	
	PHP (Lord of Joy)	
	COL (Fullness)	
	1 THESS (Coming Again)	
	2 THESS (Returning Lord)	
	1 TIM (Mediator)	
	2 TIM (Raised Saviour)	
	TITUS (Foundation, Hope)	
	PHILM (Redeemer)	
	HEB (High Priest)	
	JAS (Worker in our Faith)	
	1 PET (Living Hope	
	2 PET (Grace, Guardian)	
	1 JOHN (Light, Love, Life)	
	2 JOHN (Truth and Love)	
	3 JOHN (Hospitable)	
	JUDE (Lord Protector)	

This beautifully expresses grace. God doesn't love us after we have overcome major sins and tried to change. He sent his Son to die for us when we were ungodly sinners. Jesus freed us from sin and made us right with God, not on account of anything we do, but because he loved us to death. This is why the *focus of scripture is not us but Christ*!

A Trap. Yet, there is a danger of making the same mistake made by many religious leaders in Jesus' day. What is this trap? Note Jesus' words directed to them in John 5:39-40,

"You examine the Scriptures because you think that in them you have eternal life; and it is those very Scriptures that testify about Me; and yet you are unwilling to come to Me so that you may have life".

William Barclay commented, "They read it not to search for God but to find arguments to support their own positions. They did not really love God; they loved their own ideas about him".

So it is possible to study the Bible thoroughly for years, memorise many passages, and even know the original Bible languages, yet not know Jesus in a personal saving relationship. You see, the Bible is really the Spirit's biography of the Son. It is not a painting to glance over superficially, nor to forensically investigate the paint used in each brush stroke, but to enjoy as a window to view the beauty of Jesus. Then let Him transform us by the Spirit into His image. As D. L. Moody commented, "The Bible was not given for our information but for our transformation".

The Bible is the unshakeable and infallible Word of God. It is God's message to us here on earth to be understood by his Holy Spirit. It is the main resource God has given us to know Him more. It is meant to be bread for daily use, not cake for special occasions. Someone aptly remarked, "The Bible is the only book whose author is always present when one reads it". Also, "The Bible is the only book where the Author is in love with the reader".

In the question sheet, you will find encouragement to follow a daily Bible reading plan that suits your personal needs.

But some object to its authenticity. So, our next article will answer the question, 'Is it True?'

"The Bible is the cradle wherein Christ is laid".
- Martin Luther

Digging Deeper - What is the Bible All About?

Scan the QR code for informative links to each of these questions.

1. Try this ten-question **quiz** 'How the Bible Came To Be.' What two facts didn't you know?

2. How many parts comprised the original **Hebrew Bible** (OT)? What is the Tanak?

3. Summarize the Bible's message in **one sentence.** (1 John 5:11-12).

4. What are the main differences between Bible **translations**?

5. Eph 1:6-11. What stands out to you in this "Look at the Book"?

See Suggested Answers at the end of this book.

Action Point

Have you chosen a good Bible that you find especially helpful? Or perhaps a couple of Bibles; one for its literal translation and another that is paraphrase? It is helpful to establish a daily Bible reading schedule.

Prayer

> Lord, now as I open up your Word, please open up my mind by Holy Spirit to understand your words. Give me understanding so that I can know you better and wisdom to live out what I read. In Jesus' Name I pray, Amen.

THE TRUTH
Jesus is the greatest affirmation of Scripture
- John 17:17

Q5. IS THE BIBLE TRUE?

A British poll conducted in 2017 revealed that only 6% of British adults read or listen to the Bible, while 55% of Christians in the country never do so. Many turn to it for comfort in times of trouble; others refer to it for answers to crosswords and quizzes. What do you personally believe? Is the Bible true? Reliable? Inspired?

It is very popular to question its accuracy based on certain historical and scientific criticisms. Others believe the Bible contains *some* truth because of personal experiences, the testimony of others, or the fulfilment of some biblical prophecies. Adding to the mix, there are numerous Christians who seem willing to deny reality by ignoring, stubbornly evading, any *critical thinking* in regard to the Bible's historicity or canonicity. The faith of a genuine Christian, though, does not suppress the evidence, or refuse to acknowledge the data, but encompasses it, incorporates it. In the words of Hebrews 11:1, "Now faith is the assurance (the confirmation, the title deed) of the things [we] hope for, being the proof of things [we] do not see and the conviction of their reality [faith perceiving as real fact what is not revealed to the senses]". (Amplified, Classic Edition)

Yes, there remain many Christians who still view the Bible as the inspired Word of God - the facts matter. They are persuaded that: "All Scripture is inspired[19] by

---

[19] **Inspired by God** (theopneustos, from Theos = God + pneo = to breathe or blow) means divinely breathed or given by inspiration of God. The Greek word for "inspired" describes ships' sails filled, and the vessels being carried along over the seas. In the OT alone, the human writers refer to their writings as the words of God over 3800 times! On April 18th, 1521, at the Diet of Worms, when Martin Luther was called on by Johann von Eck, Official General of the Archbishop of Trier, to renounce his errors, Luther replied, "Unless I am convinced by testimonies of Scripture or by evident reason-for I believe neither the Pope nor Councils alone, since it is established that they have often erred and contradicted themselves-I am the prisoner of the Scriptures cited by me, and my conscience has been taken captive by the Word of God. Here I stand. I can do no other. God help me. Amen".

Taking a leaf out of Luther's book, we need to be careful of religious organisations that control all interpretations of scripture. This is the claim of Jehovah's Witnesses, "The Bible is an organisational book and belongs to the Christian congregation as an organisation, not

God and beneficial for teaching, for rebuke, for correction, for training in righteousness; so that the man or woman of God may be fully capable, equipped for every good work" (2 Tim 3:16-17). "That no prophecy of Scripture becomes a matter of someone's own interpretation, for no prophecy was ever made by an act of human will, but men moved by the Holy Spirit spoke from God" (2 Pet 1:20-21). Do you believe the Scriptures are remarkable in their prophecies[20], principles, and publishing? In this article, we will touch upon just three lines of evidence listed in ascending order of importance: the *accuracy* of detail, the *alteration* of lives, and the *affirmation* of Christ.

Accuracy of Detail

Although not in itself proving the inspiration of the Bible, its accuracy in historical detail and harmony is remarkable. Remember that we are talking of about 40 writers[21], including farmers, fishermen, soldiers, and kings, from differing cultures, over a period of 1600 years. We can take as an example Luke 3:1-2. Luke flagged the year of two events: the start of John the Baptist's ministry and the baptism of Jesus. "Now in the fifteenth year of the reign of **Tiberius Caesar**, when **Pontius Pilate** was governor of Judea, and **Herod** was tetrarch of Galilee and his brother **Philip** was tetrarch of the region of Ituraea and Trachonitis, and **Lysanias** was tetrarch of Abilene, in the high priesthood of **Annas** and **Caiaphas**, the word of God came to John, the son of Zechariah, in the wilderness". The ESV Study Bible points out that "Luke's precision in naming five Roman officials with their specific titles shows concern for detailed historical accuracy, and his accuracy is confirmed by historical records outside of the Bible". Luke adds two other names from the priesthood, making seven names in all, each corroborated by secular historians. For now, let us sketch out the first three names: Tiberius, Pilate, and Herod.

---

to individuals, regardless of how sincerely they may believe that they can interpret the Bible. For this reason, the Bible cannot be properly understood without Jehovah's visible organisation in mind". – Watchtower 1967 Oct 1 p587 par. 9

[20] **Prophecy,** at its most basic definition, is "a message from God". So, to prophesy is to proclaim a message from God. Although foretelling is often associated with prophecy, revealing the future is not a necessary element of prophecy; however, since only God knows the future, any authoritative word about the future must of necessity, be a prophecy, that is, a message from God.

[21] **Quran**. Contrast this with the Islamic Qur'an. One individual, Zaid bin Thabit, compiled it under the guidance of Mohammed's father-in-law, Abu-Bekr. Then, in AD. 650, a group of Arab scholars produced a unified version and destroyed all variant copies to preserve the unity of the Qur'an. The Bible was unified from the time of its writing. The Qur'an had unity forced upon it by human editors.

Tiberius Caesar is well-known, and his physical appearance has been depicted in artwork. The Roman Senate appointed him emperor on September 15th of 14 AD., when Jesus was in his mid-teens. A 48cm marble bust of this Caesar is exhibited in the British Museum.

Pontius Pilate's name was recorded by Roman historian Tacitus shortly after the Bible was completed. There is also an Inscription discovered in 1961 at Caesaria. The Latin reads: "Pontius Pilate, Prefect of Judaea, made and dedicated the Tiberium[22] to the Divine Augustus". The inscription uses the title of "Prefect" (equivalent to the New Testament's ἡγεμών, hēgemōn, "governor") for Pilate, not "Procurator" (for which the Greek term was ἐπίτροπος, epitropos). The prefect functioned more in the realm of the military than the procurator. Thus, this inscription supports the historical accuracy of the Scriptures.

Herod Antipas ruled from 4 BC–39 AD. A tetrarch was a ruler with the rank and authority lower than a king who ruled with the approval of the Roman authorities. It was this Herod who imprisoned and later executed John the Baptist. He also had a hand in the unjust trial of Jesus.

'Yes,' someone may object, 'but there are many contradictions in the Bible.' It may appear so, but these alleged, apparent contradictions are largely discrepancies which revolve around relatively trivial inconsistencies, like certain numbers in different OT books, and minor translation and copying errors of old manuscripts. Also, some accounts are not contradictory but complementary. Have you ever known of eyewitness reports of an accident which seemed to be at variance with each other? Upon investigation, they are discovered to be in fact, complementary, but just seen from different angles. It has been said that no serious doctrinal dispute within the church has ever been caused by such. Our salvation does not depend on such things. Wayne Grudem, a renowned NT scholar, candidly observes: "Our understanding of Scripture is never perfect, and this means that there may be cases where we will be unable to find a solution to a difficult passage at the present time. This may be because the linguistic, historical, or contextual evidence we need to understand the passage correctly is presently unknown to us". (Systematic Theology, Zondervan, 1994, p. 99).

You will have opportunity to consider a number of these apparently conflicting verses in the Digging Deeper page.

- If Adam and Eve had only two sons, where did Cain find his wife?

---

[22] **Tiberium.** A Tiberium was a temple dedicated to a Roman emperor, considered a deity.

- Doesn't 'baptism for the dead' contradict that people must believe individually? (1 Cor 15:29).
- If Paul says we are 'saved by faith, not works'; why does James insist works are involved?

Granted that the historical and harmonious accuracy of a book does not prove inspiration; nevertheless, we would expect anything written under God's inspiration to have been originally perfect and precise.

Alteration of Lives

Yes, the Word of God has the power to transform lives. 'Fine', some may say, 'but even non-believers can make changes to their life, and without a book'. Agreed. In this case, though, we are talking about profound personal and behavioural alterations. Even more than that – the Scriptures point to a brand-new life in a relationship with Christ – a new creation! Christianity isn't turning over a new leaf; its receiving a new life.

We can reread 2 Timothy 3:15-17, but from a paraphrase Bible: "There's nothing like the written Word of God for showing you the way to salvation through faith in Christ Jesus. ..... Every part of Scripture is God-breathed and useful one way or another - showing us truth, exposing our rebellion, correcting our mistakes, training us to live God's way. Through the Word we are put together and shaped up for the tasks God has for us". (Message Bible)

"I believe the Bible is true because it gives me the experience that it claims it will give me. For example, the Bible says that God will forgive my sins. I believe that. I accepted God's forgiveness and it happened. How do I know? I have a sense of freedom from guilt... yes, the Bible really changes lives. Millions of people - from great heads of state to brilliant educators and scientists, from philosophers and writers to generals and historians - could all testify about how the Bible has changed their lives". (Why Believe the Bible? - John MacArthur). Additionally, evangelist D L Moody commented, "The Bible was not given for our information but for our transformation".

Yes, the Bible is like a love letter from God. Imagine receiving a love letter from your fiancé overseas, but you never bother to open it. Or alternatively, you become so engrossed in dissecting and analysing every word that when your fiancé makes a surprise visit in person – you ignore her as she stands in the room so that you can continue scrutinising her letter!

A final quote to encourage us to read our Bible as a vital connection with God: "When you read God's Word, you must constantly be saying to yourself, "It is talking to me, and about me. ... Complaining about a silent God with a closed Bible, is like complaining about no text messages with a turned off phone". (Soren Kierkegaard)

54

Affirmation of Christ

We move on to our third and important evidence of the Bible's authenticity: how Scripture affirms Christ through numerous prophecies. A quarter of the Bible is predictive prophecy, which makes it distinctive from all other Holy books. Some estimate that at least a sixth of these prophecies are Messianic, pointing to Jesus. Revelation 19:10 proclaims, "For the essence of prophecy is to give a clear witness for Jesus". (NLT) Think of just eight of these prophecies, which, apart from the first one, predicted events surrounding Jesus' death. These were written hundreds of years in advance.

PROPHECY		WRITTEN
Micah 5:2	His birth in Bethlehem	c. 735-710BC
Zechariah 9:9	As king he enters on a donkey	c.480-470 BC
Zechariah 11:12	Thirty pieces of silver	c.480-470 BC
Zechariah 11:13	Temple and potter	c.480-470 BC
Zechariah 13:6	Wounds in hands	c.480-470 BC
Isaiah 53:7	No defence; innocent	c.700-681BC
Isaiah 53:9	Died with the wicked; grave with the rich	c.700-681BC
Psalm 22:16	Crucified – hands and feet pierced	c.1410-450 BC

It has been estimated that the chances of just these eight prophecies relating to Jesus' death are 10^{17}. Yet throughout the OT there are over 300 such Messianic prophecies. (See Question sheet). Notice Isaiah 53 listed in the chart. This whole chapter is worth examining.

We could rightfully conclude that since Jesus is who he said he was – the Messiah, the risen Son of God – he is trustworthy and speaks with full authority when he testified on numerous occasions to the integrity of Scripture. For example, Jesus said, "the Scripture cannot be nullified" and "Your word is truth". (Matt 4:1-11; 5:15; Luke 18:31; John 10:35; 17:17). So, without a doubt, the primary evidence of the Bible's authenticity is, not the accuracy of detail, nor the alteration of lives, but rather the *affirmation* **of** *Christ* – not only in him fulfilling prophecy but more importantly still, in that he gave **his personal testimony to the truthfulness of scripture** – the affirmation **by** Christ to their authenticity.

On a side note, I generally like to study from the NASB of 2020 with its formal equivalence. The NET Bible with its many footnotes and its combination of formal equivalence with functional equivalence is useful too. Also, a valuable addition is the "Analytical – Literal Translation of the NT" by Gary F Zeolla. However, rather than getting overly bogged down in scholarly debates with the minutia of manuscript comparisons, my focus is being taught by the Holy Spirit through the overarching message of God's grace in Christ (John 5:39-40; Rev 1:4-6). Yes, open the Bible daily – it is reliable, inspired, and can transform your life. It may well cause you to fall in love even more deeply with our Lord Jesus Christ. Next, we will consider a few recommended methods of personal Bible study.

> *"I've read the last page of the Bible;*
> *it's all going to turn out alright".*
> *-Billy Graham*

Prayer

I kneel in your presence Father, praising you. Through Christ's shed blood, I no longer feel dirty and distant, but clean and close. O how I long to know your Son better. That's why, Lord, I read and treasure your Word, for "the revelation of Your words brings light and gives understanding to the inexperienced". Lord, I pray for this illumination and direction from your Word by the Spirit, so that I can reflect your glory. Amen. (Ps 119:130)

Digging Deeper - Is the Bible True?

Scan the QR code for informative links to each of these questions.

1. In addition to the **Pilate** stone, what other evidence proves his existence?

2. Which one of these nine **archaeological** finds confirms the Bible's accuracy most to you?

3. Here is a list of over **800 scriptures** that may puzzle us, among them some which appear to be contradictory. Solutions are suggested. Can you answer the following 4 scriptures?
   a. Gen 4:17 ... where did Cain get his wife?
   b. John 20:22 ... was the Holy Spirit received by the disciples before Pentecost?
   c. 1 Cor 15:29 ... doesn't 'baptism for the dead' contradict a personal belief?
   d. James 2:21 ... does James contradict Paul by saying we are justified by works?

4. a. How does one theologian reason on the Bible's authenticity of the **Old Testament** stories?

   b. Which of these five prophecies convinces you that the Bible is inspired?

5. This video clip estimates the chances of **Messianic prophecies** being fulfilled. What fact or two may help you reason with others?

See Suggested Answers at the end of this book.

Action Point

How about listening to this moving testimony of a former JW Floyd Erwin, recorded at age 73? Find inside the QR below, under Action Point.

Q6. HOW DO YOU STUDY THE BIBLE?

Have you ever felt inferior to some other Christians who seem to know their Bibles inside out? Some Bible readers can instantly recall scripture references from memory in answer to complex questions. But you flounder in fumbling to find the book of Ruth or Esther. Take heart. God is more interested in our hearts bursting with love than our minds bursting with knowledge. These words from 1 Corinthians may be relevant here, "But while knowledge makes us feel important, it is love that strengthens the church. Anyone who claims to know all the answers doesn't really know very much. But the person who loves God is the one whom God recognises" (1 Cor 8:1-2 NLT).

So do not view Bible reading and study merely as an academic exercise, an accumulation of knowledge. A seminary professor studying in the Holy Land met a man who claimed to have memorised the OT - in Hebrew! Astonished, the professor asked for a demonstration. A few days later, they sat together in the man's home. "Where shall we begin?" asked the man. "Psalm 1," replied the professor, an avid student of the Psalms. Beginning with Psalm 1:1, the man began to recite from memory while the professor followed along in his Hebrew Bible. For two hours, the man continued word for word without a mistake as the professor sat in stunned silence. When the demonstration was over, the professor discovered something even more astonishing about the man - he was an atheist!

Here the Pharisees may come to mind. Though some of that dedicated exclusive group may have genuinely sought to piously follow God's law, they were generally more concerned with their own status, power and legalism. To them, study was an end in itself. They studied Scripture to know Scripture and impress others with their religious lifestyle. Look what Jesus said to them: "You have your heads in your Bibles constantly because you think you'll find eternal life there. But you miss the forest for the trees. These Scriptures are all about ME!" (John 5:39 Message).

That said, all Christians should have the desire to steadily deepen their grasp of God's Word, to see Christ more clearly (1 Pet 2:2). Yet it has to be acknowledged that one person's level of understanding differs from another because of their background, religious grounding, education, ability, and many other factors. Furthermore, there are different levels or layers of Bible interpretation, from literal to symbolic. Symbolic meaning could include the usually shorter and simpler metaphors and the longer, more complex allegories. However, we should be aware of at least three basic dangers:

a) Jumping immediately to personal applications without starting at the baseline of the context.

b) Fixating on academic information (historical, geographical, cultural etc) without any effectual transforming power. "And we also [especially] thank God continually for this, that when you received the message of God [which you heard] from us, you welcomed it not as the word of [mere] men, but as it truly is, the Word of God, which is effectually at work in you who believe [exercising its superhuman power in those who adhere to and trust in and rely on it]". (1 Thess 2:13, Amplified).

c) ignoring the scripture focus on Christ (Rev 19:10).

Sadly, it is this focus on Christ, in relationship with Him, that many Christians in today's society miss out on. Instead, they view the Bible mainly as a handbook of moral guidelines to help improve their lives. This usually results in feelings of condemnation and guilt. They are "always learning but never able to arrive at the truth" (2 Tim 3:7). The truth - who Is Jesus, the personification of "truth". Indeed, the Bible is not a manual for life but about Immanuel, who is eternal life!

What, then is the primary purpose of studying the Bible? It is first to comprehend how much God, as our Father, loves us in Christ. Then we, in turn, come to know, love, and obey[23] God and His Son more fully. As we prayerfully ponder scripture, we begin to see Christ on every page and, through the Spirit, enjoy oneness with Him. Knowledge about him is the tool to knowing him. And to know him is to love him! Please note, this is a far cry from merely repeating what a particular group's material declares as the 'Truth'.

How can we study the Scriptures effectively to focus on the grace of God through Christ? There are several acronyms representing different methods of studying. Among them are:

PLANT – Prepare Your Heart, Learn from the Word, Ask Questions, Name the Truth, Take Action.
SOAK – Scripture, Observation, Application, Kneeling in Prayer.

---

[23] **Obedient.** See footnote 105 on page 133.

OIA – Observation, Interpretation, Application. This Inductive Bible Study[24] is very popular.

Please permit me to introduce my acronym for a method of personal study.

GRACE - God, Read, Analyse, Christ, Engage. There follows a short comment about each step:

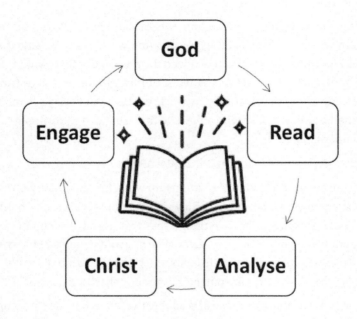

G. *GOD*

God comes first. Prayer to Him is the priority before studying the Word. Take time to still yourself in God's presence. Give your distractions, worries, and concerns to him. Wait in silence, listening to the still, small voice of his Spirit. One of the Psalmists memorably said, "Open my eyes, that I may behold wondrous things out of your law" (Ps 119:18; Jer 33:3). We ask God to open our spiritual eyes to show us the glimpses of glory we cannot see by ourselves. Without his help, we are simply "natural" persons with natural eyes. "The natural person does not accept the things of the Spirit of God, for they are folly to him, and he is not able to understand them because they are spiritually discerned" (1 Cor 2:14). Approach him boldly, humbly, and expectantly. It is, therefore, imperative to pray before we

---

[24] **Inductive Bible Study**. The word inductive implies collecting information and drawing logical conclusions from what you observe. Inductive Bible Study, therefore, is a method of studying Scripture that, by focusing on three basic steps, seeks to find meaning in the original context and apply it to everyday life today.

start to study His Word. We can also season and conclude our study times with prayer.

R. *READ*

Here are several suggestions to make the most of your reading of God's Word: Some choose one of the many *Bible reading plans*[25] that are readily available. Others select a Bible book or chapter they wish to consider more closely. Read your chosen passage of Scripture slowly, perhaps a few times from your chosen translation or Study Bible.[26] How about *comparing translations* – a literal with a paraphrase[27]? As you read, *mark the text* in your study Bible. Especially note key words[28] or phrases that are repeated in the section or may be unique to the passage but arouse your curiosity. You may begin to see a structure or outline emerge by linking phrases together. I have included an example of how a chapter could be marked out, using 1 Peter 5 from the NASB. It is good to be creative and develop your own system. A word of caution at this point. Initially, after prayer for the Holy Spirit's enlightenment and reading the text, use your own thinking and reasoning ability. Resist the temptation to immediately dive into scholarly works, whether online or on your bookshelf. Yes, these can provide invaluable insights, but don't let academia rule you.

Many find *reading aloud* beneficial because it slows them down, allowing them more time to think things through. Another suggestion is to select a verse or two from the passage and *write* it/them on a card or in a notebook. Carry the written note with you so that you can accurately memorise and mull over the words during the day. Some enjoy listening to *online audio*[29] recordings of scripture, so that their senses become immersed in the text.

---

[25] **Bible Reading plan**s: see two links inside the QR below under Action Point.

[26] **Bible translations**. And 'Choosing a Good Study Bible' - see links below in this section - Question 2

[27] **Paraphrase Bibles** takes the meaning of a verse or passage of Scripture and attempts to express the meaning in "plain language" through a modern author's eyes. This contrasts with more literal translations, which communicate as "word-for-word" or as "thought-for-thought". One of the most popular examples of a Bible paraphrase would be "The Message" by Eugene Peterson. A paraphrase of the Bible may contain many helpful renderings but should not be used as a Christian's primary Bible.

[28] **Key words**. Mark the text in your study Bible using a pencil or non-bleed pens (e.g. micron) and coloured highlighters. Alternatively, Bible Gateway facilitates the printing out of Bible pages. If you prefer to multicolour highlight through a Bible app, the free Blue Letter app is helpful and allows the writing of personal notes.

[29] **Audio recordings**. Biblegateway; YouVersion; Bible.is; ESV.org; Audible. Biblestudytools.com/audio-bible/

Unit 2: Bible

A. *ANALYSE*

Here are three aspects to consider under the heading of Analyse:

1. Context. Whatever way you read God's Word, it is of utmost importance to consider where this passage or chapter fits in with the whole Bible book it is part of. In other words, keep context king. (see <u>Additional Information</u> below.) A good Study Bible with an introduction to each Bible book may help in this regard. How did the culture of that historical period influence the writer's word choice? Ask, 'what did this mean to listeners at that time?' - *before* asking, - 'what does it say to me right now?' In this way, the tendency to egocentric eisegesis[30] will be avoided, that is, reading into the text what you wish to see.

2. Questions. When analysing scripture, we should assume a detective's role by constantly asking questions. Imagine you are interviewing the writer. 'What was your intention and main point in writing this?' To whom were you directing this? Why? Where? When?

3. Research. There is an array of Bible Study tools available to help - many free and online - including Study Bibles, encyclopaedias, and lexicons of Hebrew and Greek. I have listed some on the attached question sheet. These can provide, not only cross references and glossaries, but also historical, geographical, cultural, archaeological, and linguistic background information. Don't myopically confine yourself to just one Christian website, translation, or sectarian interpretation.

C. *CHRIST*

To highlight again John 5:39-40, "You search the Scriptures because you think they give you eternal life. But the Scriptures point to me! Yet you refuse to come to me to receive this life". In these two verses, Jesus not only claims to be the subject of Scripture and so greater than Scripture, but the giver of eternal life. Later, after his resurrection, Jesus taught that he is the Bible's closest thing to a skeleton key for unlocking the meaning of every text, every book, every plot twist - the whole story. How patiently, "he interpreted to them in all the Scriptures the things concerning himself" and "opened their minds to understand the Scriptures" (Luke 24:27,44-45). The great goal of Bible reading and studying is this: knowing and enjoying Jesus. See him on every page (Rev 19:10b).

---

[30] **Eisegesis** denotes "to lead out of". That means that the reader jumps to his own conclusions by mishandling a text. He makes the scripture fit in with his preconceived ideas, being concerned only with making a point, even at the expense of the meaning of words. Exegesis, on the other hand, though more time-consuming, is the preferred manner of exposition or explanation of a text based on a careful, objective analysis of its grammar, syntax, and setting.

Here is a simple illustration of a JIGSAW. You shake the over 1000 pieces out of the box and as you slowly fit it together it forms a wonderful face (the face of Christ). The unalterable picture is already there, you don't need to add or take away any pieces. So the 1,189 chapters of the Bible all form the complete picture of Christ with whom we can have a face-to-face relationship (Gal 4:19). The light of the Holy Spirit (like the sunlight falling on our jigsaw) will only serve to make the pieces and the colours clearer but will not alter the picture - just reveal Christ to us more fully from scripture. But sects and cults have the pieces turned on the obverse side on which there is a contrasting dull picture featuring themselves as an organisation, their buildings or logo. There is only artificial light shining in this case.

E. *ENGAGE*

At this point, we may feel, to at least some extent, that we have mastered the text, but we need to let the text *master us*. The purpose of engaging what you learn is in order to become more like Jesus. Engage with the passage you are considering with a view to employing (implementing, applying) the meaning into your own life. How? Take time to meditate on the meaning.

J. I. Packer says that meditation is "the practice of turning each truth we learn about God into matter for reflection before God, leading to prayer and praise to God. .... It is an activity of holy thought, consciously performed in the presence of God, under the eye of God, by the help of God, as a means of communion with God". (Knowing God).

Reading the Bible without meditating on it is like trying to eat without swallowing. Chew key phrases over, especially with a view to implementing, that is, engaging at least one 'action point', the same day, if possible, to your specific circumstances of life. This would include situations at work, home, school, or church. Can you share a recent insight with someone? Why not start a personal journal of reflections? Note therein any specific points that God opens to you.

A word of caution, however. Hebrews 4:12 tells us that, "the word of God is alive and active. Sharper than any double-edged sword, it penetrates even to dividing soul and spirit, joints and marrow; it judges the thoughts and attitudes of the heart". Treating God's Word like a warm and cuddly toy when it is really a double-edged sword would be condescending. So come to the Bible ready to be challenged, to be brought to your knees, to be asked to change – not just in external behaviour, but internal attitudes. Turn the things you have learned, and wish to engage with, into prayers. Thank God for his greatness and love.

In Summary

The takeaway is that this GRACE personal study method emphasises prayerful consideration of the context and Christ. If you want a similar but reduced form of this approach, you could use the alliteration **C**-**C**-**C**, representing Context + Christ + Character. Later in this course, in Unit 4 (Q11), you will have the opportunity to put the GRACE study method into practice. A few final tips:

- Find a plan that fits you. Avoid focusing so much on the mechanics of the process that you miss the Person behind it.

- Choose a place and time when you can concentrate. For many this is first thing in the morning. But you don't need hours. Just 15-30 minutes is fine. Decide to begin today.

- Don't beat yourself up if you fail at first; rather than feel angry, feel hungry! Remember, God really loves you. He wants to meet with you. Don't focus on guilt for not "paying your dues" to God. Instead, in whatever time you have, focus on receiving his love and expressing your devotion to him – praising him. Soon you will find yourself feeling less guilty and more excited about meeting with God.

Whatever personal study method you adopt, may it help you to enjoy your Lord and to break out in spontaneous praise to His glorious name. "Be constantly growing in the sphere of grace and an experiential knowledge of our Lord and Saviour Jesus Christ. To Him be glory both now and to the day of eternity" (2 Pet 3:18, K. Wuest). So, fittingly, our next two units (**3**-a,b,c & **4**- a,b,c) will consider questions relating to God and Christ.

> *"A Bible that's falling apart*
> *usually belongs to someone who isn't".*
> *- C Spurgeon*

Prayer

O Lord, as I open the scriptures today, open my heart to your words of truth. May your words come alive within me. Help me make your words the very fabric of my life as they heal, teach, inspire, restore, and cleanse my heart. May you help me to grow and learn so that I may bring your light, O Lord, to the world. Amen.

DIGGING DEEPER - HOW DO YOU STUDY THE BIBLE?

Scan the QR code for informative links to each of these questions.

1. What is the **goal** of Bible Study?

2. Explain the differences between formal equivalence, functional equivalence, and paraphrase Bibles. Which **Bible versions** do you prefer?

WORD-FOR-WORD Formal Equivalence	MEANING-FOR-MEANING Closest Natural Equivalence	THOUGHT-FOR-THOUGHT Functional Equivalence	PARAPHRASE Retelling
NASB KJV TRB ESV NKJV	GW	NIV CSB NLT	NIRV MSG CEV

CSB	Christian Standard Bible	KJV	King James Version
CEV	Contemporary English Version	MSG	The Message
ESV	English Standard Version	NASB	New American Standard Bible
GW	GOD'S WORD Translation	NIRV	New International Reader's Version

NIV	New International Version
NKJV	New King James Version
NLT	New Living Translation
TRB	The Readable Bible

3 **a**. What is the **OIA** Inductive Bible Study?
   b. What is the **GRACE** Bible Study Method?

4 Which of these 12 **Bible tools** would you recommend?

Bible.org	Crosswire	Lumina
Biblehub	Desiring God	Steps
Blueletter	Got Questions	Studybible
Carm	Logos	Studylight

5 How are these scriptures often taken out of **context**?
   E.g. 1. "For where two or three are gathered in my name, there am I among them". – Matt 18:20
   E.g. 2. "Judge not, that you be not judged". – Matt 7:1

See Suggested Answers at the end of this book.

Action Point

The QR link has a list of daily Bible reading plans. Which one do you prefer to try?

**By Him [Christ] all things were created
in all their complexity - Col 1:16-17**

Q7. DOES GOD EXIST?

Theism, atheism, agnosticism? Where do you align yourself presently? Or are you undecided? After all, belief in God is a deeply personal and subjective matter, and there is no one definitive line of evidence that can be used to prove the existence of a deity to convince everyone. Those who do believe find sufficient evidence, ranging from personal experience and feelings of spiritual connection to philosophical arguments, scientific evidence and religious texts.

Sadly, there are both unbelievers and believers who outspokenly accuse, even ridicule, those taking an opposing view, calling them delusional and irrational. Of course, it is your right to firmly hold an opinion, but should our personal viewpoint descend to insulting others or expressing ridicule? For example, if someone is dedicated to the philosophical idea that nothing can exist outside of the natural realm (ie. no supernatural God), no amount of evidence, especially if presented in a contemptuous manner, could convince them otherwise because anything which God might have done - any supernatural act which might serve as evidence for His existence - would have to be explained away in terms of natural causes. So, we sometimes hear of the ten plagues in Egypt, Jesus' miracles, or even the resurrection of Jesus, being given a naturalistic spin. But that is their right to hold such an opinion, and the same goes for those in the opposing camp. C. S. Lewis, for example, reasons, "When you are arguing against God you are arguing against the very power that makes you able to argue at all".

In our short discussion today, time will only allow us to touch very lightly on three lines of 'evidence' that many believers in God find personally convincing: *causation*, *complexity*, and *conscience*.

1. CAUSATION

This is often called the *cosmological* argument. Discoveries in astronomy have shown beyond a reasonable doubt that the **universe did have a beginning**. This is underscored by the second law of *thermodynamics*[31], the *radiation echo* of the

---

[31] **Thermodynamics** is the field of physics that deals with the relationship between heat and other properties (such as pressure, density, temperature, etc.) in a substance. A creationist

'big bang' (known as the cosmic microwave background (CMB), provides strong evidence for the expanding universe), and *Einstein's* theory of relativity. Although we await total confirmation of the 'big bang' theory, this does not alter the fact that the universe has had a beginning.

This inevitably leads to the kalam[32] cosmological argument: **whatever has a beginning has a cause**. One of the earliest formulations is in the Islamic philosophical tradition comes from Al-Ghazali, who expressed it in his way: "Every being which begins has a cause for its beginning; now the world is a being which begins; therefore, it possesses a cause for its beginning".

Visualise a railway train. Each car is being pulled by the car in front of it. The "cause" of movement for any car is the next car ahead. However, if the train were extended forward infinitely, how could it be moving? If the train has an unending succession of cars, nothing would provide force to move the cars. At some point, there must be an engine - something that pulls but is not itself being pulled. In other words, causes and effects.

Experience teaches us that nothing comes into existence out of nothing. Simply put, if some assert there was a big bang – what went bang? How did life come from non-life? William Lane Craig wrote, "To suggest that things could just pop into being uncaused out of nothing is to quit doing serious metaphysics and to resort to magic" (Reasonable Faith, p. 111). Or, as the apostle Paul asserted, "By faith we understand that the universe was created by the word of God, so that what is seen was not made out of things that are visible" (Heb 11:3).

Someone told this imaginary story: A scientist argued with God. "You're not the only creator," he declared. "I also can make a man". So God said, "Let's see you do it". The man walked over to some dirt. But God stopped him and said, "Get your own dirt!" Creating is making something out of nothing; manufacturing is making something out of something else! Only God can create.

---

would point out that the Second Law can be stated in many different ways, eg that the entropy of the universe tends towards a maximum (in simple terms, entropy is a measure of disorder); usable energy is running out; information tends to get scrambled; order tends towards disorder; a random jumble won't organise itself.

[32] **Kalam.** A part of the reasoning is something cannot come from nothing – that would sound more like magic. If something can come into being from nothing, then it becomes inexplicable why just anything or everything doesn't come into being from nothing. Think about it: why don't bicycles, Beethoven, and beer just pop into being from nothing? Why is it only universes that can come into being from nothing? What makes nothingness so discriminatory? There can't be anything about nothingness that favours universes, for nothingness doesn't have any properties. Nor can anything constrain nothingness, for there isn't anything to be constrained!

2. COMPLEXITY

This is often called the **teleological**[33] argument. Teleology is a broad category that includes several narrower ideas, namely: *fine-tuning*[34], *intelligent design*[35], and *irreducible complexity.*[36] Teleological arguments suggest that God's deliberate choices are the most reasonable explanations for certain observations. Some marry intelligent design with irreducible complexity. In other words, life comprises intertwined parts that rely on each other to be useful.

i.   An **eye** is only a useful system if all its parts are present and functioning properly at the same time. The complexity of creation is a massive problem for those who deny the existence of God.

ii. The **DNA**. Molecular biology has revealed vast amounts of information encoded in each and every living cell and thousands upon thousands of exquisitely designed machines at the molecular level. Information requires intelligence, and design requires a designer.

iii. The **bacterial flagellum** are helical filaments, each with a rotary motor at its base which can turn clockwise or counter-clockwise. What are the possibilities that this biological motor arose by chance? The figure is asserted to be 1 in 2^{234} (2 followed by 234 zeros). But given enough time, could such a device occur by chance? Let's say that every atom in the universe is devoted to the sole task of evolving the bacterial flagellum at the fastest

---

[33] **Teleology** is the study of evidence of design in nature; the fact or character attributed to nature or natural processes of being directed toward an end or shaped by a purpose. This argument has been formulated in various ways throughout history, with the most famous version being William Paley's watchmaker analogy.

[34] **Fine-tuning** arguments focus on the universe's specific nature and how it appears to have been carefully arranged to allow for intelligent life. According to the fine-tuning argument, the exact quantity of each physical constant and the respective ratios must all be precise as they are in order for life to exist. In most cases, the tiniest change to one of these constants would not only prohibit life as we know it, but it would also make most forms of matter impossible.

[35] **Intelligent design** is the theory that intelligent causes are necessary to explain biology's complex, information-rich structures and that these causes are empirically evidenced. Even the atheist zoologist Richard Dawkins says that intuitively, "Biology is the study of complicated things that give the appearance of having been designed for a purpose".

[36] **Irreducible complexity** is the argument that certain biological systems cannot have evolved by successive minor modifications to pre-existing functional systems through natural selection because no less complex system would function. Generally, the scientific community regards intelligent design as pseudoscience and rejects the concept of irreducible complexity.

possible speed physics allows since the literal beginning of time. The chances would be 10^{150}. And because 40 parts are necessary for its function, the flagella of this bacillus cannot simply have evolved gradually.

Perhaps you have heard of an illustration similar to the following. As you walk on the beach one day, you notice what looks like a number '7' shaped in the sand. Of course, you likely write it off as the motion of the waves and wind on the shore. The next day, however, you notice not just an image of a number in the sand but are amazed to observe a whole stanza of poetry neatly inscribed on the beach in evenly spaced lines. Do you now write off this ode as a natural oddity, or more likely, do you attribute the poem to *someone* (though presently unseen to you) having skilfully written it in the sand? Biochemists and mathematicians have calculated the odds against life arising from nonlife naturally via unintelligent processes. The odds are astronomical. If life did not occur by chance, how did it originate? Evolution[37] and the theories of abiogenesis[38] leave this unresolved.

Before we leave the beautiful complexity that we see in life around and within us, there is a fundamental question: What about beauty? Is it nothing more than a chemical reaction in the brain? Is the beauty of a sunset and wonder of a newborn baby's precious life somehow a chance by-product of the survival of the fittest?

3. CONSCIENCE
If you believe in right and wrong and then ask yourself - why? Who gave you your conscience? Why does it exist?

---

[37] **Evolution**. When many Christians say they don't believe in evolution, they are not talking about microevolution, a credibly scientific phenomenon. Instead, they are usually referring to macroevolution that requires the introduction of new genetic information. No amount of rearrangement, corruption or loss of existing genetic information will produce macroevolution. There are also Christians who are evolutionary creationists, calling into question the Genesis 1-3 account and the words at Hebrews 11:3, "By faith we understand that the universe was created by the word of God, so that what is seen was not made out of things that are visible".

[38] **Abiogenesis** is the idea that life arose from nonlife more than 3.5 billion years ago on earth. Abiogenesis proposes that the first life forms generated were very simple and, through a gradual process, became increasingly complex. Biogenesis, in which life is derived from the reproduction of other life, was presumably preceded by abiogenesis, which became impossible once earth's atmosphere assumed its present composition. Although many equate abiogenesis with the archaic theory of spontaneous generation, the two ideas are quite different.

This is often called the *moral* argument.[39] You could argue that murder is bad not because of God but because it hurts society. But we could, in turn, ask, why is hurting society bad? Let's raise a hypothetical situation. Suppose the Nazis had won World War II and successively generation after *generation, were taught from childhood that killing Jews, gipsies, black people, and disabled people was the right thing to do to preserve the gene pool. If society adopted this way of thinking, would such killing then indeed be 'right' and moral? If morality was built just from society, then anyone's standard is no better than someone else's.*

C.S. Lewis, in his book 'Mere Christianity,' and elsewhere, raised a different argument - that of our **desires**. *He posited that all natural desires have* a natural object. One thirsts and there exists water to quench this thirst; one hungers and there exists food to satisfy this hunger. He then argued that the human desire for perfect justice, peace, happiness, and other intangibles, strongly implies the existence of such things, though they seem unobtainable on earth. He further stated that the unquenchable desires of this life strongly imply that we are intended for a different life, necessarily governed by a God who can provide the desired intangibles.

Finally, people of every race, creed, colour, and culture claim to have personally experienced something of the supernatural. Ignorance and imagination may have played a part, to be sure, but is there something more?

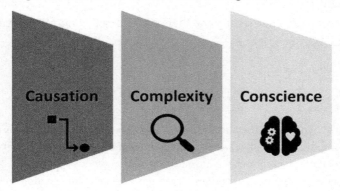

---

[39] **Moral Argument** holds that the existence of morality, including our sense of right and wrong, points to the existence of a moral lawgiver or God, who is the source of objective moral values and duties. Critics argue that naturalistic or evolutionary processes can explain the existence of morality and that there is no need to appeal to a divine being to explain it. Ultimately, whether or not the existence of morality proves the existence of God is a matter of personal belief and interpretation.

CONCLUSION

Former atheist Lee Strobel commented, "Essentially, I realized that to stay an atheist, I would have to believe that nothing produces everything; non-life produces life; *randomness produces fine-tuning*; chaos produces information; unconsciousness produces consciousness; and non-reason produces reason. Those leaps of faith were simply too big for me to take, especially in light of the affirmative case for God's existence ... In other words, in my assessment, the Christian worldview accounted for the totality of the evidence much better than the atheistic worldview".

So, is there a God? Causation, complexity, and conscience cry out in the affirmative. Personally, I believe there is, and that He has revealed himself to us, not only in **creation**, and the **Bible**, but even more specifically in the person of **Jesus Christ**. After all, it is by Him [Christ] that all things were created in all their complexity (Col 1:16-17).

To end on a note of humour. Comedian Frank Skinner related, "I have friends who are atheists. There's this mate of mine. He says, 'It's such rubbish. Come back to my flat, and I'll make a cup of tea, and we'll talk the whole thing through.' So I go back with him and he puts the kettle on. 'The thing is, Frank, the universe – it just happened. A big bang, an accident, no one made it happen. There's no great designer, no thought went into it or planning, it just happened – do you get it? ... Anyway, that cup of tea won't make itself.' ..... I said, 'Why not?'"

In our next article in this three-part unit, we will continue our discussion of God by asking the question, is He "One or Many"? Is God a trinity?

"You may deny the existence of God, but always remember that God will never deny being your loving Father".
- Gift Gugu Mona

Digging Deeper - Does God Exist?

Scan the QR code for informative links to each of these questions.

1. Where does the **Bible** attempt to prove that God exists?

2. What facts impress you about the **bacterial flagellum?**

3. What is there about structure of the **DNA** that convinces you that we have a designer?

4. If evolution doesn't explain the origin of life itself, does **abiogenesis**?

5. When someone **questions the existence** of God, what should we try and ascertain?

See Suggested Answers at the end of this book.

Action Point

Do you remember the THREE 'C' lines of evidence we considered?
Could you relate and discuss them with a friend?

Prayer

How about framing your own prayer, praising Him as the majestic Creator?
You may wish to view two links to music videos in the QR code.

"What God was the Word was" - John 1:1, NEB; NET footnote

Q8. ONE OR MANY?

In today's society, many consider themselves **atheistic**, an absence of any belief in any gods. Others call themselves '**spiritual**,' in contrast to being religious. 'Spiritual' is a broad term but generally means holding a strong connection, to yourself, to the earth, and all its inhabitants. Perhaps, though, you have a deep desire to **know God** more fully, to worship him in spirit and truth.

In this section, we will study the question of who God is, more specifically, whether He is one or many. What do various *religions* teach? What are three major *concepts*? Finally, we will reflect on a few key *scriptures*.

We must start by agreeing with the statement of Elihu, "Take a long, hard look. See how great he is—infinite, greater than anything you could ever imagine or figure out!" (Job 36:26 Message; also, Job 11:7-9; 26:14; 37:23). Although one day we will see Him as he really is, now in the present, would it not be presumptuous to dogmatically assert that our limited definitions and dogmas are perfect, inerrant? After all, God exists outside the confines of our time and space dimensions. God operates and exists in ways beyond our experience and comprehension.

Naturally, you are free to see different sides and reach your own conclusions. We hopefully have escaped the manipulative mind control of cults. Have you, though, ever found yourself reacting to contrary opinions with inflexible *automatic learned responses*[40] based on your *preconceived ideas,* or indoctrination? How much better to listen nonjudgmentally with the spirit of an open mind – after all, you could be wrong on this matter! Avoid derogatively feuding over words with an air of theological smugness. "Warn them before God to stop their useless bickering over words. After all, splitting hairs does no good; it only ruins those forced to listen to their meritless arguments" (2 Tim 2:14, Voice).

Or, an associated trap, at this stage, is to become so wrapped up in *analysis*, *definitions*, and absorbing heaps of *information* that we lose sight of our goal – that of receiving and reflecting, a love relationship with our Father through Jesus by the Holy Spirit. So, with those advisories in mind, we can begin by presenting

---

[40] **Automatic learned responses** are conditioned reactions learned through repetition, positive reinforcement, negative reinforcement, or punishments.

a sample summary in chart form of alternative *religious* opinions about who God is.

	WHO IS GOD?
BUDDHISM	No belief in a personal God; but rather 'gods' as supernatural entities who can bestow benefits such as health or wealth.
CHRISTADELPHIAN	Reject the trinity; God created Christ who had a sinful nature.
CHRISTIANITY	Trinitarian: Father, Son, and Spirit are one in essence, but exist eternally in three distinct persons; monotheistic.
CHRISTIAN SCIENCE	Pantheistic; God is not a deity, but an all-embracing force or principle living in everything.
IGLESIA NI CRISTO	Rejects the traditional Christian belief in the Trinity as heresy, adopting a version of unitarianism.
HINDUISM	Belief both in one God and many gods expressing this one Deity; combination of monotheism, polytheism, and pantheism.
ISLAM	Allah, the one true God; monotheists, no secondary gods.
JEHOVAH'S WITNESSES	Jehovah is almighty God, who is worshipped; Jesus a lesser mighty god, an archangel, but not worshipped.
JUDAISM	There is only one God (name left unspoken), monotheistic; no other gods.
MORMONS	God, once a man, now exalted, living near star Kolob; Father, Son, Holy Ghost are three separate Gods (tritheism), so deny the trinity.
NEW AGE	An impersonal force in everything.
SCIENTOLOGY	No set dogma about God; only by reaching to the eighth dynamic (infinity) can one's relationship to the Supreme Being be fully understood.

Most Christians reason that if God isn't three in one, then he couldn't have loved until he created other beings, since love is between two beings. They conclude that within God there is a community of persons enjoying each other. Marriage is a picture of this. Let's try unwrapping just three major concepts about God and an example of each:

a. **Monotheism**. One true God is recognised and worshipped; *all other gods are regarded as false* — whether just human fantasies or demons pretending to be

Unit 3: God

gods. Islam and Judaism are monotheistic. Mainstream Christians, in that they define the trinity as recognising only one true God, though in three persons, are also monotheistic. They believe that all three equally possess 'God-ness,' divine nature, reasoning that Adam and Eve were separate persons yet of the same human nature as "one flesh". And just as submission doesn't make a wife less human than her husband, nor does submission make Jesus less God than the Father.

b. **Polytheism** describes belief systems in which *several gods are acknowledged and worshipped*. Throughout the course of human history, polytheistic religions of one sort or another have been the dominant majority. For example, the classic Greek, Roman, Indian, and Norse religions were all polytheisms.

c. **Henotheism** (commonly called monolatry) has been described by some as a variant type of polytheism in which just a single God is worshipped but *where other lesser gods[41] are accepted as existing elsewhere, but not to be worshipped*. Many tribal religions fall into this category. Some would argue that Jehovah's Witnesses also do because they assert that there are other gods like Jesus ("a

---

[41] **Lesser gods**. In the context of the OT, the term "elohim" is used to describe a range of powerful beings, including God, angels, and even human judges. However, it is clear from the overall biblical narrative and the teachings of mainstream Christian churches that there is only one true God who is the creator and ruler of all things. The mainstream Christian belief in monotheism rests, for example, on Deuteronomy 6:4, it is written: "Hear, O Israel: The Lord our God, the Lord is one". This belief in the oneness of God is affirmed in the Nicene Creed, which declares belief in "one God, the Father Almighty". The mainstream Christian view is that there is only one true God, and all other beings, including angels, are subordinate to him.

A quick read of Psalm 82 informs us that God (Elohim, here singular) called a council meeting to judge the elohim (plural) for the corrupt rule of the nations. Verse 6 of the psalm declares that these elohim are sons of God. God says to them: I have said, "You are gods [elohim], and sons of the Most High [beney elyon], all of you". These corrupt elohim are sentenced to die like humans (v. 7). In English, the word 'god' tends to be used very narrowly. It is most often used in specific reference to the god of the Bible, usually called simply 'God' (ie, YHWH, the God of Israel). In Hebrew, the word elohim essentially means "strengths" or "powers," This word-family (e.g., 'elohim, 'eloah, 'el, 'elah) has a wide semantic range.

Psalm 82:5 could literally be read as: "Powers stands in the assembly of power; he judges among the powers". But which powers? There are a number of views: (a) The council or assembly refers to the Canaanite religion's pagan gods (Deut 4:28; 1Kings 11:33); (b) human judges to represent God but who became corrupt (Exod 4:16; 7:1 [as god, or like a god LXX]; 21:6; 22:8-9; cf. John 10.33-35) or, (c) as angelic beings (Ps 8:6 LXX; Isa 14:12-15).

god"- John 1:1), angels, Moses, and the devil[42], but not to be worshipped. Mainstream Christianity, though, assert that the other 'gods,' like idols, are false and not approved by the Lord, YHWH. Psalm 96:4-5 reads, "For great is the Lord, and greatly to be praised; He is to be feared above all gods. For all the gods of the peoples are idols, But the Lord made the heavens". There will be opportunity to examine a few more scriptures on this matter later. The best recommendation is to read the New Testament for yourself – preferably from a translation that may be new to you, perhaps the Amplified Translation, New American Standard Bible, NET Bible, or the New Living Translation, etc.

Here are a final three Scriptures to think over regarding the identity of God. We are not studying them in depth here but showing that alternative interpretations exist to consider. As you deliberate over the context, can you think of arguments and counterarguments for these texts?

1. The Holy Spirit?

How were Barnabas and Saul (Paul) selected for the first missionary journey? "While they were serving the Lord and fasting, the *Holy Spirit said*, "Set Barnabas and Saul apart for Me for the work to which I have called them" (**Acts 13:2**).

Did the Holy Spirit speak? Later, what triple guidance did the apostolic band receive on their second missionary journey? "And they went through the region of Phrygia and Galatia, having been forbidden by the *Holy Spirit* to speak the word in Asia. And when they had come up to Mysia, they attempted to go into Bithynia, but the Spirit of *Jesus* did not allow them. So, passing by Mysia, they went down to Troas. And a vision appeared to Paul in the night: a man of Macedonia was standing there, urging him, and saying, "Come over to Macedonia and help us". And when Paul had seen the vision, immediately we sought to go on into Macedonia, concluding that *God* had called us to preach the gospel to them" (Acts 16:6-10).

The brothers were obviously being guided – but how? By the Spirit, or/and Jesus, or/and God? How would you reason on this? You may also notice the different ways the Spirit is referred to in the following scriptures: Romans 8:9-11; Galatians 4:6; 1 Peter 1:11.

2. Jesus Christ?

When Thomas saw his resurrected Lord and evidence of his crucifixion, he exclaimed: "My Lord and my God!" (**John 20:28**). Compare a footnote in the

---

[42] **Devil.** Since Christadelphians do not believe in either the devil or the Holy Spirit as persons, they are forced to admit that the only passage where the devil is called a god (2 Cor 4:4) is to be classed as figurative language, like idols are called gods.

Jehovah's Witnesses RNWT reference Bible with a footnote from the NET Bible. First, the RNWT:

> Thomas may have addressed Jesus as "my God" for the following reasons: He viewed Jesus as being "a god" though not the almighty God. (See study note on Joh 1:1.) Or he may have addressed Jesus in a manner similar to the way that servants of God addressed angelic messengers of Jehovah, as recorded in the Hebrew Scriptures. Thomas would have been familiar with accounts in which individuals, or at times the Bible writer of the account, responded to or spoke of an angelic messenger as though he were Jehovah God. (Compare Ge 16:7-11, 13; 18:1-5, 22-33; 32:24-30; Jg 6:11-15; 13:20-22.) Therefore, Thomas may have called Jesus "my God" in this sense, acknowledging Jesus as the representative and spokesman of the true God.

Alternatively, now the note in the NET Bible:

> "Thomas' statement, while it may have been an exclamation, does in fact confess the faith which he had previously lacked, and Jesus responds to Thomas' statement in the following verse as if it were a confession. With the proclamation by Thomas here, it is difficult to see how any more profound analysis of Jesus' person could be given. It echoes 1:1 and 1:14 together: The Word was God, and the Word became flesh (Jesus of Nazareth). The Fourth Gospel opened with many other titles for Jesus: the Lamb of God (1:29, 36); the Son of God (1:34, 49); Rabbi (1:38); Messiah (1:41); the King of Israel (1:49); the Son of Man (1:51). Now the climax is reached with the proclamation by Thomas, "My Lord and my God," and the reader has come full circle from 1:1, where the author had introduced him to who Jesus was, to 20:28, where the last of the disciples has come to the full realization of who Jesus was".

3. Deity?

Paul, in the book of Colossians, focuses on the supremacy of Christ and our submission to him. Let's look at **Colossians 2:9** from two contrasting translations; noting the words I have italicized.

"See to it that no one takes you captive by philosophy and empty deceit, according to human tradition, according to the elemental spirits of the world, and not according to Christ. For in him the whole fullness of *deity* dwells bodily" (ESV).

"Look out that no one takes you captive by means of the philosophy and empty deception according to human tradition, according to the elementary things of the world and not according to Christ; because it is in him that all the fullness of the *divine quality* dwells bodily" (RNWT)

A footnote in the RNWT reference Bible reads,

> "The "divine quality" includes all the excelling qualities of Jesus' heavenly Father and God, and these also dwell in Christ. The Greek word (the·o'tes), which occurs only here in the Christian Greek Scriptures, is derived from the Greek word for "god," the·os', but is different in meaning. Many lexicons give such definitions as "divine character; divine nature; divinity". The term was used by ancient Greek writers to describe a quality or condition that could be obtained or lost as a result of one's behavior. Obviously, then, such a term was applied to created beings and not exclusively to the almighty and eternal God, Jehovah. So there is solid basis for rendering the·o'tes to refer to a divine quality rather than to God himself". (NB. In the Watchtower's own Greek translation (KIT, 1985 edition) the word theiotes is rendered 'divinity' in the literal English translation under the Greek text).

Now compare this with Vine's Expository Dictionary, just one of the lexicons defining this word:

> "Theiotes [Rom 1:20] ... divinity ... is to be distinguished from theotes, in Colossians 2:9, "Godhead" ... [in this passage] Paul is declaring that in the Son there dwells all the fullness of absolute Godhead; they were no mere rays of Divine glory which gilded Him, lighting up His Person for a season and with a splendor not His own; but He was, and is, absolute and perfect God; and the Apostle uses theotes to express this essential and personal Godhead of the Son" (Vines, Vol 1, pp.328-329).

Additionally, reading prayerfully through Isaiah 48:16-17 and Hebrews chapter 1 has given many pause for thought regarding the deity of Christ.[43]

---

[43] **Deity of Christ**. To look at just one expression today from Heb 1:3, when describing Jesus, it says, "He is the radiance [apaugasma] of His glory". A possible translation of the word can be 'reflection' and so the NWT and the NRSV render it, "He is the *reflection* of God's glory"- but by far most translations use words like radiance, brightness, or beaming, for example, JW's Greek Interlinear says, "beaming forth light"; Byington - "beam of his glory"; Vincent - "out-raying"; NET - "radiance of his glory". We could reason that light beams forth from a torch, but that is not a reflection, joy beams forth from a face, and that is not a reflection. 'Apaugasma', radiance, is what is in the person coming out. Jesus is no mere pale reflection in a mirror, but from his very being, he shines forth that which is God, as the sun emits rays. "The Person of the Son is thus represented, not as of one apart from God, irradiated by His glory, but as Himself the sheen of his glory". (The Pulpit Commentary) "I do not separate Christ from God more than a voice from the speaker or a beam from the sun. Christ is the voice of the speaker. He and the Father are the same thing, as the beam and the light, are

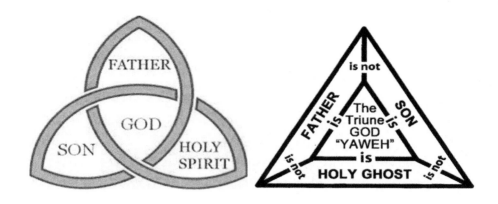

Does this mean that we must accept the Trinity as essential to become saved?

Did the Samaritan woman, having left Jesus at the well, run into the city telling everyone about systematic theology? She simply expressed her discovery of Christ. There is no theology exam on which a person needs a passing score before God will accept that person's trust in him for salvation. We are saved by God's grace through faith, that is, through our trust and reliance on God's gift of salvation in Christ (Rom 3:21-26; Eph 2:8-10; Titus 3:5-8).

On the other hand, deviation from the basics[44] of sound Christian doctrine can be evidence that a person is either immature in faith (see Acts 18:25-26) or has not genuinely come into a saving faith relationship with Christ (Rom. 16:17-18). We should always approach a study of such matters prayerfully as a truth seeker because, as I'm sure you will agree, we are to keep growing in our understanding, and this takes time.

"The amazing grace of the Master, Jesus Christ, the extravagant love of God, the intimate friendship of the Holy Spirit, be with all of you" (2 Cor 13:14 Message).

Next? God - What is His Name and Nature?

---

the same light". (Michael Servetus, a Spanish physician and theologian, was executed for his anti-trinitarian views!) Some would go further in reasoning that the brightness issuing from the sun is the same nature to that of the sun; it is of as long continuance as the sun: and though the brightness cannot be separated from the sun, they are distinct from one another.

[44] **Basic doctrine**. The more important things are written down for us in 1 Corinthians 15:1-8. Our attention is drawn to the expression 'en protos' in verse 3, rendered in many translations as "of first importance". Or, as the Contemporary English Version reads, "I told you the most important part of the message exactly as it was told to me". See also Hebrews 5:12; 6:1, where the elementary things and the primary doctrine of the Christ are referred to without mention of the trinity.

Prayer

'O the depth of the riches of both your wisdom and knowledge Lord! How unsearchable are your judgments, and inscrutable your ways!' You are both incomprehensible and knowable at the same time. I praise you my Lord for revealing so much about yourself through your written Word so that I have come to know you personally. Thank you that you have multiplied your grace and peace in my life.

"Bring me a worm that can comprehend a man, and then I will show you a man that can comprehend the Triune God".
- John Wesley

Digging Deeper - One or Many?

Scan the QR code for informative links to each of these questions.

1. Can you name at least four 'Christian' **denominations** that do NOT believe the Trinity?

2. **a.** How would you **define the trinity**? Does it mean that the Father, Son, and Holy Spirit are parts of God? Could we illustrate the trinity by using the example of a 3 elders Bishopric (LDS) or a 3 elders Service Committee (JWs)?

   b. What is **modalism**?

3. What would you say to the objection, "The trinity teaching is both illogical and **incomprehensible**"?
   Please watch the *second* video "The Trinity Explained" in this series of twelve.

4. Would you say that the trinity is taught in the **New Testament or by the early church fathers**?
   Please watch "The Trinity in the NT," the *fourth* video in the same series referred to in Q3 above.

5. **a.** What is **henotheism**?

   b. But isn't **Satan** called the "god of this world" in 2 Corinthians 4:4?

See Suggested Answers at the end of this book.

Action Point

Jot down your responses to these seven Jehovah's Witnesses key objections to the trinity: (a) the word, "Trinity" is not in the Bible; (b) the Trinity is derived from pagan sources; (c) the church Fathers did NOT believe in the doctrine of the Trinity. (d) the trinity doctrine did not emerge until fourth century; (e) the Early Christian church fell into Complete Apostasy after the death of the Apostles; (f) the Trinity is three separate Gods; (g) the trinity is illogical.

Q9. WHAT IS HIS NAME AND NATURE?

Do you wish to know God more intimately? That's the overall purpose of this simplified course - to deepen our relationship with the Father and Son. To know God, to have a personal present acquaintance with the great unseen reality who is God, as his regenerate loved children, is our goal, not merely to sort through various opinions or religious creeds (Job 42:1-6; Ps 63:1; Hos 6:1-3; Heb 12:22-24).

Let's start with the names of God. In the Bible, the word 'name'[45] is usually more than just a label but identifies a person's character and reputation – who they are: Noah means one who brings relief and comfort; Anna means grace; Isaac means laughter; Leah ... weary. What about the names of God?[46]

There are in fact, dozens of ways in which the people of Israel referred to the transcendent God, like Creator, Elohim, El Shaddai, El Roi, Adonai, Saviour, Redeemer, and so on. But the distinctive name, Yahweh appears thousands of times in the OT, derived from the four Hebrew consonant YHWH[47]. What do these four Hebrew letters mean? Take a look at Exodus 3:14-15. "Then Moses asked God, "If I go to the Israelites and say to them: The God of your fathers has sent me to you, and they ask me, 'What is His name?' what should I tell them?"

---

[45] **Name**. We use a name as little more than a distinguishing mark or label to differentiate one person from another. But in the ancient world, a name signified not only the person's identity, but the inherent character of the person designated by the name. In ancient times, one's whole character (reputation, person, and authority) was implied in the name (Matt 1:21; Mark 3:17; John 17:26; 3 John 7). In the earlier period of Biblical history, names were given to children at birth which often reflected the circumstances associated with their birth or the feelings of the father or the mother. But later, Hebrew boys were named when they were circumcised on the eighth day (Luke 1:59; 2:21). There were times when parents received divine direction about the name to be given to their children. Among those getting their names in this way were Ishmael (God hears) - Gen 16:11; Isaac (laughter) - Gen 17:19; Solomon (from a root meaning "peace") - 1 Chron 22:9.

[46] **Names of God** – a chart summary; see the Additional Information in Question document linked to this article.

[47] **YHWH**. See the Additional Information in Question document linked to this article.

God replied to Moses, "I AM WHO I AM. This is what you are to say to the Israelites: I AM (הָיָה *ha.yah*) has sent me to you" (HCSB).

This phrase "I AM" refers to God's *constant presence* in all eternity. He has always been, is and always will be, present and involved with people. Now notice a few verses later, God said, "Go and assemble the elders of Israel and say to them: Yahweh (יְהֹוָה *ye.ho.vah*) the God of your fathers, the God of Abraham, Isaac, and Jacob, has appeared to me". This name speaks of God's revelation of His majesty and glory; His progressively communicating, interconnecting with men.

This name Yahweh uses the same Hebrew letters as "I am" to mean "He is". So, God says of himself, "I am," and we say of Him, "He is". The NET Bible comments:

> "Some commentators argue for a future tense translation, "I will be who I will be". ... But a translation of "I will be" does not effectively do much more except restrict it to the future. The idea of the verb would certainly indicate that God is not bound by time, and while he is present ("I am") he will always be present, even in the future, and so "I am" would embrace that as well (see also Ruth 2:13; Ps 50:21; Hos 1:9). The Greek translation of the OT used a participle to capture the idea, and several times in the Gospels Jesus used the powerful "I am" with this significance (eg, John 8:58). The point is that Yahweh is sovereignly independent of all creation and that his presence guarantees the fulfilment of the covenant (cf. Isa 41:4; 42:6, 8; 43:10-11; 44:6; 45:5-7). Others argue for a causative Hiphil translation of "I will cause to be," but nowhere in the Bible does this verb appear in Hiphil or Piel".

It is true to say that although we cannot ascertain the exact pronunciation of this name, it was never said as 'Jehovah.' Jehovah is a hybrid form of Yahweh originally used in the 13th century by a Spanish monk, Raymundo Martini, and first appeared in an English Bible in the 16th century. This is something like persistently calling a person *Howard* when their name is really *Harold*. So the name Yahweh is preferred by most scholars, rather than a popularised distortion like Jehovah.

As already noted, this name appears thousands of times as the four letters YHWH (tetragrammaton) in the Hebrew text of the OT. Many English translations render it as capitalised LORD and point out in their preface or footnote the original Hebrew tetragrammaton. Some view this as a deficiency in certain translations of the OT – perhaps so. However, the Jehovah's Witnesses inserted the name Jehovah 237 times in the Greek NT in their own Bible translation (RNWT 2013). For example, they render Romans 10:13 as "Everyone who calls on the name of Jehovah will be saved". They insist on this practice even though the

Tetragrammaton (YHWH) does not (with perhaps a dubious exception or two, see Question Sheet) occur in over 5,000 extant Greek manuscripts of the New Testament. Nor, we can add, does the name Jehovah occur even once in their own Greek Kingdom Interlinear translation. Greek New Testament manuscripts contain the Greek word Kyrios (Lord) in Old Testament quotes, where the Hebrew has the YHWH.

What name did Jesus use?

Whenever Jesus talked about God's "name," that name is always Father, not Yahweh. We see this clearly in John 14-17, where Jesus is quoted as referring to or addressing the 'Father' 50 times. Even in the NWT, the name Jehovah does not occur once anywhere in the High Priestly prayer of John 17, but rather six times Jesus spoke directly to "Father". The evidence indicates that when Jesus, for example, said, "I have manifested your name to the men whom you gave me out of the world" and "I have made your name known to them" (17:6,26), he was not telling them the tetragrammaton, Yahweh. Or as William Barclay explained, "He is saying: "I have enabled men to see what the real nature of God is like". It is, in fact, another way of saying: "He who has seen me has seen the father" (John 14:9). The Jews occasionally referred to God as Father before Jesus came, but Jesus was unique in making this practice central to the faith life of his disciples. Will this affect the way you pray to God?

What about the Nature or Character of God?

Three things are told to us in Scripture concerning the nature of God.

   i. 'God is **SPIRIT**,' therefore as a *person*, He has no visible substance (John 4:24).

   ii. 'God is **LIGHT**,' in *expression*, He has no darkness of evil dwelling in Him (1 John 1:5).

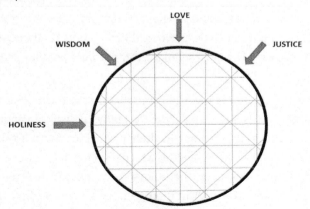

   iii. 'God is **LOVE**,' in *essence*, He is infinitely unselfish; beneficence flows from Him (1 John 4:8).

When we are brought back to God the Father, in fellowship with Him, we can start to enjoy real life, divine light, and divine love! We may enjoy God's nature.

We will just graze the very surface of God's united array of vast qualities. But first, please realise that God's being is not a mere collection of attributes added together, as though we could split off love from justice as more important. Rather God's whole being includes all of His attributes, like a rainbow, in entirety, in complete unity. In the diagram, imagine the vertical lines represent His love, the horizontal His holiness, one of the diagonal lines His wisdom, and another diagonal His Justice. We can add innumerable other lines, but we can see that each attribute is simply one aspect of God's total character or being. He himself is a unity, a completely integrated whole.

Let's go a little further to consider just three of God's **incommunicable** attributes; that is, His qualities which we do not share in common with Him. Later in the notes, you will have the opportunity to search out three of his many communicable attributes, that is, the qualities he does share with us. Here are listed three of the numerous incommunicable attributes we have started with the letter "I".

INDEPENDENT

He is *self-existent*. John 5:26 says, "He has life in Himself". God does not need us or the rest of creation for anything; He is self-sufficient (no need for food or sleep). Acts 17:24-25 makes this clear, "The God who made the world and everything in it, being Lord of heaven and earth, does not live in temples made by man, nor is he served by human hands, as though he needed anything, since he himself gives to all mankind life and breath and everything" (ESV). Note 'aseity' in Additional Information.

In contrast, we are dependent - dependent on God. He is the "I am" – eternal, always existing before creation. Without creation, God would still be infinitely loving, just, omniscient, and so forth.

INFINITE

This means He is *unlimited*. The infinite nature of God means that God exists outside of, and is not limited by, time or space. When God is referred to as infinite – without limits – terms are used like 'omniscience' (all-knowing), 'omnipotence' (all-powerful), and 'omnipresence' (always present). This indicates that God is so infinitely above and beyond us and our ability to comprehend Him fully, that, had He not revealed Himself, we would not know or understand what He is like. Although God is transcendent, infinite – he is also personal, wanting to draw close to us.

IMMUTABLE

The immutability of God means He is *unchanging*. This is taught throughout Scripture. For example, in Malachi 3:6, God affirms, "I the Lord do not change". Why must this be true? If anything changes, there must be a point in time before the change and a moment in time after the change. However, God is eternal and exists outside of the constraints of time. Also, if anything changes, it must change for the better or the worse, but since God is perfect, He does not need anything. Therefore, He cannot change for the better; cannot become more perfect, wiser, or 'improve with age'. Such a change would mean that He is not what He said He was eternally - God!

Independent – Infinite – Immutable. This is an infinite study that transcends our finite understanding. How grateful we are that Jesus reassures us, "All things have been handed over to Me by My Father; and no one knows the Son except the Father; nor does anyone know the Father except the Son, and *anyone to whom the Son determines to reveal Him*" (Matt 11:27). A theologian, Lenski (1864-1936), in commenting on this passage in Matthew, wrote, "Jesus here has reference to the "infants" mentioned in verse 25. ... They shall know with real experimental heart knowledge as children know their Father on the basis of all the manifestations of his fatherhood and his love. This is supreme spiritual blessedness but a closed book to the wise and intelligent of this world. Only by the Son's revelation can any man really know the Father and by no wisdom of his own". Then Lenski quotes Luther, "Here the bottom falls out of all merit, all powers and abilities of reason, all the free will men dream of, and it all counts nothing before God; Christ must do and must give everything". Jesus wills to reveal the Father only through his own person, work, and Word; for in no other way can a poor sinner ever come to know God.

As Romans 11:33-36 says, in describing the depths of God's wisdom and mercy in saving people of all nations through Christ, "We cannot wrap our minds around God's wisdom and knowledge! Its depths can never be measured! We cannot understand His judgments or explain the mysterious ways that He works! For, Who can fathom the mind of the Lord? Or who can claim to be His advisor? Or, Who can give to God in advance so that God must pay him back? For all that exists originates in Him, comes through Him, and is moving toward Him; so give Him the glory forever. Amen". (Voice) Can we not trust this Great God? The "I am"! Then pause now to give Him the glory!

"There (in the Psalms) ...
I find an experience fully God-centred,
asking of God no gift more urgently than His presence,
the gift of Himself, joyous to the highest degree,
and unmistakably real" - C S Lewis

Prayer

Abba Father, I love you because you are God, and there is no other. I love you because you first loved me, gave Jesus as a sacrifice and redeemed my life from sin and death. I love you in response to your great love - the only love that will never let go of me. Father, there's no safer place to be than in Christ - in life or in death. My heart will forever proclaim, "My God has done all things well". Please hear my prayer about..... I pray, with gratitude and humility, in Jesus' worthy name.

Digging Deeper - What is His Name and Nature?

Scan the QR code for informative links to each of these questions.

1. What is the **Name** which we hallow or sanctify in the Lord's Prayer?

2. Is the regular use of the name **Jehovah** a mark of true Christians?

3. What does "**a people for his Name**" mean in Acts 15:14 (17)?

4. Is there any **manuscript evidence** that indicates that the Hebrew name of God was used in the New Testament?
    a. How about the Greek Septuagint?
    b. What is the scroll from Nahal Hever?

5. A few questions about two of God's **communicable** attributes:
    a. God is **Holy** – what does holiness mean? How can we share in His holiness?
    b. God is **Love**. Should we say that God's love is unconditional? Do you agree with this preacher's conclusions?

See Suggested Answers at the end of this book.

Action Point

Paul wrote to the Galatians: "Because you are sons, God has sent the Spirit of his Son into our hearts, crying "Abba, Father!" So you are no longer a slave, but a son, and if a son, then an heir through God" (Gal 4:6–7). As a child of God, pray today to "Abba, Father" with a sense of intimacy and deep respect, pouring out your heart in praise and tell him about your chief concerns.

THE TRUTH
"No-one can say 'Jesus is Lord' except by the Holy Spirit" - 1 Cor 12:3

Q10. WHO IS JESUS?

Twenty centuries have passed, and today Jesus is still the central figure of the human race and all history. He continues to change the lives of millions, bringing them into a living relationship with Himself.

His biography was written in prophecy before he was born. Yet, he had no credentials but Himself. Consider that he never travelled more than 200 miles from the place he was born. He preached from a borrowed boat, borrowed a coin to make a point in a sermon, rode to Jerusalem on a borrowed donkey, has his final meal in a borrowed room, and was buried in a borrowed tomb (Matt 8:20).

Most accept that Jesus was unquestionably a man who lived in Israel 2,000 years ago. The debate begins with a discussion of Jesus' full identity. As we see from this chart, almost every major religion teaches that Jesus was a *prophet*, a *good teacher*, or a *godly man*. In this brief overview, we will refer to numerous scriptures you may wish to note for later consideration.

	Who is Jesus?
BUDDHISM	A good man
CHRISTADELPHIANS	No pre-existence; possessed a sinful nature
CHRISTIANITY	Eternal Son of God; affirms deity; died for our sins; to come again
CHRISTIAN SCIENCE	Deny his deity; his death was insufficient payment for sins
HINDUISM	A 'holy man;' an empowered incarnation
IGLESIA NI CRISTO	Jesus as God's highest creation; he is a man and denies his deity
ISLAM	A prophet, though less than Mohammed
JEHOVAH'S WITNESSES	The first created being; a lesser god; the archangel Michael
JUDAISM	A great teacher or false messiah
MORMONS	A created being; one of many sons of God
NEW AGE	A leader having the 'Christ spirit'
SCIENTOLOGY	A good teacher; deny sin atoning value of his death
WAY INTERNATIONAL	Deny the deity of Jesus Christ. He had no pre-existence

The question is, was he just a prophet, or a good teacher, or a godly man? The Bible tells us that Jesus was infinitely more than that. But first, we raise a related question:

Why focus on Jesus so much?

Firstly, because, in Jesus' words, "that all may honour the Son according as they honour the Father; he who is not honouring the Son, doth not honour the Father who sent him" (John 5:23, Youngs). Or, as the Expanded Bible renders this verse, "that all people will honor the Son *as much as* they honor the Father who sent him".[48]

Secondly, we need to realise that God has placed Jesus centre stage, the source and goal of our faith and love – the "name above every name". Like a proud Father, God loves that the attention, the limelight, falls on His beloved Son.[49]

Thirdly, as the theologian John Stott expressed it, "A Christian is, in essence, somebody personally related to Jesus Christ.[50] Christianity without Christ is a chest without a treasure, a frame without a portrait, a corpse without breath".

What is his Identity?

The Holy Spirit uses the *Scriptures* to reveal the truth about who Christ is. But in the final analysis, a proper understanding and confession of his identity as 'divinity' is possible only through the supernatural ministry of the Holy Spirit in the *heart.* So the apostle Paul said, "No-one can say "Jesus is Lord" except by the *Holy Spirit*" (1 Cor 12:3; cf. Matt 16:17; Luke 10:22).

After studying John 5:17-47, many have been led to the conclusion that Jesus makes five claims to equality with God: in His person (vs 17-18); in His works (vs

---

[48] **As much as**. The Greek word is here καθώς (kathôs), having the basic meaning of 'according as, just as,' - but with the nuance of 'according as, ie in proportion as, in the degree that.' (Thayer's Greek Lexicon).

[49] **Beloved Son**. "The Father loves the Son and has entrusted all things to His hand. The one who believes in the Son has eternal life; but the one who does not obey the Son will not see life, but the wrath of God remains on him" (John 3:35-36).
"While he was still speaking, a bright cloud overshadowed them, and behold, a voice from the cloud said, "This is My beloved Son, with whom I am well pleased; listen to Him!" (Matt 17:5; Luke 10:22).
"If we receive the testimony of people, the testimony of God is greater; for the testimony of God is this, that He has testified concerning His Son" (1 John 5:9). Are you acceptable to God? God's view of Jesus reflects his view of you. "To the praise of the glory of His grace, by which He made us accepted in the Beloved". (Eph 1:6, NKJV)

[50] **Related to Jesus Christ**. John R.W. Stott; Understanding Christ, pp. 155-156.

Unit 4: Jesus

19-20); in His power (vs 21); in His judgment (vs 22); in His honour (vs 23). You may reason differently.

Does this mean that we must accept and understand the ins and outs of the Trinity to become saved? As we mentioned in lesson 8, neither the Samaritan woman in John 4 nor the evildoer next to Jesus had a grasp of detailed theology to be saved. God's grace saves us through faith, God's gift of salvation in Christ (Rom 3:21-26). God wishes for us to continue to grow. He "wishes all men to be saved and [increasingly] to perceive and recognise and discern and know precisely and correctly the [divine] Truth". (1 Tim 2:4, Amplified Bible, Classic Edition). Refer to Q8 regarding views of Christ's deity.

Is Jesus revealed as being the Jehovah of the Old Testament?

'No way!' - you may immediately respond. Some denominations, named earlier, take exception to this concept, dismissing such a meaning by saying Jesus is merely acting as God's agent. Yet the majority of Christians see Jesus as fitting the description given to Jehovah. If this is the case, we should note this does *not* make Jesus the Father. They understand the name Jehovah (Yahweh) applies to the whole Godhead which has the three persons. Notice just seven titles, or roles, of Jehovah in the OT. Judge for yourself as you read the following scriptures.

TITLE	JEHOVAH	JESUS
God	Ps 45:6-7 **"Your throne, O God**, is for ever and ever. The sceptre of your kingdom is a sceptre of uprightness; you have loved righteousness and hated wickedness. Therefore God, your God, has anointed you with the oil of gladness beyond your companions". (see Isa 9:6) Also, note Isa 40:3-4, "highway of our *God*".	Heb 1:8-9 But **of the Son he says, "Your throne, O God**, is for ever and ever, the sceptre of uprightness is the sceptre of your kingdom. You have loved righteousness and hated wickedness; therefore God, your God, has anointed you with the oil of gladness beyond your companions". (see John 20:28; Col 2:9) Also in reference to Isa 40:3-4, compare Matt 3:1-3, "highway of our Lord".
Creator	Isa 44:24 "I am Jehovah, **who made everything**. I stretched out the heavens **by myself**, And I spread out the earth. Who was with me?" (see Ps 102:25-27)	Col 1:16 For by him **all things** [not, "all *other* things" as NWT; cf.. Byington, ASV, KJV, Rotherham] **were created**, in heaven and on earth, visible and invisible,

		whether thrones or dominions or rulers or authorities, all things were created through him and for him. (Jo 1:3,10; Heb 1:10-12)
First and Last	Isa 44:6 This is what Jehovah says, The King of Israel and his Repurchaser, Jehovah of armies: '**I am the first and I am the last.** There is no God but me".	Rev 1:17 When I saw him, I fell as dead at his feet. And he laid his right hand on me and said: "Do not be afraid. **I am the First and the Last".**
Lord of Lords	Deut 10:17 Jehovah your God is the God of gods and the **Lord of lords**, the God great, mighty, and awe-inspiring, who treats none with partiality and does not accept a bribe.	Rev 17:14 These will battle with the Lamb, but because he is **Lord of lords** and King of kings, the Lamb will conquer them. Also, those with him who are called and chosen and faithful will do so".
Rock	Deut 32:4 The **Rock**, perfect is his activity, for all his ways are justice. A God of faithfulness who is never unjust; righteous and upright is he. (See Isa 8:13-14)	1 Cor 10:4 All drank the same spiritual drink. For they used to drink from the spiritual **rock** that followed them, and that rock meant the Christ. (in reference to Isa 8:13-14, cf. 1 Pet 2:7-8)
Saviour	Isa 43:11 "I—I am Jehovah, and besides me there is no **saviour**". (See Isa 45:21; Hos 13:4)	Luke 2:11 "For today there was born to you in David's city a **saviour**, who is Christ the Lord". (Titus 2:13; 3:4-6)
Forgiver	Mic 7:18-19 Who is a God like you **pardoning error** and passing over the transgression of the remnant of his inheritance? He will not hold onto his anger forever, for he delights in loyal love. He will again show us mercy; he will conquer our errors. You will throw all their sins into the depths of the sea.	Mark 2:5-7,10 "Child, your sins are forgiven". Now some of the scribes were there, sitting and reasoning in their hearts: "Why is this man talking this way? He is blaspheming. Who can **forgive sins except one, God**?" … But in order for you to know that the Son of man has authority to forgive sins on earth…"

Is it proper to pray to Jesus?

It is a common practice among most Christians. They enjoy praying directly to Jesus. But have they any scriptural basis to do so? Here are a few references to think over from the New Testament:

"If you **ask me** anything in my name, I will do it". (John 14:14). The word "me" is found in the oldest and most reliable manuscripts.

"And as they were stoning Stephen, **he called out, "Lord Jesus**, receive my spirit" (Acts 7:59).

"All those who in every place **call upon the name of our Lord Jesus** Christ, both their Lord and ours" (1 Cor 1:2). In the OT, "to call upon the name of the Lord" usually referred to prayer to God. See 1 Kings 18:24,37; Ps 116:4.

"Three times I **pleaded with the Lord** about this, that it should leave me" (2 Cor 12:8). In Paul's writings "Lord" (kurios) usually signifies Jesus (2 Cor 11:31; 13:14), whereas the title of "God" usually referred to the Father.

Is it proper to worship Jesus? What scriptures help us draw that conclusion?

"And they came up and took hold of his feet and **worshipped** ('proskenyo') him" (Matt 28:9). The two Marys first caught him by the feet, the respectful act of bowing, and then further they 'proskenyo' him; cf.. Acts 10:25-26; Rev 19:10).

"All may honor the Son, **just as** (καθώς -'in proportion as, in the degree that') they honor the Father" (John 5:23).

"To him who sits on the throne **and to the Lamb** be blessing and honor and glory and might forever and ever!" And the four living creatures said, "Amen!" and the **elders fell down and worshipped**" (Rev 5:8,12-14).

As we sincerely search through the Scriptures to understand the TRUTH about Jesus, pray for the Holy Spirit, the Spirit of truth, to shed light on Christ. "No-one can say "Jesus is Lord" except by the Holy Spirit" (1 Cor 12:3). No one has ever truly recognised Jesus without the aid of the Holy Spirit. It is the Holy Spirit that opens our eyes to the Lordship of Jesus, and it is the Spirit who is our pledge or guarantee of what is to come (2 Cor. 1:22).

In the Question sheet, you will be able to review these points, along with the question, 'Is Jesus the archangel Michael?'

" Jesus was God spelling himself out
in language humanity could understand".
- S.D. Gordon

DIGGING DEEPER – WHO IS JESUS?

Scan the QR code for informative links to each of these questions.

1. Certain **prepositions** focus on our relationship with Jesus.
Please read the scriptures and write a brief comment in response to the questions.

a. THROUGH him Rom 5:1-2,11	What do we receive **THROUGH** Christ?
b. IN him John 15:1-8	How do you abide **IN** Jesus?
c. UNDER him Eph 1:19-23	What results when we come **UNDER** his authority?
d. FOR him 2 Cor 5:14-15	What happens first before we can live **FOR** Christ?
e. WITH him Eph 2:4-6	Are we **WITH** Jesus now or in the future?

2. Is Jesus the archangel **Michael**?
   JWs, like the Seventh-day Adventists, believe that Michael is another name for the Son of God in heaven. A JW textbook states, "Scriptural evidence indicates that the name Michael applied to God's Son before he left heaven to become Jesus Christ and also after his return. Michael is the only one said to be "the archangel," meaning "chief angel," or "principal angel". The term occurs in the Bible only in the singular. This seems to imply that there is but one whom God has designated chief, or head, of the angelic host. At 1 Thessalonians 4:16 the voice of the resurrected Lord Jesus Christ is described as being that of an archangel, suggesting that he is, in fact, himself the archangel". (Insight 2 p.393) How would you use the following scriptures to reason on this teaching?
   a. Hebrews 1:5-6? **b.** Daniel 10:13 **c.** 1 Thessalonians 4:16

3. Who did the **earliest Christian** writers say Jesus was?

4. What can we say to the explanation that Jesus is just a **representative** of God?

5. What is a simple way to understand **John 1:1** and the absence of the definite article "the" in the final clause?

See Suggested Answers at the end of this book.

Action Point

Scan the QR to check out and ponder over the two tables under 'Action Point'.

Prayer

How we praise and magnify the name of Jesus, Father. He set aside the glory he had in heaven with you before the world was made, so that through His perfect life and sacrificial death, sinners such as I may be redeemed from the pit of destruction, forgiven and have peace with you Father. (Dear Jesus, you deserve all our honour and glory and worship and praise, and I confess you as my Lord and Saviour, now and for evermore. Praise Your holy name.)

Q11. WHAT DO YOU LOVE ABOUT JESUS?

Where do we start? Many people, regardless of their religious beliefs, often recognise Jesus as an exemplary figure, a role model, worth emulating. He was loving, unselfishly compassionate, humble, just, and prayerful. We could easily list many more of his divine qualities and spend time exploring each.

Examine just one Gospel account from Mark 4. "The Great Storm". Let's use the **GRACE** personal study method we considered in Question 6, ie God + Read + Analyse + Christ + Engage. Don't worry if you don't pick up on every detail, nuance, or application in your personal study. This just underlines the value of group discussion when different ones can join together in voicing their perspectives.

Step 1. **G - GOD**

Prayer is a priority before we study. We can pray for understanding by the Holy Spirit, "Open my eyes, that I may behold wondrous things out of your law" (Ps 119:18; Jer 33:3). With what goal in mind? Genuine *fellowship* with God and His Son. In John's words, "We know with an absolute knowledge that the Son of God has come and is here, and that He has given us permanent understanding in order that we may be *knowing in an experiential way the One who is genuine*. And we are in the Genuine One in His son Jesus Christ. This is the genuine God and life eternal" (1 John 5:20 Wuest). We can pray, not only at the start of our study period but throughout, in thanksgiving and praise.

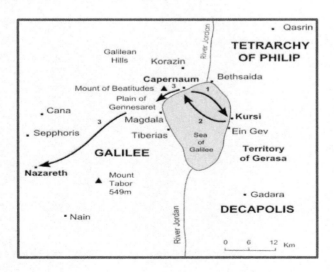

Step 2. **R -READ**

We take as an example the reading from NASB Translation (2020) of Mark 4:35-41. In addition. you will find handy links in the question sheet to other translation tools, including the Greek text.

---

35 On that day, when evening came, He said to them, "Let's go over to the other side".

36 After dismissing the crowd, they took Him along with them in the boat, just as He was; and other boats were with Him.

37 And a fierce gale of wind developed, and the waves were breaking over the boat so much that the boat was already filling with water.

38 And yet Jesus Himself was in the stern, asleep on the cushion; and they woke Him and said to Him, "Teacher, do You not care that we are perishing?"

39 And He got up and rebuked the wind and said to the sea, "Hush, be still". And the wind died down and it became perfectly calm.

40 And He said to them, "Why are you afraid? Do you still have no faith?"

41 They became very much afraid and said to one another, "Who, then, is this, that even the wind and the sea obey Him?"

Can you imagine the scene as these skilled fishermen battled into the storm from Capernaum (Jewish territory) to Gergesa (Gentile territory; Kursi on the map, arrow 1) to the southwest?

Sometimes a Bible map, as above, can help us understand the account with more clarity.

To help us further involve our senses, we can sometimes locate an appropriate clip on YouTube. (Find such a link to a 2 mins film on the question sheet in the QR below).

What words or expressions stand out to you that could be underlined? You can develop your own system of underlining but take a look at this example from biblearc.com.

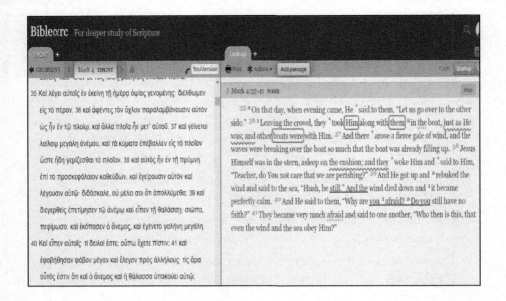

[In the right hand pane of the graphic above: **boxes** (people involved); **zigzags** (details about Jesus); **straight lines** (certain words of Jesus); **dots** (Greek details)]. Notice the numerous details: the people involved, the time of day, Jesus' state - "just as he was," his position in the boat, the cushion, the disciple's terror, and finally, the "other boats," These suggest the report of an eyewitness, likely Peter.

Step 3. **A – ANALYSE**

Context is king. What about the background[51], symmetry[52], culture and overall context of the book of Mark itself? Even more than Jesus' teachings, Mark highlights his mighty works, bearing a similarity to the miracles of Elijah and Elisha. Jesus is also shown to provide deliverance greater than that of Moses in the exodus and through the Red Sea. He proves to be the ultimate 'suffering servant' for all people, including the outcasts of society - in this case, to help demon-possessed Gentile Gerasenes across the sea. Mark portrays Jesus as a **subversive figure** who challenges and overturns societal norms through his

---

[51] **Background**. As professors Blackwell, Goodrich, and Maston explain: "Failure to immerse oneself within the religious environment of the New Testament world will likely result in not only unconscious imposition of alien meaning onto the biblical text but also a poorer understanding of the person and work of Jesus Christ". Also, Bruce Metzger comments, "Though it would be altogether extravagant to call the Apocrypha the keystone of the two Testaments, it is not too much to regard these intertestamental books as an historical hyphen that serves a useful function in bridging what to most readers of the Bible is a blank of several hundred years. To neglect what the Apocrypha have to tell us about the development of Jewish life and thought during those critical times is as foolish as to imagine that one can understand the civilization and culture of America today by passing from colonial days to the twentieth century without taking into account the industrial and social revolution of the intervening centuries. (Metzger, An Introduction to the Apocrypha, 151–152)

[52] **Symmetry in Mark**. A suggested pattern (chiastic structure) of the Gospel of Mark is:

A Beginning – John the Baptist points to Jesus 1:4-8
　B Jesus' baptism – The splitting of the heavens, "You are my son," 1:9-11
　　C Jesus is tested in the wilderness 1:12-13
　　　D The parable of the sower 4:1-9
　　　　E Raising of the young girl 5:21-43
　　　　　F The death of John the Baptist 6:14-29
　　　　　　G Stilling of the second storm (exorcism of deep) 6:45-52
　　　　　　　H Peter's confession 8:27-30
　　　　　　　　I – Jesus' first passion prediction 8:31-33
　　　　　　　H' Transfiguration 9:2-10
　　　　　　G' Exorcism of possessed boy 9:14-29
　　　　　F' Appearance of the rich (young) man 10:17-22
　　　　E' Raising of the young man in Secret Mark (followed Mark 10:34)
　　　D' Parable of the vineyard 12:1-11
　　C' Jesus is tested in the temple 12:13-27
　B' Jesus dies, the temple veil is split "Truly this was God's son". 15:33-39
A' The "post-runner" the young man, points to Jesus 16:1-8

teachings and actions. Here are some examples that highlight this subversive nature of grace, particularly in relation to his focus on the poor and marginalized: Mark 2:13-17; 3:1-6; 10:17-27; 12:41-44. He is the *Son who serves and saves*!

a. How about the closer context in Mark 4 and 5? Mark seems to love a certain symmetry to his structure in his gospel. So, Mark 4 relates three main 'seed' parables: the sower and the seed, the growth of a seed, and the mustard seed. Then starting at 4:31 to the end of chapter 5, Jesus draws attention to his four-fold victory over danger (the storm), the demons, disease, and death.

b. Study tools. Biblehub, for example lists 40 commentaries on this passage alone! By making use of the Blue Letter Bible site, we find that when we compare the two uses of the word "afraid" - one in Mark 4:40 and the other in the next verse, 4:41 - we discover that they are different Greek words, namely, δειλός (vs 40) and φοβέω (vs 41). The first word is always used in a bad sense meaning 'cowardice' (2 Tim 1:7); the second word, in verse 41, can have the meaning of to treat with deference or reverence. Hence verse 41 is rendered in the Phillips Translation as, "But sheer awe swept over them and they kept saying to each other, "Whoever can he be? - even the wind and the waves do what he tells them!"

Step 4. C- CHRIST

a. The humanity of Jesus is seen in his exhaustion after a long day's teaching. He was sleeping so hard that this storm didn't even wake him up - the only place in the Gospels where Jesus is said to have slept. This is reminiscent of a similar account of Jonah, who, on an aborted assignment to a gentile city, slept in a storm, then spent three days in a 'grave.' But in contrast to that prophet, Jesus did not run away from his mission to the Gentiles. However, like Jonah[53], he also spent three days in the grave. Our Lord fully

---

[53] **Jonah**. How Jonah may parallel Jesus:

1. Jonah arrived in the city of Nineveh in the belly of a fish (Jonah 2:10); Jesus arrived in the city (the World) in the belly of a virgin (Luke 1:31,34).
2. Jonah spent three days in the belly of a fish, a symbol of death (Jonah 1:17); Jesus died and spent three days in the earth (Matt 12:40).
3. Jonah was regurgitated alive on the shores of Nineveh, a symbol of resurrection (Jonah 2:10); Jesus was resurrected and returned alive (1 Cor 15:4).
4. Jonah completed his mission but hated the inhabitants of the city - the Ninevites (Jonah 4:1,4); Jesus completed His mission and loves the inhabitants of the city – humankind (John 15:13).

Unit 4: Jesus

understands our need for rest too, if we are to continue serving others. In Mark 6:31, Jesus said to his hard-working disciples, "Let's go off by ourselves to a quiet place and rest awhile". A footnote in the Power New Testament says regarding the word 'rest', "Anapausis is a temporary rest, like a coffee break at work... The verb anapaouo is used in Matthew 11:28 when Jesus says, "I will give you rest". Jesus understands our need to take breaks so that we do not overextend ourselves to our physical and, especially, spiritual detriment".

b.   Jesus said to the waves, "Quiet! Be still!" It could be that Jesus was quoting from Psalm 46:10, which discusses trusting God in the face of international wars and turmoil because He is in charge of history and will, in his appointed time resolve matters to bring peace through his kingdom. But don't miss the deeper point. In that verse which the disciples would have learnt, the Psalmist said, "Be still ... and know that I am God". In the Old Testament, it is only God who stills the storms at sea (Ps 107:23-32); here it is Jesus!

Step 5. **E - ENGAGE**

a.   The disciples were in this fix because they accompanied Jesus. "His disciples followed him" into the boat. To follow Christ doesn't exempt us from the tempests of life. He can allow and use such rough times to fulfill his purpose and teach us to **trust in him fully**. The purpose of venturing across the sea eventually became apparent: a) to teach them to trust him fully in rough times. Do you see Jesus as entirely trustworthy, especially when facing unexpected storms? And b), to help demon-possessed Gentile outcasts who lived in the country of the Gerasenes across the sea (Matt 8:28-34). Are you ready to 'cross to the other side' of the street to help the excluded, vulnerable outsiders?

b.   These skilled fishermen were "very much afraid". and asked the sleeping carpenter Jesus for help. Jesus is sufficient in all circumstances. Reliance on

---

5. Jonah went out of the city to wait for its destruction (Jonah 3:4-5); Jesus went out of the city to die for its redemption (John 19:17).

6. Jonah's tree is called 'Ricinus or castor' - modern name: Palma Christi (Jonah 4:6); Jesus' tree is called the 'Cross' on Calvary (Gal 3:13).

7. Jonah sat under his tree for his own protection (Jonah 3:6b); Jesus was nailed to his tree for man's protection (Isa 53:5).

8. Jonah went outside the city and waited for God to punish and kill the inhabitants of the city (Jonah 4:5); Jesus went outside the city and asked God to forgive and give life to the inhabitants of the World (Luke 23:34).

Unit 4: Jesus

our own experiences and skills can impede our complete trust in him. At first, they had been afraid of the storm but now became more fearful of the stiller of the storm! When over-whelmed at a tragedy, sense the Lord's **presence**, and become overwhelmed by his love and power.

c. Mark 4:36 adds, "other boats were with him". When Jesus stilled the tempest for those in his boat, it became calm for all other people in other little boats too. **Jesus sees all**. We can be so preoccupied with what's going on in our own little boat that we forget there are other boats in the sea of life. For example, as parents, how we react to stormy challenges with Jesus in our life has a profound effect on our children. Everyone has a sphere of influence.

So what do *you* love about Jesus?

As you continue to study the scriptures, may the Spirit grant you a deeper revelation of the beauty of Jesus. He appeals to us individually to come to Him, to believe on Him, to repent (Matt 11:28-30; John 3:16; Acts 17:30). Or, as Peter said, "You must repent and every one of you must be baptised in the name of Jesus Christ, so that you may have your sins forgiven and receive the gift of the Holy Spirit. For this great promise is for you and your children—yes, and for all who are far away, for as many as the Lord our God shall call to himself!"

Maybe you live by the maxim "what *would* Jesus do?" (WWJD). But have you thought that as He lives in you, it's not just a case of trying to copy Jesus but that He is *reproducing himself in you*, so it's more a case of WIJD... "what *is* Jesus doing" - in me and through me?

> " *A Muslim person may say: I worship the true God just like you worship the true God. Jesus would say: You don't know the true God if you don't receive the Son of God*".
> – *John Piper*

Prayer

"Worthy are You to take the scroll and to break its seals; for You were slaughtered, and You purchased people for God with Your blood from every tribe, language, people, and nation. You have made them into a kingdom and priests to our God, and they will reign upon the earth. Worthy is the Lamb that was slaughtered to receive power, wealth, wisdom, might, honor, glory, and blessing". (Rev 5:9,12)

DIGGING DEEPER - WHAT DO YOU LOVE ABOUT JESUS?

Scan the QR code for informative links to each of these questions.

The following five questions are based on various visual or audio recordings:

1. **Water into wine** (John 2:1-12) Bible Study Tools audio Bible (NLT)
   What does this scene impress on your mind in regard to Jesus' first miracle?

2. **The Loaves: one, five and seven** (Mark 8:16-21)
   Noting verses 16-21, what do you think Jesus was trying to teach to his disciples?

3. **The Samaritan woman at the well** (John 4:1-42)
   What barriers did Jesus break through to help this woman?

4. **Jesus Heals the Leper** (Matt 8:1-3)
   How did Jesus' compassion contrast to the customary way Jews viewed lepers ? Can you identify with his situation?

5. **Jesus and the children** (Matt 18:1-6)
   What do you take away from Jesus' words here?

See Suggested Answers at the end of this book.

Action Point
Scan the QR code and enjoy listening to a selection of CHRISTIAN SONGS that honour our Lord Jesus Christ. You may have a collection of similar songs already – if not, why not start a list of your personal choices?

Q12. JESUS' DEATH, RESURRECTION, AND KINGDOM?

These topics relating to Jesus have been the subject of tens of thousands of books, articles, and films. So rather than get snowed under with wordy detailed analysis, we would like to present fundamental scriptural teaching, along with the question – how do these events involve you? We will touch on three points under each subject.

HIS DEATH

Why did Jesus die? It is essential to get this straight because we could easily be caught in the anti-grace trap of trying to earn salvation through our personal performance or doing penance for forgiveness. Several denominations fall into this works-salvation snare.[54] For example, Jehovah's Witnesses, although they give lip service to Jesus dying as the atonement[55] and ransom for sins, ultimately

---

[54] **Works-salvation**. Many groups preach salvation by grace alone but then have to rely on their own works to ensure their eternal security. These include the Church of Christ, Methodism, Mormonism and Judaism. Only Biblical Christianity puts the greatest emphasis on faith that saves but still calls for works to show that faith (Eph 2:8-10). Yet, without faith, those works are empty. If one is to accept what is written in the Bible, then a person is reckoned as righteous by their faith. If you are saved, your old self is dead - finished with. You have been reckoned as righteous in Christ and, by grace alone, have been given eternal life. This is not a fleeting "temporary eternal life" here today, gone tomorrow causing a person to live in constant fear of losing their salvation. Jesus said, "And I give unto them eternal life, and they shall never perish, neither shall any man pluck them out of my hand". See Question 20.

[55] **Atonement**. In the Hebrew Scriptures, the concept of atonement was connected with sacrifices offered to allow people to approach God and worship him. Under the Mosaic Law, sacrifices were made, particularly on the annual Day of Atonement, to effect reconciliation with God despite the sins of individuals and the whole nation. William Tyndale first used the word atonement in 1526 when working on his translation. In the Revised Standard Version the word reconciliation replaces the word atonement. Atonement (at-one-ment) is the reconciliation of men and women to God through the death of Jesus. To be reconciled means to be made "at one" with God, having fellowship and peace with Him, where once there was enmity. Those sacrifices pointed to Jesus' sacrifice, which completely atoned for humanity's sins once for all time. Isaiah 53:5, "But he was pierced for our transgressions, he was crushed for our iniquities; the punishment that brought us peace was upon him, and

believe that they will atone for their own sin when they die (a misapplication of Romans 6:7), and eventually, after a thousand years of striving for perfection in paradise on earth, will merit being called sons of God. So, the idea that by believing in Jesus as the substitutionary scapegoat for *them personally*, bringing present *justification*[56], is not on their radar or is very much secondary. They claim that justification as sons of God is presently reserved for the final members of the 144,000 yet remaining on earth, who are all Jehovah's Witnesses.

Consequently, they and other similar groups live in constant insecurity - a fear of never doing enough or of failing to 100% obey the 'directions' (rules) set out by their 'Governing Body' leadership. In such a case, Jesus' death merely becomes a temporary backup, a safety net, when they fail by their self-efforts. This would be like a patient in dire need of an immediate transplant deciding to apply his own home remedies and exercises to cure himself. This is just one example showing the importance of grasping the meaning, and personally accepting, Jesus' death and resurrection.

Further, we need to be aware that different Bible scholars often have their particular emphatic viewpoints, which they defend vigorously. Let's touch on three of the key ideas that are stressed: victor, substitute, and ransomer.

a. Victor. Indeed, Jesus is! He has already conquered sin, death, and the devil, through his death! On a personal level, he cleaned house and has moved in. The Devil may stand outside threatening, but we have our resident conqueror on the inside. Satan is powerless over us, having no hold on us.

"Death has been swallowed up in *victory*. Where, O Death, is your victory? Where, O Death, is your sting?" (1 Cor 15:54-55). We can face the process of dying and death itself with confidence as we meet our Victor. "Therefore, since the children share in flesh and blood, He Himself likewise also partook of the same, so that through death He might destroy the one who has the power of death, that is, the devil, and free those who through *fear of death* were subject to slavery all their lives" (Heb 2:14-15).

b. Substitute. God's wrath is his holiness and love stirred into action against sin. Jesus was punished in our place as our substitute. He took our punishment.

---

by his wounds we are healed". Notice the substitution. Here again, we see that Christ paid the price for us! —Lev 5:10; 23:28; Col 1:20; Heb 9:12. See 'Systematic Theology' by Wayne Grudem for a deeper explanation (p586-607).

[56] **Justification**, see footnote 16, page 27.

"He was pierced for our *offenses*, He was crushed for our *wrongdoings*; the *punishment* for our well-being was laid upon Him, and by His wounds we are healed. All of us, like sheep, have gone astray, each of us has turned to his own way; but the Lord has caused the wrongdoing of us all to fall on Him" (Isa 53:4-6).

This goes much further than any annual Atonement Day in ancient Israel in that Jesus did not merely *cover over* their sins until the following year, but once-for-all-time *removed* our sins. "He appeared in order to *take away sins*; and in Him there is no sin" (1 John 3:5).

This substitutionary arrangement is sure grounds for our forgiveness, and even more - "we become the righteousness of God"[57] as His sons! "He made Him who knew no sin to be sin *in our behalf*, so that we might become the righteousness of God in Him" (2 Cor 5:21).

c. **Ransom.** Jesus died to settle a ransom[58] and buy us back from sin's clutches. "... Just as the Son of Man did not come to be served, but to serve, and to give

---

[57] **Righteousness** (dikaiosune). Manmade religion defines righteousness as morally good behaviour or holy and right living according to God's standard. This would suggest we can become righteous through proper performance, but in reality, this is practising self-righteousness (Rom 10:1-4). Although God's laws are righteous, no one is made righteous by keeping his laws because none of us can. We all fall short of God's glory (Rom 3:10; 7:12). If sin is missing the mark, righteousness is hitting the bullseye. It's being able to say, "Because God has been good to me, I am good with God". We are not made righteous because of our sacrifices, but because of the sacrifice Jesus made (Rom 5:18-19; 1 Cor 6:11; 2 Cor 5:21). Righteousness is a gift. How do we receive the gift of righteousness? The moment we believe in Jesus Christ, we are credited with his righteousness (Rom 3:28; 5:17). We stop trusting in our own righteousness, and receive by faith the righteousness that comes from the Lord. It means we have had a complete renovation, a Holy Spirit renewal, an entire rebuild. We have been straightened out. We are no longer the crooked person we used to be in Adam. Now, in Christ, we are inclined to walk straight and true, with a new desire to please the Lord. We don't pursue and practice righteousness to become righteous but because we are righteous. It's who we really are. We all need to receive the grace of God that teaches us how to live righteously (Titus 2:11-12).

[58] **Ransom** (luton) is a noun which literally refers to the payment (purchase price) which is necessary to free a slave from their bonds or a prisoner from captivity (such as a prisoner of war). The unbeliever is a slave to sin, the flesh, Satan, and death, and it was to redeem men from those slaveries that Jesus gave His life a ransom in exchange for sinners. Christ's sacrifice repurchased us from the slavery of sin. Jesus' ransom was paid to God to satisfy His holy justice, and it was *more than sufficient* to cover the sins of everyone who has ever lived and ever will live. The problem was Jesus hated sin and wickedness with all his heart. But he loved us, sinners. Therefore, some way of forgiveness must be found that allowed God to remain perfectly just while justifying those who have faith in Jesus (Rom 3 26). The

His life as a *ransom* for many" (Matt 20:28). "Or do you not know that your body is a temple of the Holy Spirit within you, whom you have from God, and that you are not your own? For you have been *bought for a price:* therefore glorify God in your body" (1 Cor 6:19-20).

Please note that according to Romans 5:10, 15, 17,   this grace "abounded much more" (huperperisseuō). Paul, by adding the prefix hyper to 'super-abundant' is emphasising the idea that God's grace is even more abundant than the sin that entered the world through Adam's disobedience; more than balancing the scales of what Adam lost. To speak of 'the *perfect* man Adam in the garden' is to confuse innocence with perfection and to misunderstand the nature of the perfection of Christ that qualified him to redeem. The statement "like should go for like" refers to temporal punishment for sin (Deut 19:21), and has no application to redemption in the case of Adam and Christ. Adam's sin was limited, though far-reaching in its effects; Christ's sacrifice is infinite in its embrace. Further, God's grace in Christ not only covers our sin and makes us right with God, but it also, through faith in Jesus, imparts righteousness and empowers us to live a life by the Spirit that is pleasing to Him (Gal 5:22-23).

Sometimes we think, "What am I worth?" Answer: you are worth Jesus! He willingly paid the price for you. But why does the scripture say, "*therefore* glorify God in your body"? Does the "therefore" imply – because Jesus has done so much for you, are you doing enough, in payback, for him? *No.* That would not be grace but bargaining on God's part. He paid and possesses your life ... to *transform* it and to *inspire* it! He works in you and through you, not in some works-demand-policy but grace-filled-Spirit-led life in glorifying God. Yes, because of the ransom paid by Christ, we can be filled with His Spirit.

---

answer to the problem was Jesus' voluntary acceptance of the cross where 'God made him who had no sin to be a sin offering for us so that in him we might become the righteousness of God (2 Cor 5:21).

The result? Paul explained to believers in Rome, "So now there is *no condemnation* for those who belong to Christ Jesus. And because you belong to him, the power of the life-giving Spirit has *freed you from the power of sin* that leads to death. The law of Moses was unable to save us because of the weakness of our sinful nature. So God did what the law could not do. He sent his own Son in a body like the bodies we sinners have. And in that body God declared an end to sin's control over us by giving his Son as a sacrifice for our sins". (Rom 8:1-3 NLT) In 1 Timothy 2:6, Paul adds the preposition anti (instead) to lutron (ransom), which intensifies the meaning of Christ's ransom payment. He did not merely pay a ransom to free us; He became the *victim in our place.* He died our death and bore our sin. He gave Himself.

To summarise so far: Why did Jesus die? Rather than decide between the above three options (and there are other views[59]) we could accept them *all* as aspects of his death.

As the **VICTOR**, he defeated sin to FREE us.

As the **SUBSTITUTE**, he took our punishment to FORGIVE us.

As the **RANSOMER**, he bought us back to FILL us.

Spurgeon in commenting on Romans 5:8 said, ""Oh!" said a little boy once to his mother, "I do not think so much of Christ dying for men, I think I would be willing to die if I could save a hundred men by dying". But his mother said," Suppose it was a hundred mosquitoes, — would you die for them?" "Oh, no!" he said, "I would let the whole lot of them die". Well, we were much less, in comparison with Christ than mosquitoes are in relation to men, yet he died for us, good-for-nothing creatures that we are. Well does one say, "God shows part of his love to us in many different ways, but he shows the whole of his love in giving Christ to die for us". Here you see his heart laid bare, the very heart of God laid open for the inspection of every believing soul".

---

[59] **Ransom views**. The atoning sacrifice and ransom of Christ is a central belief in Christianity and has been understood in various ways throughout history. Here are some of the most prominent understandings:

Ransom to Satan: This understanding dates back to the early church fathers and is based on the idea that Christ's death was a ransom paid to Satan to release humanity from his grip.

Satisfaction Theory: First articulated by Anselm of Canterbury in the 11th century, it argues that Christ's death satisfied the demands of divine justice for the sins of humanity. According to this view, humanity had offended the honour of God, and Christ's death was the only way to restore the honour of God and bring about reconciliation between God and humanity.

Penal Substitution Theory: Developed in the 17th and 18th centuries, it asserts that Christ's death was a substitutionary punishment for the sins of humanity. God the Father punished Christ on the cross in place of humanity so that those who believe in Christ can receive the forgiveness of their sins and escape the punishment they deserve.

Moral Influence Theory: 18th-century German theologian Friedrich Schleiermacher asserts that Christ's death was an example of love and self-sacrifice that moved humanity to repent and turn back to God. Christ's death served as a moral influence that inspired humanity to lead a better life and seek reconciliation with God.

These are just a few of the many understandings of Christ's atoning sacrifice and ransom that developed over the centuries. While there are differences in how these views understand the mechanics of atonement, they all agree that Christ's death was a pivotal event in the history of salvation and that it had a profound impact on the relationship between God and humanity.

HIS RESURRECTION

When he died, so did your sin. When he rose, so did your hope. The entire Christian faith hinges on the resurrection of Jesus.[60] As 1 Corinthians 15:14, 17 asserts, "If Christ has not been raised, then our *preaching* is in vain, ... and if Christ has not been raised, your faith is worthless; you are still in your *sins*". In the words of Bob George, "Jesus Christ 'died for my sins' is the half-gospel. Jesus 'died for my sins and rose to give me life' is the Full Gospel". For when he rose, your own grave was changed from a final resting place to temporary housing.

Consider three 'T' lines of evidence verifying his resurrection:

- **Testimony**. At least three times, Jesus prepared his followers by predicting his death and resurrection. The four independent biographies of Jesus were all written by eyewitnesses or based on eyewitness testimony, many of whom (500 on one occasion) were still alive. The 11 recorded post-resurrection appearances were in different locations and at different times of the day. He was touched, heard, seen, and he ate food in the presence of witnesses – likely all of whom knew him before his death.

- **Tomb**. Roman soldiers had guarded the grave, yet the stone had been rolled away; and no one ever claimed to have stolen the body. All the Jewish authorities needed to do to put an end to Christianity was to produce the body of Jesus; it was never found. Grave robbers would not have neatly left behind the grave clothes.

- **Transformation**. While Jesus was on trial, the Apostles deserted Him in fear, yet three days after the crucifixion, the disciples were suddenly willing to die a martyr's death. What accounts for their transformation into men willing to die for their message? They had nothing to gain from concocting such a story.

Why are His death and resurrection relevant to us?

He would only be King through crucifixion and resurrection. The disciples could scarcely comprehend that, especially before his death. However, not only is His death a guarantee of the future resurrection, but Scripture describes a similar pattern of us individually *dying and being raised* to a new life when we come to believe:

"When we were baptized, we were *buried* with Christ and shared his [and participated in his; into] death. So, just as Christ was raised from the dead by the

---

[60] **Resurrection**. See Q18 – footnote 4.

Unit 4: Jesus

wonderful power [glorious power; glory] of the Father, we also can *live a new life*" (Rom 6:4, Expanded Bible).

His death removes the *penalty* of sin; his resurrection delivers from the *power* of sin and imputes Christ's righteousness. A housewife wants to preserve some fruit in jars. She sterilises the jars, fills them with preserves, and seals them. Cleansing, filling, and sealing are a picture of salvation. Cleansed by the blood, filled with His life and righteousness, and sealed[61] by the Spirit.

THE KINGDOM

What is the Kingdom of God, which Jesus talked and prayed about so much? The word kingdom is the short version of the 'king's domain.'

a. The eternal Kingdom of God. Broadly speaking, the kingdom of God is the reign of the eternal, sovereign God over all the universe, or multiverse.

b. The present Kingdom of the Son. An expression of the kingdom of God is the kingdom of God's Son, who started ruling as king from 33 AD. Jesus came to save believing ones and rule in their hearts and lives, imputing His righteousness.

"[The Father] has delivered and drawn us to Himself out of the control and the dominion of darkness and *has transferred us* into the kingdom of the Son of His love". (Col 1:13 AMPC ... note: the past tense).

"For the kingdom of God is not a matter of eating and drinking, but of *righteousness, peace and joy* in the Holy Spirit" (Rom 14:17 ... describes the present Spirit-gifted qualities).

Initial repentance[62] and new birth are absolutely necessary to be a part of Jesus' present kingdom. We could call this kingdom, *the kingdom of grace,* which deals with the salvation of our souls, whereas the gospel of God's Kingdom, like a giant umbrella, deals with all things that the cross affected, including salvation and restoration of all things.

c. The future Kingdom of Glory. In a parable, Jesus spoke of himself leaving to receive a kingdom (Luke 19:12). Revelation chapter 20 mentions a 1000-year

---

[61] **Seals** were used to make something secure, to guarantee the contents' correctness, to indicate authenticity, and to indicate ownership. Sacrificial animals were examined and sealed if perfect. Jars, sacks of fruit or grain were sealed, and sometimes it took the form of a mark or a brand, as on livestock. Later the seal became a mark of royalty. There are five verses in the Bible that refer to a "seal of God" or an object or person sealed by God (John 6:27; 2 Tim 2:19; Rev 6:9; 7:2; 9:4). The gift of the Spirit to believers is a down payment on our heavenly inheritance, which Christ has promised us and secured for us at the cross. It is because the Spirit has sealed us that we are assured of our salvation. No one can break the seal of God.

[62] **Repentance**, see Question 2, footnote 2.

Messianic kingdom six times. It appears that the future kingdom is a glorious manifestation of the kingdom of grace. So, what do we preach? Early Christians were witnesses of Jesus as Lord:

"But the Holy Spirit will come upon you and give you power. Then you will tell everyone *about me* in Jerusalem, in all Judea, in Samaria, and in the world" (Acts 1:8, CEV).

"They cannot see the light of the Good News - the message about the divine greatness of Christ. Christ is the one who is exactly like God. everywhere We don't tell people about ourselves. But we tell people that *Jesus Christ is Lord*" (2 Cor 4:4-5, ERV).

Rather than preach about a particular religious denomination or focus only on Armageddon[63] or the future physical restoration in the 1000-year kingdom, we have the clear commission to bear witness about our saviour and king Jesus and preach complete reconciliation.[64] This is the Gospel of Grace. The heart of the gospel is always the person and work of Jesus. His beauty! Those focused on Him and submitting to His reign in their lives will inherit the earth as part of God's eternal Kingdom, rather than being assigned to a hell[65] of separation from God.

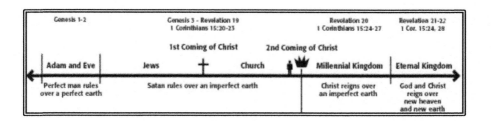

---

[63] **Armageddon**. See Additional Information on the Question sheet.

[64] **Reconciliation** means having fellowship and peace with God where once there was hostility. Our sin alienated us from Him. Jesus Christ's death on the cross is the basis of our forgiveness and justification. Formerly dead in sin, we are raised to new life. The love of God has been poured out in our hearts through the Holy Spirit whom he has given to us (Rom 5:5). It is a change in the total state of our lives. God does not change. He remains perfect. But He changes us. As a result, our relationship with Him changes. "For if while we were enemies we were reconciled to God through the death of His Son, much more, having been reconciled, we shall be saved by His life. And not only this, but we also celebrate in God through our Lord Jesus Christ, through whom we have now received the reconciliation" (Rom 5:10-11).

[65] **Hell** – see link in Additional Information.

In summary:

Do you recall the first Passover[66] when the blood of a slain lamb daubed on the doorposts saved those inside? Yet, the one represented by the lamb, also was alive to lead Israel to the Promised Land. Similarly, we can see the connection between our *crucified lamb of God,* who was resurrected and brings us to God and into His *kingdom* (1 Pet 3:18). The kingdom is the ultimate goal of the cross, and the cross is the means by which the kingdom comes. We have a cruciform kingdom!

> *"The Kingdom of God is a kingdom of paradox,*
> *where through the ugly defeat of a cross,*
> *a holy God is utterly glorified.*
> *Victory comes through defeat;*
> *healing through brokenness;*
> *finding self through losing self".*
> *- Charles Colson*

---

[66] **Passover** was the annual Hebrew festival on the evening of the 14th day of the month of Abib or Nisan. It was instituted to commemorate God's sparing the Jews when He destroyed the firstborn of the Egyptians (Exodus 12; Lev 23:5; Num 9:2-6).

Digging Deeper -
What do Jesus' Death, Resurrection, and Kingdom mean to you?

Scan the QR code for informative links to each of these questions.

1. Was Jesus **raised bodily** from the dead?

2. Read Titus 2:14. How does Jesus being the redeemer
   relate to **works**?
   Write your own thoughts. If you wish to research
   further, here in the QR is a Bible Tool with numerous
   commentaries in the right-hand column; click on
   "all commentaries". ('view all')

3. Using cross references from 2 Corinthians 4:5 can you find other verses
   which encourage us to **preach Christ**?

4. Is the **Kingdom** present or future?

5. What is the connection between the **cross and the Kingdom**? Col 1:13-14 and
   Rev 1:5-6

See Suggested Answers at the end of this book.

Action Point
Have you fully given your heart to Jesus?
Please take time to prayerfully consider these two articles behind the QR code.

Prayer

(We don't need to pray a sinner's prayer to be saved, but it is certainly appropriate, especially when in private, to express heartfelt contrition and repentance. The publican prayed, "God, be merciful to me, a sinner". (Luke 18:13) The thief on the cross said to Jesus, "Remember me when you come into your kingdom". So, if someone comes to believe in Jesus as their saviour, they can use their own words in prayer. The following few sentences may help).

'Lord Jesus, be merciful to me, a weak sinner. I believe you are the Son of God, that you died on the cross and were raised to rescue me from sin and death and to restore me to the Father. I confess my sinfulness and choose now to turn from my sins, my self-centeredness. I give myself to you. I receive your forgiveness and ask you to take your rightful place in my life as my Saviour and Lord. Come reign in my heart, fill me with your love and your life, and help me to become a person who is truly loving - a person like you. Live in me. Love through me. In Jesus' name I pray. Amen.'

THE TRUTH
Jesus promised another Helper
who would glorify the Son - John 16:14

Q13. Is the Holy Spirit a Person?

The Old Testament contains 88 specific references to the Holy Spirit. The New Testament refers to the Spirit 264 times and uses 39 names. He is called the Holy Spirit, the Spirit of God, the Spirit of Christ, the Spirit of Jesus, the Spirit of his Son, of Truth, Grace, Holiness, Glory, and of Adoption.

Jehovah's Witnesses, Christadelphians, Unitarians, New Ageists, Spiritualists' and Christian Scientists, all teach that the Holy Spirit is God's active and impersonal force (like radar or electricity), and not an actual person. Mormonism is viewed by many as resembling tritheism[67]. We will reference a number of pertinent scriptures in today's discussion.

Jehovah's Witness	"The invisible energizing force that God puts into action to accomplish his will. It is holy because it comes from Jehovah, who is clean and righteous to the highest degree, and because it is God's means to accomplish what is holy." - Glossary; RNWT 2013.
Christadelphian	"The Spirit is not a "separate" or "other" person. It is God's own radiant power, ever outflowing from Him, by which His "everywhereness" is achieved. The Spirit is personal in that it is of God Himself: it is not personal in the sense of being some other person within the Godhead". — christadelphia.org
Unitarian	"Is the Spirit really anything other than God's energy, inspiring human beings to perform extraordinary feats of valor, endowing them with special artistic skill or miraculous powers, and especially communicating divine truth?" Sir Anthony Buzzard, Unitarian theologian.

---

[67] **Tritheism** is the concept of three separate and independent divine beings or gods. It stands in contrast to monotheism, which asserts the belief in a single, unified God. For example, the Trinity of the Father, Son, and Holy Spirit are understood to be distinct persons but also part of the same divine essence or substance.

New Ageist	Beliefs may differ among individuals. Some may view the Holy Spirit as an aspect of the broader universal energy or consciousness that pervades the universe (Monism). Others perceive the Holy Spirit as an internal guiding force, an aspect of their own higher self or inner wisdom.
Spiritualist	Their 'Declaration of Principles' sets out their general view of God: God is the creative force in the universe is what Spiritualists know as God. That force created life in the beginning and still does so today (a form of pantheism or panentheism).
Christian Scientist	Mary Baker Eddy understood the Holy Spirit as a divine influence, synonymous with divine Science, and playing a vital role in revealing Truth, restoring spiritual awareness, and facilitating healing and salvation through Christian Science teachings.
Mormon	The Church "teaches that the Holy Ghost is a spirit man, a spirit son of God the Father. ... The Holy Ghost is the third member of the Eternal Godhead, and is identified also as the Holy Spirit, Spirit of God, Spirit of the Lord, and the comforter".- Encyclopaedia of Mormonism (2:649)

Does the Holy Spirit have the attributes of personhood? Well, we could raise the question: What do you believe the **Devil** is? Some, like the Jehovah's Witnesses, will readily say that he is a real spirit person that rebelled against God. In which case, we could reason: how do you know for sure that the Devil is a person, not just a "force for evil" - as Christadelphians and followers of Christian Science teach? Then, whatever ways they use to identify the Devil as spirit person, we can adopt their line of reasoning to show the Holy Spirit is likewise a person!

1. First, we turn to **1 Timothy 4:1** where the personality of the Spirit appears to be doubly implied:

> "Now the **Spirit expressly says** that in later times some will depart from the faith by devoting themselves to deceitful spirits and teachings of **demons**".

First, the Spirit speaks. This may remind us of the passage in John 16:13 where, in reference to the Spirit, it says, "he will not *speak* of his own initiative, but what he *hears* he will speak..." (NWT- the JW Bible). Do you notice the correspondence to Jesus words in John 12:49? "For I have not *spoken* of my own initiative, but the Father who sent me has himself given me a commandment about what to say and what to speak" (NWT). The Son heard and spoke the words of the person of God, but can a non-person hear and speak?

Additionally, we again refer to 1 Timothy 4:1, the warning given by the Holy Spirit against deceitful spirits or demons. These demonic spirits are real personalities and so likewise is the Holy Spirit who expressly speaks out in warning. On a side note, here the NWT, as opposed to all other translations, obscures the personality of the Holy Spirit by rendering this verse, "However, the *inspired word clearly says* that in later times some will fall away from the faith, paying attention to misleading inspired statements and teachings of demons". Yet in their Bible's footnote and their Greek "Kingdom Interlinear," they admit that "*spirit*" could be an alternative rendering to "inspired word".

2. Next, we can read verses from **John 14** that refer to the Spirit as "**he**". For example:

> "I will ask the Father, and he will give you **another** (allos) **Helper** to be with you forever, even the Spirit of truth, whom the world cannot receive, because it neither sees him nor knows **him**. You know him, for he dwells with you and will be in you". ... "**he** will teach you all things" (John 14:16,17, 26).

W.E. Vine says of the word Helper: "It was used in a court of justice to denote a legal assistant, counsel for the defense, an advocate; then, generally, one who pleads another's cause, an intercessor, advocate". The word "another" (allos) means 'another of the same kind; the same kind of Helper as the person of Christ. Secondly, the "He ... him" are masculine pronouns used of the Holy Spirit despite the fact that "Spirit" (Greek–pneuma) is neuter. In connection with this, we need to know that in Greek, the gender of a noun or pronoun is a matter of grammar; it has nothing to do with actual gender. For example, think about the words translated as "little girl" in Mark 5:41, "Taking her by the hand he said to her, "Talitha cumi," which means, "Little girl, I say to you, arise". Here "little girl" is a neuter Greek word 'korasion,' but no one, including the NWT would render this as., "taking *it* by the hand ... Jesus said to *it*, arise". Likewise, the fact that the Greek word for "spirit" is neuter does not make a "spirit" an "it". The Watchtower agrees, for example, that demonic spirits are persons, and the Bible even says that "God is a Spirit" (John 4:24).

3. Adding to this are scriptures saying that Holy Spirit can think, evaluate, and choose. Let's take these one at a time, with two scripture references in each case.

   a) **MIND.** The Spirit can think.

   > "And He who searches the hearts knows what the **mind of the Spirit** is, because the Spirit intercedes [before God] on behalf of God's people in accordance with God's will" (Rom 8:27 Amplified).

   Sadly, again the NWT, in contrast to almost all other translations, changes the expression "the *mind* of the Spirit" to "the *meaning* of the spirit" (spirit with a lowercase 's'), although contrariwise in their Greek "Kingdom Interlinear" the word "minding" is used. The Spirit knows the very mind of God too.

   > "For who knows a person's thoughts except the spirit of that person, which is in him? So also no one **comprehends the thoughts** of God except the Spirit of God" (1 Cor 2:11, ESV).

   b) **EMOTIONS**: Does the Holy Spirit have feelings? Yes, at times he is made to groan and grieve. Here are a couple of references.

   > "Now in the same way the Spirit also helps our weakness; for we do not know what to pray for as we should, but the Spirit Himself intercedes for us with **groanings** too deep for words" (Rom 8:26, NASB).

   Does this describe an invisible active force? Or, rather, a spirit person who can and does participate in our feelings? To quote the Message Bible, the Holy Spirit prays on our behalf "with unspeakable yearnings and groanings too deep for utterance". The word for groanings literally means sighs.

   > "Also do not be grieving the Holy Spirit" (Eph 4:30).

   Some would argue that Paul used a figure of speech called personification, saying that the Holy Spirit, an impersonal force, can be grieved as if it were a person. But a few sentences earlier, in verse 27, Paul refers to our bad conduct providing a foothold for the Devil, the *unholy spirit person*. Now here, in verse 30, he adds that our misconduct - especially in unchristian speech - may also lead to grieving a person, the Holy Spirit.

   d) **WILL**. Can the Holy Spirit make **CHOICES** and actions? The Holy Spirit has a will.

   > "But one and the same Spirit works all these things, distributing to each one individually just as **He wills**" (1 Cor 12:11, NASB).

It is clear from the context that it is the Holy Spirit who makes the decision about what gift each respective Christian receives. An impersonal force does not have the ability to make decisions. This is an attribute of persons, not impersonal forces.

> "For to us God revealed them through the Spirit; for the **Spirit searches** all things, even the depths of God" (1 Cor 2:10, NASB).

If the Holy Spirit has a *mind* that thinks, *emotions* that feel, and a *will* that decides, it may prove difficult to maintain the view that the Holy Spirit is merely an impersonal force.

The Holy Spirit is called by a number of different titles. They include the "Spirit of Jesus Christ," the "Spirit of Jesus," and "the Spirit of the Son".

Finally, you may find it interesting to refer to three references from 2 Corinthians in summary. Paul's words in 2 Corinthians 3:17-18 from the NWT:

> "Now **Jehovah is the Spirit**,
> and where the spirit of Jehovah is, there is freedom".

Yes, you read that right! "Jehovah is the Spirit" – not *a* Spirit. Sadly, they have inserted the name "Jehovah" with no support. It does not relate to any OT quotation or any manuscript evidence. In fact, the context points to Jesus as the Lord (kyrios), which means that Jesus is the Spirit, and that Christians reflect Jesus' glory. Something that no JW could affirm.

Of interest too, note that 2 Corinthians 6:6–7 indicates that when listing elements of his personal ministry, Paul called attention to the "holy spirit" as something distinct from "God's power". "In purity, in knowledge, in patience, in kindness, in the **Holy Spirit**, in genuine love, in the word of truth, and in the **power of God**; by the weapons of righteousness for the right hand and the left".

And finally, also in 2 Corinthians, but his final greeting:

> "The grace of the Lord Jesus Christ,
> and the love of God, and the **fellowship of the Holy Spirit**,
> be with you all" (2 Cor 13:11, NASB).

> *"As the sun can be seen only by its own light,*
> *so Christ can be known only by His own Spirit".*
> *- Robert Leighton*

DIGGING DEEPER - IS THE HOLY SPIRIT A PERSON?

Scan the QR code for informative links to each of these questions.

1. Do you agree or disagree that when John chapters 14 to 16 calls the Holy Spirit "he," it is using **personification**, similar to wisdom (Luke 7:35) and sin (Rom 5:21)?

2. Can you suggest why the Holy Spirit lacks a **name** if it is a person?

3. Please watch these two short videos within the QR, and then answer the questions:
   a. What does the Holy Spirit do for **unbelievers**?
   b. What does the Holy Spirit do for **believers**?

4. Can you list some **gifts** of the Holy Spirit? How does Paul describe their purpose? (1 Cor 12:4-31; Eph 4:12)

5. Can you summarise different viewpoints of **speaking in tongues**? What is your take on tongues?

See Suggested Answers at the end of this book.

Action Point

Prayer in the Spirit. This is mentioned in Eph 6:18 and Jude 20. It has three aspects: (1) admitting our inability to pray as we ought (Rom 8:26), (2) enjoying the presence of God; living communion with Him (Heb 4:16), and (3) plead, but do not demand, the promises of God with boldness and assurance (Matt 7:7-11).

Additional Information

(These scriptures can also help establish the personality of the Holy Spirit: Acts 10:19-20; Acts 13:2; Rev 22:17. The Spirit is said to speak, to call to assignments, and along with the members of the Bride and new believers, invite people to take the water of life.)

Prayer

Holy Father, thank you for sending your Holy Spirit to comfort me in my weaknesses. He gives me strength when I cannot take another step. I know He guides me into all truth and will give me boldness to testify about what you're doing in my life. I pray Father that your Spirit will shape and mould me into a purer reflection of your Son.

THE TRUTH
Jesus sends the Spirit to testify about Him - John 15:26

Q14. DOES THE SPIRIT AFFECT YOU

What does "walking by the Spirit"[68] mean to you? To some, it means endeavouring to read the Bible, help their neighbours, and pray that God will help them each day to suppress sin, or simply put, trying to do the best they can. That is the way many Christians try to conduct their lives. They may feel the Spirit will especially bless them when engaging in serious Bible research, notable evangelistic enterprise, or partaking of the bread and wine (communion).

Before we go any further, let's ask, just what does the Holy Spirit do, and how are we affected? Considering together three of the many activities of the Spirit will undoubtedly reinvigorate us:

1. He imparts **LIFE**.

Pinocchio is the story of a wooden puppet who was manipulated by strings but was brought to life. No longer impeded by cords, he enjoyed an autonomous life. Yet he still had much to learn. Have you been liberated from religious entanglements and received life from the Holy Spirit? Are you growing under the Spirit?

The NT teaches that the Spirit can replace our old heart with a new one. Imagine you have a heart failure leading to death but are saved by a heart transplant. You can experience a new life thanks to the donated *indwelling heart* beating inside you! So, Christ died to freely donate his life, which now dwells in each believer by the Holy Spirit. Your new heart beats with new passions and they are the passions of the Holy Spirit. Romans 8:1-11 sheds light on this. Here is verse 11:

> "If the Spirit of the One who resurrected Jesus from the dead lives inside of you, then you can be sure that He who raised Him will cast the light of life into your mortal bodies through the **life-giving power of the Spirit residing in you**" (Voice; cf. Ezekiel 11:19-20).

---

[68] **Walking by the Spirit** (Gal 5:16,25). Before the point of being saved, we were IN Adam, but then we were placed IN Christ. We may at times, be tempted to WALK in the old ways of thinking and acting. But as we are now located permanently IN Christ, we are to walk in the Spirit. See Question 2 below in Digging Deeper.

Unit 5: Spirit

Yes, as Jesus said,

> "Truly, truly, I say to you, the one who hears My word, and believes Him who sent Me, has eternal life[69] and does not come into judgment, but has passed out of **death into life**" (John 5:24).

In other words, at one time, we were located in dying Adam, but now we are located in the living Christ through the indwelling Holy Spirit.

Michael Reeves explains the work of the Holy Spirit in this way: "The life the Spirit gives is not an abstract package of blessing; it is his own life that he shares with us, the life of fellowship with the Father and Son. Thus the Spirit is not like some divine milkman, leaving the gift of 'life' on our doorsteps only to move on. In giving us life he comes in us to be with us and remain with us. Having once given life, then, he does not move on; he stays to make that life blossom and grow." ('The Good Life' - 2012, p77)

The indwelling Spirit certainly affects our *prayers* – bringing life to them. We can begin a son-to-Father (Abba) dialogue relationship. The indwelling Spirit also moves us to live in *service of others* as never before. You will recall what Jesus said regarding his commission:

> "The Spirit of the Lord is upon me, because he has chosen me to bring good news to the **poor**. He has sent me to proclaim liberty to the **captives** and recovery of sight to the **blind**, to set free the **oppressed**" (Luke 4:18, GNB).

---

[69] **Eternal Life**. Does everlasting life refer only to the duration or longevity of life? Most commentators draw attention to the aspect of everlasting life, which means sharing the life of God and His Son in our spirit– the 'God quality' of life enjoyed by the Sons of God forever. The aspect of duration or longevity allows us the opportunity to enjoy this divine quality of life forevermore. William Barclay comments, "Let us remind ourselves of what eternal means. In Greek, it is aionis. This word has to do, not so much with the duration of life, for life which went on forever would not necessarily be a boon. Its main meaning is quality of life. There is only one person to whom the aionis can properly be applied, and that is God. Eternal life is, therefore, nothing other than the life of God. To possess it, to enter into it, is to experience here and now something of the splendor and the majesty, and the joy, and the peace, and the holiness, which are characteristic of the life of God". (The Daily Bible Study Commentary: John – by W Barclay (Vol 2, p 207). This new God quality of ainois life begins the moment a person puts faith in Christ. It is our current possession. John 3:36 says, "Whoever believes in the Son HAS eternal life". We find similar present-tense constructions in John 5:24 and John 6:47. The focus of eternal life is not on our future but on our current standing in Christ – 'receiving God's own life'. This life-giving knowledge, or knowing the Father and the Son, is true, personal knowledge, not just an academic awareness (John 17:3). See also Q 20 - 'Is our Salvation secure?'

So, we are moved, impelled, by this same Spirit to serve others – whether in seeing to the physical needs of the poor and oppressed or being empowered to courageously witness[70] - as Jesus later said, "But you will receive power when the Holy Spirit has come upon you, and you will be **my witnesses** in Jerusalem and in all Judea and Samaria, and to the end of the earth" (Acts 1:8).

Yes, it's true that some unbelievers can be altruistic, but they are not motivated internally by the Spirit of Christ so that all glory goes to the Lord.

2. He empowers **PURITY**.

Purity is to be expected as he is called the HOLY Spirit. He performs an initial cleansing work in us, making a decisive break with the patterns of sin that were in our lives before. Paul wrote the Corinthians, "You were washed, you were sanctified[ ], you were justified[ ] in the name of the Lord Jesus Christ and in the Spirit of our God" (1 Cor 6:11, see Titus 3:5; Heb 10:10, 14).

Thereafter, the Spirit produces in us growth in holiness of life. Those who yield to His dealings will be graced to develop patterns of Spirit-empowered self-discipline. When God gives a breakthrough, we must be faithful to follow through. Remember the defeat of the nation of Israel after their great breakthrough victory at Jericho. The little village of Ai whipped them because Achan hid accursed things in his house (Josh 7:1-12). Abandon any idols. Have you thought that whining and worrying can become idols in our life? Out with the old whine, in with the new wine! No more being crisis-centred because we are Christ-centred!

He brings forth the fruitage of the Spirit within us. Men may try to produce the "fruit of the Spirit" before new birth, but it will only be a manufactured glimmer of the real thing until they become regenerated ones, belonging to Christ (Gal 5:22-25). Or, as 2 Corinthians 3:18 beaut-ifully expresses it, "Now all of us, with our faces unveiled, reflect the glory of the Lord as if we are mirrors; and so we are being **transformed, meta-morphosed**, into His same image from one radiance of glory to another, just as the Spirit of the Lord accomplishes it" (Voice).

John MacArthur comments: "If I had my choice of being obedient to an external

---

[70] **Witness.** See Q21 – 'How can we share the Gospel?'

list of rules, or simply walking by the energy of an internal power, I would choose the latter. I am glad I live under the New Covenant, where practical holiness is the product of *living by the energy of the indwelling Spirit*, who empowers me to do the things that I couldn't force myself to do, no matter what the outside rules were".

As we are now IN the Spirit, does it not make sense to walk BY that Spirit? In other words, live out who you really now are, exercising our conscience[71]. As evidence of having been born again, we will display, at least to some degree, the fruitage of the Holy Spirit. True, we may dabble in some sin, but now it just doesn't feel right; you have become a new creation! So you repent - that is, are "transformed by the renewing of your mind" – of these daily sins, which Jesus called 'feet' sins, knowing the Father has forgiven you because you have already 'bathed' once for all in his blood. The goal of the Holy Spirit's work is to make us more like Jesus (Rom 12:2; John 13:8-10; 1 John 3:3).

1. He gives **ENLIGHTENMENT.**

The Spirit constantly points to Jesus. This is made clear in the Gospel of John:
"The Helper will come - the Spirit, who reveals the truth about God and who comes from the Father. I will send him to you from the Father, and **he will speak about me**" (John 15:26, GNB).

Yes, to see Christ, His identity and reality, is only possible by the ministry of the Holy Spirit, not just by referring to a pre-packaged string of 'proof texts' or engaging in academic study of the Bible. Through the ministry of the Holy Spirit bringing us to the reality of the person of Christ, we are inevitably led into a deeper intimacy with the Father. He gives evidence of Father's presence and love to us. For example, He bears witness with our spirit that we are children of God, and only by the Spirit can we appreciate God as "Abba[72], Father!" In this way, He

---

[71] **Conscience**. The word conscience appears about 30 times in the NT, and in the original Greek (suneidesis) it is made up of two words that loosely translate as "with knowledge". Your conscience knows when you have crossed the line and missed the mark. How does it know? From where does your conscience acquire the knowledge of right and wrong? For some, this knowledge is defined by cultural norms. For others, it may come from some religious code, such as the Law of Moses. But ultimately, any definition of right and wrong is grounded in the character of God. God alone defines what is good, and it is his morality that is hardwired into creation. A healthy conscience is one that is in tune with the Holy Spirit. "I am telling the truth in Christ, I am not lying, my conscience testifies with me in the Holy Spirit" (Rom 9:1). The law is a shadow, but the Spirit of Christ is the true Guide by which we live.

[72] **Abba**. Children, as well as adult sons and daughters in Israel, use Abba when speaking to their fathers. It is an expression of warm intimacy. Nowhere in the Old Testament do we

provides comforting assurance. This is far more than intellectual confidence or reliance on emotionalism.

Further, the Spirit progressively reveals the Father and His will. How? By becoming our Teacher (John 16:13). In His time, he reveals enlightenment from the scriptures appropriate to our needs. This is something more than knowing our Bible well or our reflecting on biblical moral standards. This knowledge is to lead us into a knowing relationship, a communion, with God. Also, He may lead us by inner promptings in our spirit to a specific person or activity. In this regard, remember how the Spirit "drove" Jesus out into the wilderness (Mark 1:12). The word "drove" is a strong term meaning "drive out, expel" and more literally expresses "throw out". Do not stifle these impulses or write happenings off as lots of coincidences. The Holy Spirit will not leave us in confusion but will reveal the truth to us. He illuminates the dark areas of our lives to give us a clear vision of God's purpose for us.

If we truly are in Christ[73], then in a sense, His Spirit is our dance partner leading us in the right steps in sync with the rhythm of Jesus' love. It is not our job to struggle to find God's will but to rest in confidence that He will reveal his will as he holds us in his embrace, leading us across the ballroom of grace. What a gift to us is the Holy Spirit. Among many other things, He imparts LIFE, empowers PURITY, and gives ENLIGHTENMENT. When we receive the gift of the Holy Spirit, we welcome the gift and the giver, because the gift is the giver (Acts 2:38). The Holy Spirit is our unity with God, our source of communication from God, and the guarantee that we are His children.

> " If the Holy Spirit was withdrawn from the church today,
> 95 percent of what we do would go on and no one
> would know the difference."
> - A. W. Tozer

---

find the term abba used in addressing God. The pious Jews sensed too great a gap between themselves and God to use such a familiar expression. In an entirely new departure, Jesus used this intimate term to address God in prayer, thereby expressing His own unique relationship to God as Father. The early Christians carried on the use of "Abba" in prayer as indicated in Galatians 4:6 and in Romans 8:15, thereby giving expression to their own "adoption as sons of God" through Christ and their possession of the Spirit. As those "in Christ", Christians today often begin their prayers with the words "Dear heavenly Father" with the fondness of the modern English equivalents of Daddy or Papa.

[73] **In Christ**. See footnote 135 on page 159.

DIGGING DEEPER- DOES THE SPIRIT AFFECT YOU?

Scan the QR code for informative links to each of these questions.

1. Name at least three **roles** of the Holy Spirit in our lives?

2. Is being **in** the Spirit the same as walking **by** the Spirit?

3. If the Spirit indwells us, why do we need to "**be filled with the Holy Spirit**" - Eph 5:18? Please watch this clip inside the QR and see if you agree with the reasoning.

4. What lessons can we learn from the account in **Acts 16:6-10**? Please watch this clip when you scan the QR below: 'walking the thin red line.'

5. What is the unpardonable sin of **blasphemy** against the Holy Spirit? (Mark 3:22-30)

See Suggested Answers at the end of this book.

Action Point

Today, request the Spirit to stir you inside out, to direct you in pleasing the Lord every step, in every task, every major decision, in every encounter with someone. Rest in the Spirit without anxiety! Romans 8:14 "For all who are led by the Spirit of God are sons of God".

Prayer

Abba, Father, I approach you in our Saviour's precious name. Please give us spiritual wisdom and insight, flood our hearts with light. Help us to understand the incredible greatness of Your Holy Spirit's power for us who believe You – the same power that raised Jesus from the dead. Help us to comprehend that this power is living and breathing in us.

Q15. WHAT ARE THE ANGELS AND DEMONS UP TO?

Like the Sadducees in Jesus' day, many people today say that "there is no resurrection, nor angel, nor spirit" (Acts 23:8). They deny the reality of anything they cannot see. But the Biblical teaching on the existence of angels is a constant reminder that there is an unseen world that is very real. It was only when the Lord opened the eyes of Elisha's servant to the reality of this invisible world that the servant saw that "the mountain was full of horses and chariots of fire round about Elisha" (2 Kings 6:17). In all, there are references to angels in 34 of the 66 books of the Bible.

There are several modern day anecdotal accounts[74] of those claiming to have received protection in one way or another from angels Irrespective of such stories, the Bible often mentions invisible created beings who inhabit the spiritual world. These angels are variously described as sons of God, holy ones, spirits, watchers, principalities, authorities, thrones, and dominions.

Notice that some descriptions imply rank and order among them. Michael[75], for example, is called an "archangel" and "one of the chief princes. He appears to be a leader in the angelic army (Rev 12:7-8). Also, the fact that they are organised as

---

[74] **Anecdotal accounts**. Here is an account (author unknown) from a missionary who was also a medic in New Guinea. Some would question if this story is plausible. You be the judge. However, there are many similar accounts in writing. "I was stopped by a man, one of a violent gang. He informed me that he and his friends knew that I carried money and drugs, so they followed me into the jungle with the purpose of robbing and killing me. As they approached my campsite, they said that I was asleep, but I was surrounded by 26 armed guards. I assured him that I was very much alone that evening but did have the opportunity to lead him to the Lord. As I returned to the States for furlough, I was sharing this story with a church. During the middle of the story, a gentleman jumped up and asked me what date that would have been. I gave him the date. He stated that he had been on the golf course that day and was overcome by the desire to pray for me and my protection. He called some men of the church and they met at the church and started to pray for me. He asked all the men that came that day to stand up. Twenty-six men stood up!" A real-life event or merely a parable?

[75] **Michael** - see page 180.

"armies" implies their great power. 2 Peter 2:11, says they are "greater in might and power" than human beings, but not infinite in power.

What is the place of the Angels in God's Purpose?

The angels are never described as being made "in the image of God," whereas humans are mentioned several times as being in God's image. Can we conclude then that those 'in Christ' are more like God even than the angels are? Yes - though we are at present, "a little while lower than the angels" - when our salvation is completed in glorification, we will be exalted above the angels and rule over them. In fact, even now, angels already serve the elect: "Are they not all ministering spirits, sent forth to provide service, for the sake of those who will inherit salvation?" (Heb 1:14). The Roman Catholic church teaches that angels intercede for us[76]. This is very debatable. Yet, we can say with certainty that Jesus, as our Saviour, comes alongside to assist His brothers. So, Hebrews continues in chapter 2:16, "For clearly He does not give help to angels, but He gives help to the descendants of Abraham".

When certain angels chose to rebel, God decided to redeem none of them. This is perfectly just for God to decide, and no angel can ever complain that God has treated him unfairly. However, in the case of fallen man, God decided to go beyond the demands of justice in order to redeem and save them. If He had decided to save only one hundred out of the whole human race, it would have been an amazing demonstration of mercy and love, but God is saving a great crowd from all nations. This is truly abundant grace!

How are angels an example to us?

An example of *obedience*: "Praise the LORD, you angels of his, you powerful warriors who carry out his decrees and obey his orders" (Ps 103:20, NET). Each one delights in carrying out their assigned tasks, whether acting as messengers, carrying out judgments, or serving God's chosen people. We can respond to God with the same obedience in whatever assignment he chooses to lay on our hearts. An example in *worship*: John sees a great angelic army saying with a loud voice, "Worthy is the Lamb who was slain, to receive power and wealth and wisdom and might and honor and blessing!" This reminds us of the verse in Hebrews chapter 1, when the Lord ... "brings the firstborn into the world (Jesus, probably referring to His second coming), he says, "Let all God's angels worship him". We, too, should worship the Father and the Son with similar open fervour. It is the wicked angels

---

[76] **Angelic intercession**. The Catholic understanding of angelic intercession is based on their interpretation of such scriptures as Zechariah 1:12 and Revelation 8:3-4. Note: Clarke's commentary on Rev 8:3-4, "It is not said that the angel presents these prayers. He presents the incense, and the prayers ascend with it. The ascending of the incense shows that the prayers and offerings were accepted".

– the demons – who promote disobedience and undermine honour and worship to Jesus. On the other hand, worship of angels (or angelolatry) primarily relates to excessive honouring (or possibly invoking the names of) angels,

Are you alert to demonic influences?

1 Kings 13 describes a lying prophet who deceived the man of God by claiming, "an angel spoke to me by the word of the Lord, saying, 'bring him back with you into your house that he may eat bread and drink water' – But he lied to him" (1 Kings 13:18). In a similar vein, Christians are warned against receiving false doctrine from supposed angels:

> "But even if we, or an angel from heaven, should preach to you a gospel contrary to that which we preached to you, let him be accursed" (Gal 1:8; 2 Cor 11:14).

For example, the Mormons claim that an angel (Moroni) spoke revelations to Joseph Smith. Many are drawn into New Age channelling[77] — when a person's body is taken over by a spirit for the purpose of communication. These may sound extreme, but there is the clarion call found at 1 Timothy 4:1-2,

> "But even so, the Spirit very clearly tells us that in the last times some will abandon the true faith because of their devotion to spirits sent to deceive and sabotage, and mistakenly they will end up following the doctrine of demons. They will be carried away through the hypocrisy of liars whose consciences have been branded with a red-hot iron" (The Voice).

What is our spiritual armour?

Not all evil and sin originate from Satan and demons, but some of it does. For example, if there is a pattern of persistent sin in the life of a Christian in one area or another, the primary responsibility for that sin rests with the individual Christian. Nevertheless, there could be some demonic influence contributing to, and intensifying, that sinful tendency. But according to 1 John 5:18 from the Amplified Bible (Classic edition),

---

[77] **New Age channelling** has similarities to old-fashioned seances. This occultic practice involves the alleged contact with spirits of the dead who are temporarily invited inside the body of a practitioner to speak through the vocal cords of the host and give special messages from beyond the grave. Called Spiritism in the 19th century, today, this procedure is named Channelling.

"We know [absolutely] that anyone born of God does not [deliberately and knowingly] practice committing sin, but the One Who was begotten of God carefully watches over and protects him [Christ's divine presence within him preserves him against the evil], and the wicked one does not lay hold (get a grip) on him or touch [him]".

What does this mean? No one born of God continues in a practice of sin because he carries the sinless nature of Christ, the seed (or DNA) of Jesus. He is a new creation and has become – not just given – the righteousness of God (2 Cor 5:21; 1 John 3:9; also Question 160). Sinning is abnormal behaviour for the child of God. When we sin, we feel rotten because we are acting contrary to our true identity.

Because we belong to Jesus, and his Spirit indwells us, he who touches his people touches the Lord. Satan is unable to possess (take control of) the inner spirit of a born-again Christian. However, he will try to wreak havoc in our life, to harm ourselves. One of the ways he does that is by trying to deceive and distract us from the grace of God and fill us with fear. If he can get us to agree with his lies, a stronghold may form in our *mind* giving ground to the enemy. This is why we need to resist his fiery darts with the shield of faith along with other parts of the whole suit of armour, to bring "every arrogant obstacle that is raised up against the knowledge of God, and we take every *thought* captive to make it obey Christ (2 Cor 10:5, NET; Eph 6:16).

You see, as discussed elsewhere in this series of notes (Question 18), many students of the Bible believe that we are composed of three parts; a body, a soul (mind, will, and desires) and a spirit (1 Thess 5:23). The spirit of a man belongs to God. Their spirit is united with the Holy Spirit, but their bodies and souls can still be susceptible to the influence of evil spirits. Just like you can turn a light on in one room, and the next room in the house can be dark, the same is true in the spirit realm. This is why we are told to be transformed by renewing our minds (souls) through the Word of God. Our spirits are instantly made new the moment we are saved, but our souls can take time to renew and 'clean up'.

We cannot allow ourselves to be unaware of Satan's schemes or caught off guard in this spiritual warfare, nor should we allow fear and anxiety to get the best of us. Instead, we must pray to be strong and courageous because the Lord is with us, for us, and in us. We know that God is sovereign, and we know that for those who love God and are called according to his purpose, all things work together for our good, according to the good pleasure of God's will and for God's glory" (Rom 8:28).

We can take heart in this battle. Let's read Colossians 2:15, where Jesus at the cross ... "defeated all powers and forces. He let the whole world see them being led away as prisoners when he celebrated his victory" (CEV).

Yes, because of Jesus' death on the cross, our sins are completely forgiven, and Satan has no rightful authority over us. One day these losers will be gone forever!

> *"While we do not place our faith directly in angels,*
> *we should place it in the God who rules the angels;*
> *then we can have peace".*
> *- Billy Graham*

Digging Deeper -
What are the Angels and Demons up to?

Scan the QR code for informative links to each of these questions.

1. **How many** angels are there?
   (Deut 33:2; Heb 12:22; Rev 5:11)

2. What contrasting views do Christians, Muslims, and Hindus have regarding **guardian angels?**

3. Should we **pray to, or worship,** angels?
   (Matt 4:10; Col 2:18; Rev 22:8-9)

4. Can angels or demons **read our mind?** (Dan 2:27-28; Luke 6:8; 11:17)

5. Where does Satan attack – what is his **battlefield?**

See Suggested Answers at the end of this book.

Action Point
Daily over the next week consider and apply the parts of the Christian's suit of armour (Eph 6:10-18). Each day read the appropriate few paragraphs from the following webpage in the QR.

Prayer
> Father, your word says that we will never perish and that we cannot be snatched from your hands. Lord, in this moment, I am struggling to hold on to this. Wrap me in your arms and hold me closer to you Lord. In Jesus' name, Amen.

Q16. HOW DO WE DEFEAT SIN?

What is Sin?

Perhaps we have been associated with a religion which defined sin as law-breaking; for example, breaking the Ten Commandments[78], other Bible commands, or even some church policies and protocols. Or, maybe we tend towards a definition of sin as immoral behaviour. But this is not how the Bible defines sin.

The original verb for sin[79] means to miss the mark and not share the prize. But what is the mark that we are supposed to hit, and what is the prize? Some verses

---

[78] **Ten Commandments**. After rescuing the Hebrews from Egyptian slavery, God, through Moses, established a covenant with them that included hundreds of laws for living as His chosen people. The centrepiece of this Old Covenant was the 10 Commandments. The New Covenant of Jesus has completely replaced the Old Covenant, including those 10 Commandments. However, Jesus did not say that the Old Covenant would last forever, only that it wouldn't pass away until everything was accomplished (Matt 5:17-18).

The scriptures plainly state that we are not under law (Rom. 6:14–15, Gal 5:18), we are dead to the law (Rom 7:4), and we are free from the law (Rom 7:3, 6). We have not been made lawless. Rather, we have been given something better. Instead of walking in the old way of the law, we are to walk in the new way of the Spirit (Rom 7:6, 8:4; Gal 5:18). "The old way, with *laws etched in stone* [the Ten Commandments] *led to death*, though it began with such glory that the people of Israel could not bear to look at Moses' face. For his face shone with the glory of God, even though the brightness was already fading away. Shouldn't we expect far greater glory under the new way now that the Holy Spirit is giving life? If the old way, which brings *condemnation*, was glorious, how much more glorious is the new way, which makes us *right with God*! In fact, that first glory was not glorious at all compared with the overwhelming glory of the new way. So, if the old way, which has *been replaced*, was glorious, how much more glorious is the new, which remains forever!" (2 Cor 3:7-11, NLT)

[79] **Sin.** In the OT, there are two main Hebrew words: first, chattath (Strong's H2403), first used in Gen 4:7, is "an offense,"; the second word, chata (Strong's H2398), which first appears in Gen 39:9, means "to miss". In the NT, like the Old, the word hamartia (Strong's G266) is the act of committing an offense (transgression); and hamartano (Strong's G264) is "missing the mark". Here are comments from four theologians:

Tozer stated that "The essence of sin is rebellion against divine authority".

in Romans chapter three will help us: "All have sinned and fall short of the glory of God" (Rom 3:23). To sin, to quote the Message Bible, is to fall short of "the glorious lives God wills for us". Or, to put it in another way, - sin is the absence of God, a broken relationship with Him. God has divine life; we do not. His life is whole, good, and perfect, but our lives are bruised and broken. So, how did this "falling short" come about?

In the Garden of Eden, Adam and Eve, prompted by the Devil to doubt, deny, and disobey their Creator, turned their back on God in **distrust** of His love. They chose the path of independence. Since then, humans have been operating from a baseline of **self-trust**, making themselves dominant as the centre rather than the Lord - what the Bible terms 'walking after the flesh'[80] – resulting in a multitude of daily sins, and eventually death. Another way to put this: sin is not just breaking a rule; it is breaking God's heart by failing to trust Him. It is a rebellious heart against God Himself at the root with specific sins as the inevitable fruit.

It's human nature to classify sins as big or small, as though minor sins were less serious than others. We may be tempted, for example, to categorize envy as less sinful than extortion or grade flirting far lower than fornication (cf. Matt 5:21-22, 27-28, 43-44). But from God's perspective, sin is sin. You can read the earlier verses in Romans 3, where it becomes crystal clear that every person who has ever lived - except for Jesus Christ – regardless of his or her moral or religious state, is, from head to foot, a sinner! What is affected? Our **character** (vs 10-12), **conversation** (vs 13-14, "every word they speak is a land mine; their lungs breathe

---

Ray Stedman describes sin as "self-centeredness and its companions a sense of guilt and of fear".

F F Bruce wrote regarding sin that, "There is something in man - even regenerate man - which objects to God and seeks to be independent of Him".

Spurgeon remarked that "sin is a thief. It will rob your soul of its life. It will rob God of his glory. Sin is a murderer. It stabbed our father, Adam. It slew our purity".

[80] **Flesh.** Aside from the obvious meaning of flesh, our earthly bodies, there is a deeper meaning of the word flesh. In the Bible, the flesh refers to an earthly (worldly) mindset, manner, point of view, standards, and accomplishments (Rom 8:6; 2 Cor 1:17; 2 Cor 5:16; 10:2; Php 3:4). In short, the flesh refers to things which are worldly instead of spiritual. To be IN the flesh has two meanings. The first meaning is to be "in the body" (Php 1:22,24; 1 Pet 4:1-2). The second meaning of in the flesh is to be an unbeliever (Rom 7:5, 8:8-9). Walking AFTER the flesh is when you attempt, even as a saved believer (who is now permanently IN the Spirit, and, by grace, permanently a son of God - Rom 8:9), to get your needs met independently of God. It's trusting in yourself - your abilities, your understanding. When you are walking after the flesh, even good things can be bad for you. Thankfully, your heavenly Father knows you are a work in progress.

out poison gas" – Message Bible), and **conduct** (vs 15-17, "our righteous acts are like filthy rags"- Isa 64:6), and finally, our *connection* with God (vs 18). Some people may get closer to the mark than others, but ultimately, we all fall short. We are all spiritually bankrupt, with no assets we could hand over to God as even partial payment of our debt. We all need grace. According to this definition, a sinner could just as easily be a churchgoer, a charity worker, a Pharisee, or a corrupt tax official. There are 'good' sinners and 'bad' sinners, but they are all sinners alike if they rely on themselves and live independently of God. In this state, we are spiritually dead (Eph 2:1).

As Jonathan Edwards, 18th century theologian, aptly stated, "You contribute nothing to your salvation except the sin that made it necessary".

What is God's plan for closing the gap?
Please read the next verse after Rom 3:23".[We] are being justified [declared free of the guilt of sin, made acceptable to God, and granted eternal life] as a gift by His [precious, undeserved] **grace**, through the redemption [the payment for our sin] which is [provided] in Christ Jesus" (Rom 3:24, Amplified).

The remedy for sin is to turn back in genuine heartfelt repentance[81] to God (which is gifted from God) and receive the grace he freely offers in Christ alone. God has already given the gift of His Son to the world and now it is up to us as individuals to receive Him. When prompted by God's Spirit, you may reach a personal decision day, a turning point when you come to the Lord's throne. There is no fixed wording to recite, but a prayerful recognition and expression of the fact that you are a sinner and know it is impossible to put yourself right. You can

---

[81] **Repentance**. We are called to repent of self-justification and self-righteousness. The focus is to stop our self-focus and make a 180° turn to being God-focused. We can consider the man Job in his sudden life-changing circumstances. "Job was indeed falsely accused by his friends, but the issue was not Job's good name that was at stake, but the honour of the Lord – for by falsely accusing Job, these friends were indirectly accusing God. Job came to an understanding that God can do anything and has the right to do anything without the creatures He created challenging His authority. And Job finally came to an understanding that God can do anything and nothing that He plans is impossible. But to reach this level of understanding there had to come about a deep humbling of himself, a self-loathing of who he was before God, and a true repentance - not a repentance from sin but a repentance of who he is – a recognition that in him dwells no good thing" (Knowing Jesus – Job 42:2, ISV). Yes, after 40 long chapters of an introspective pity party, Job was greatly blessed. The book of Job isn't about a good man going through bad times, but a good God who loves us broken people through thick and thin, and who desires to bless us no matter what we've said or done. The message redounds to His grace.

be forgiven[82] and saved only by His mercy and grace. You will be moved to repent of not living your life in full trust and belief in the sacrifice of the Son of God. Those who turn trustfully to Him hit the bullseye and receive the prize. They are forgiven, justified, saved, made new (born again), sanctified, and get to share in his divine life, an uncondemned and eternal life[83] (2 Pet 1:4). Thanks be to God that he is no longer in the business of holding our sins and trespasses against us (2 Cor 5:19)

It cannot be restated too many times that you can't accomplish or work up to union with God. Why? Because you've already got it. "Before the world began you were chosen, chosen in Christ to live through love in his presence" (Ephesians 1:4). You cannot ever become worthy or "perfect" by yourself; you can only reconnect to your Infinite Source. The Biblical revelation is about awakening, not accomplishing. It is about realization, not performance.

All sinners have a pile of sins, and some piles are bigger than others. But on the cross, the Lamb of God bore our sin, and now there are no more piles. True, we may have sinful regrets, and sin still has

---

[82] **Forgiven**. The original word (aphier..., is a verb that means to send away or release. Forgiveness is not merely ceasing to be angry but a deliberate action of dismissing a debt or offence. Prior to the cross, Jesus preached conditional forgiveness to those living under the old law-keeping covenant. "If you forgive, God will forgive" (Matt 6:14, Mark 11:25). However, as the messenger of the new covenant of grace, he also demonstrated and proclaimed unconditional forgiveness (Luke 7:42, 47; 15:22-24; John 8:11). On the cross the Lamb of God bore all your sins, past, present, and future. After the cross, the apostles described God's forgiveness in the past tense and as a gift to receive (Acts 13:38-39; 26:18; Rom 4:7; Eph 4:32; Col 3:13; Heb 10:18). Manmade religion says that if you turn from sin, confess, and behave right God may forgive you, but the gospel of grace simply declares you have been forgiven on account of God's great grace (Eph 1:7, 1 John 2:12). You were not forgiven once for all time because you were good but because God is good, and He longs to be good to you. As forgiven ones, we can forgive those who wrong us, even when they don't apologise. "Love your enemies ... bless those who curse you, pray for those who abuse you" (Luke 6:27–28). We must be rid of bitterness and grudges right away. We do what Jesus did on the cross. Our forgiving spirit will maintain our peace with God, peace with ourselves, and may, in time, move the other person's heart to respond, allowing restoration of a mutually peaceful relationship.

[83] **Eternal life**. See footnote 69 on page 96.

consequences. But the good news is that God chooses to remember our sins and lawless deeds no more (Rom 4:7-8; Heb 10:17). As far as He is concerned, they don't exist. "But what about the sin that I sinned just this morning?" God has no record of that sin. Your conscience, other people, and the devil may keep a record, but His love keeps no record of wrongs. When you sin, Jesus speaks to defend you. He does not do it to justify sin but to justify you and to remind you that you have been freed from sin.

Why is initial repentance so important?

Please don't forget this point. On becoming a Christian, we identify with Jesus' suffering and death - we were **co-crucified**[84] **with him**. This is clarified in Romans 6:7 and Galatians 2:20.

---

[84] **Co-crucified**. Watchman Nee tells a story, "For years after my conversion I had been taught that the way of deliverance was to count myself dead to sin and alive to God (Ro.6:11) I 'reckoned' from 1920 to 1927, and the trouble was that the more I did so the more alive to sin I clearly was. I simply could not believe myself dead, and I could not produce death. Sin was still defeating me, and I saw that something was fundamentally wrong. So, I asked God to show me the meaning of the expression, 'I have been crucified with Christ'. It became clear to me that when speaking of this subject God nowhere says, 'You must be,' but always 'You have been.' Yet in view of my constant failure this just did not seem possible, unless I was to be honest with myself. I almost turned to the conclusion that only dishonest people could make such statements. Yet whenever I sought help from others, I was sent back to Romans 6:11. I appreciated its teaching, but I could not make out why nothing resulted from it. No one, you see, had pointed out to me that 'knowing' (verse 6) must precede 'reckoning' (verse 11). For months I was troubled and prayed earnestly, reading the scriptures and seeking light. I said to the Lord, 'If I cannot be brought to see this, which is so fundamental, I will not preach any more. I want first to get clear on this.'

I remember one morning - how can I ever forget it! - I was reading Romans and I came to the words: 'Knowing this, that our old man was crucified with him, that the body of sin might be done away, that so we should no longer be in bondage to sin' Knowing this! How could I know it? I prayed, 'Lord, open my eyes!' and then, in a flash, I saw. I had earlier been reading 1 Cor 1:30: 'You are in Christ Jesus.' I turned it up and looked at it again. 'That you are in Christ Jesus, is *God's doing*!' It was amazing! Then if Christ died, and that is certain fact, and if God put me into Him, then I must have died too. All at once I saw oneness with Christ: that I was in Him, and that when *He died, I died*. My death to sin was a *matter of the past* and not the future. It is divine fact that had dawned on me. Carried away with joy I jumped from my chair and ran downstairs to the young man working in the kitchen. 'Brother,' I said, seizing him by the hands, 'do you know that I have died?' I must admit he looked puzzled, 'What do you mean?' he exclaimed, so I went on: 'Do you not know that Christ has died? Do you not know that I've died with Him? Do you not know that my death is no less truly a fact than His?' Oh, it was so real to me! I felt like shouting my discovery through the streets of Shanghai. From that day to this I have never for one moment doubted the finality of that word: 'I have been crucified with Christ; it is no longer I who live, but Christ who lives in me.'"

"Anyone who has died is made free [justified; declared righteous] from sin's control" (Rom 6:7, Expanded Bible).

"I have been crucified with Christ [in Him I have shared His crucifixion]; it is no longer I who live, but Christ (the Messiah) lives in me; and the life I now live in the body I live by faith in (by adherence to and reliance on and complete trust in) the Son of God, Who loved me and gave Himself up for me" (Gal 2:20, Amplified).

In other words, we died, and our death annulled our relationship to sin. We were born anew as new creatures in Christ! Thereafter, through Christ's Spirit, we must live out who we have become – no longer obsessed with the label 'sinner'[85] but now a son, a saint, with growing Christlikeness as our goal (Rom 6:2,14; Eph 1:4; 4:13). Imagine you work for a very demanding, harsh, boss but leave and find new work with a kind, generous employer. One morning you receive a phone call from your old boss demanding that you come into work immediately or face the consequences! Obviously, he now has no authority to order you around; you live under a new authority. Likewise, sin has lost control over you since a new Lord has authority in your life. Of course, you can foolishly choose to go back to sin's tyranny for a while, but it will never benefit you and only harm your conscience. The story is told of a new Christian who, when invited to a 'wild party,' sent back the RSVP – 'I am sorry I cannot attend your party because I recently died!'

How, thereafter, can I control a certain sin?
The answer is - YOU cannot control sin!

---

[85] **Sinners**. No longer sinners? We often say things like, "I'm a sinner, the same as anyone else". Or I'm a sinner saved by grace. "There is certainly truth in those statements. Christians have been saved, yet all still struggle with sin. However, consider this: the Bible doesn't really use the word "sinner" as a label to refer to faithful Christians. We are now declared righteous by God (Rom 5:1). You are no longer a sinner; rather, you are a saint who sometimes sins. The difference is in how God looks at you – as a child of God. When Paul says, "I am the chief of sinners" (1 Tim 1:15-16), he's alluding to an evil title he earned as a blasphemer and persecutor of Christians. He is not saying, "I still blaspheme and persecute Christians". The moment Paul became a Christian, he stopped being the chief of sinners. No matter what you've done, the moment you were placed into Christ, you became just as righteous and holy as he is (1 John 4:17). We can ask ourselves, 'Do I believe in the words of Isaiah 53:5-6, "But he was pierced for our rebellion, crushed for our sins. He was beaten so we could be whole. He was whipped so we could be healed. All of us, like sheep, have strayed away. We have left God's paths to follow our own. Yet the Lord laid on him the sins of us all"? Where are all my sins? Do I believe that God laid my sins on the Lord Jesus Christ? Or are they still on you?

When you sin, Satan will point the finger and say, "You are a sinner. Your fruit is bad because you are bad". It's not true. We need to understand that the desire to sin is not from you. "I am doing the very thing I hate" … "I am not the one doing it" (Rom. 7:15,20). 'I don't want to do it' means it is not now my new heart's desire to sin. Where does this desire come from? Sin in the flesh! Your flesh is not inherently sinful, but it is in your flesh – your body and mind – where you feel the influence of sin.

Sin tempts us through images, sounds, and thoughts - through our natural senses. This is why, by the power of the Holy Spirit, we daily need our minds transformed from the "stinking thinking" assailing us. After initial repentance at conversion, we progressively adjust and turn our sinful thinking (repentance means to 'change one's mind') to Christ's all-sufficient sacrifice and imparting HIS righteousness to us. If we have a repeat performance of certain sins, do not give up. The righteous man falls seven times and rises again. If our recovery time is shorter, we are growing in grace! (Prov 24:16).

Our thinking changes its focus – incrementally at first, yet, our life undergoes transformation. Imagine you're getting ready to migrate to Japan. You'll naturally set your mind on the things of Japan. You might try sushi, watch sumo wrestling, and even begin to learn Japanese. You think about life in Japan and set your heart on Japanese things. Paul summarises this life change by saying in Colossians 3:1-5 that "Christ is your life". He is the orienting centre of everything we do. Our priority in family life; our leisure life; our speech. Everything in life revolves around the resurrected Christ who is in heaven.

Hence, the solution to sin, sexual or otherwise, is not to focus on denial, but to revel in pleasure with Christ, your life! Consider a young man who formerly enjoyed the habit of lazing late in bed every morning. But now suddenly he awakes and goes jogging every morning at 6:00 AM. Why? He met a girl and she also jogs every morning at 6:00 AM. A greater pleasure! Seeking Christ in heaven means we have found a new pleasure. Ungodly speaking, immoral pleasures, and greediness can be killed with resurrection pleasure. Jesus' resurrection transforms our eternity, but it also transforms our lives now.

How do we live by grace in the New Covenant?

We need to learn to no longer live according to law but by grace. Imagine being married to someone who threatened to kick you out every time you made a mistake. You would be an emotional wreck. You would walk on eggshells for fear of upsetting your hyper-sensitive and ungracious partner. This is exactly how many Christians live. Since they don't understand the completed work of Christ, forgiveness, and the new covenant, they are filled with performance anxiety. They are ever fearful of enraging a temperamental God. But now we enjoy real freedom. We become not more sinful but Son-full. Sure, you still have the capacity to sin. But you don't enjoy it like you used to. Sinning makes you miserable because you know who your Father is; and who you are – His son!

We must embrace God's blood currency to understand this once-for-all forgiveness. "Without the shedding of blood there is no forgiveness" (Heb 9:22). We are totally forgiven because of blood, not by our wordy apologies – although, of course, we can express our sorrow and shame before our Father. In our human relationships, we're used to a word-based currency for forgiveness. But God has a blood-based economy for sins.

On the Day of Atonement[86], the Jews were not required to name or even remember every sin committed over the past year. How could they? Instead, they relied on the blood of bulls and goats as the covering for their sins. It was never about their memory and words. It was always about the blood. Likewise, for us today, it's about the blood of Jesus. But here's the difference: Jesus shed His blood only once. No repeat needed. Because of His one-time blood sacrifice, you're as forgiven today as you'll ever be. You can do nothing to be more forgiven than you already are! Imagine if you were only forgiven for the sins you asked forgiveness for. What if you forgot one or more? What if you passed away with 10,000 unconfessed sins? This is why it can't be about your memory or the number of prayers of confession. It is about the blood of Christ, and 'it is finished.'

Yes, maybe religion trained you to think that, like the ancient Israelites under the old Law Covenant, you are forgiven progressively or in instalments. The New Covenant is different. Jesus has already given you all the forgiveness you'll ever need. No one is 59 per cent forgiven. You're either in Adam and entirely unforgiven, or you're in Christ and completely forgiven. There's no middle ground. There's a reason it's called "the finished work of Christ" - because *you*

---

[86] **Day of Atonement** in Israel was something like an annual spiritual spring cleaning, except for the fact that this sacred day came in the fall of the year, in September-October, six months after the celebration of Passover (Leviticus 16). Unlike the other Jewish holidays, the Day of Atonement was no festive event. Instead, it was a day of national mourning and repentance. The issue at stake is whether or not God will continue to abide within the camp in the midst of His people. The uncleanness of the people contaminated the dwelling place of God, and the Day of Atonement was provided to remove these sins. The Day of Atonement foreshadowed and anticipated a greater, permanent cleansing of God's people and of His dwelling place, which was to be accomplished by a better priest, who offered a better sacrifice (Heb 7:26-28; 9:11-12).

don't have to finish it! Grace will teach us, and enable us, to live a holy life (Titus 2:11-12). Remember that we are now children of God filled with purifying hope[87].

We can, in conclusion, make two summary statements:

Sin is to fall short of "the glorious lives God wills for us". It is not just breaking the rules; it is breaking God's heart by failing to trust Him.

The remedy for sin is to repent and turn back to God and receive the grace he freely offers in the New Covenant through the blood of Jesus. John Piper writes, "I know of no other way to triumph over sin long term than ... to gain a distaste for it because of a superior satisfaction in God".

> *"There is no saint without a past, no sinner without a future".*
> *- Saint Augustine*

---

[87] **Purifying Hope** "And everyone who has this hope in him [in Christ] purifies himself, just as that one [Jesus Christ] is pure" (1 John 3:3). We are God's children with the hope of not only one day being with our Jesus but like him. In English, we often use the word 'hope' to imply 'I hope so', like, 'I hope it will become warmer today'. However, the Greek word for hope (elpidos) has a sense of absolute certainty, of "full assurance", when compared to our English word (Heb 6:11; yet note a rare exception in Acts 27:20).

Such certainty is based on what Jesus Christ has already done. It is a certain hope that is merely awaited. We are motivated by this sure hope. A child of God "is (not should be, or will be) constantly purifying himself" as Jesus is pure. As we gaze at the pure One and yield to the Spirit, we become progressively transformed. We don't live holy lives to prove we are children of God, but we live holy lives because we are children of God, possessing a new nature. We are holy, so act holy. We are God's dearly loved children, so act like it (2 Cor 7:1; Gal 5:16-26; 1 Pet 1:15). We may be struggling with a particular sort of addiction or habit. But we will find that as we abide in Christ with a new heart and mind, and fix our hope on Him, our appetites will begin to change. All this is to the glory of his grace that empowers us to say no to ungodliness and impurity (Titus 2:11-14).

Martyn Lloyd-Jones once commented on 1 John 3:3: "The tendency is for people to argue like this: 'Ah,' they say, 'there is not much point in talking to us about doctrine; you have to remind people of their practical duty.' So holiness teaching not infrequently becomes a constant repetition of certain duties which we are to carry out. I agree that we do have to do these things, but I say that the ultimate way of carrying out these duties and really practicing these things, is to have such a grasp and understanding of the doctrine that the practice becomes inevitable. And that is, of course, precisely what the New Testament always does."

142

Digging Deeper - How do we Defeat Sin?

Scan the QR code for informative links to each of these questions.

1. What could you say to those who reason, "I'm a nice person, I don't sin as badly as terrorists or drug pushers, in fact, I give to charity"?

2. How would you help someone **overwhelmed with guilt**?

3. "But surely," someone objects, "grace gives a person **license to sin**!" How would you reply?

4. What does 1 John 3:9 mean, "No one who is born of God practices sin, because His seed abides in him; and **he cannot sin** because he is born of God"?

5. Will God whip me into shape if I sin? Doesn't Hebrews 12:6 say we are "**scourged**" by God?

See Suggested Answers at the end of this book.

Action Point
Please watch this uplifting video (link behind QR code) ,
"Does God Love Me When I Sin?

Prayer
Loving Heavenly Father, I thank you for your forgiveness through your Son's blood, and the imputation of His righteousness. I surrender my whole life into your hand. May your grace and Spirit empower me today to live out a life of holiness that glorifies you name. Protect me from the Evil One and sin. I thank You Lord. "And in His temple all cry "Glory!" (Ps 29:9) Amen.

Q17. WHY DO WE SUFFER?

Where is God in this messed up, suffering world? We will not here catalogue just how much suffering people contend with – there is enough in daily TV news reports, newspapers, and more to the point, likely in your own life and that of your loved ones. The problem of reconciling how an all-powerful, all-loving God could allow such pain and suffering has led some to walk away from their faith.

We may sometimes say as did Jacob – as he experienced Rachel's death, Joseph's apparent untimely demise, the disgrace brought by Reuben, Judah, Simeon, Levi, and Dinah, along with a famine – "all things are against me." (Gen 42:36) How wrong he was! "These things" were secretly working together to his own good, as the end of the story proved.

We will touch on three **C**'s: The creator, the crash, and the cross.

1. THE CREATOR

Why do we suffer? The simple reality is **we do not know** the full answer! When we were infants, did we fully understand our parents (just or unjust) handling of matters? Or, imagine a fly hitting a window pane within a CEO's office. The fly cannot conceive either the mind of the executive or the building's architect. Nor can we fully know our sovereign Creator and His ways, especially as related to humanity's suffering. He and His ways are beyond our present comprehension. So, how can we presume to challenge God's ineffable and perfect will?

> "Behold, these are but the outskirts of his ways, and how small a **whisper** do we hear of him! But the thunder of his power who can understand?" (Job 26:14).

> "For my thoughts are not your thoughts, neither are your ways my ways, declares the Lord. For as the heavens are **higher** than the earth, so are my ways higher than your ways and my thoughts than your thoughts" (Isa 55:8–9).

> "Oh, the depth of the riches and wisdom and knowledge of God! How **unsearchable** are his judgments and how inscrutable his ways! "For who has known the mind of the Lord, or who has been his counsellor?" (Rom 11:33–34).

"But surely," many reason, "isn't God to blame, either directly or indirectly?" Imagine if someone stormed into the Louvre and defaced, ruined, or stole Da Vinci's Mona Lisa, worth an estimated $900 million. The culprit would be held accountable for this act of terrorism and be severely punished. Suppose, though, it was Leonardo himself, the masterpiece's owner, who decided to make alterations to it, paint over it, or even have it removed shortly after finishing the original painting. Of course, as the owner, he would not be held accountable. In a small way, this illustrates that our Creator, as Sovereign, has his own perfect will, and He is above reproach and questioning (Jer 18: 18:7-10; Ps 81:12; Hos 4:17). Romans chapter 9 helps us with this line of reasoning by using a different illustration. It says in part:

> "Who in the world do you think you are to second-guess God? Do you for one moment suppose any of us knows enough to call God into question? Clay doesn't talk back to the fingers that mold it, saying, "Why did you shape me like this?" Isn't it obvious that a potter has a **perfect right** to shape one lump of clay into a vase for holding flowers and another into a pot for cooking beans?" (Rom 9:20-21, Message Bible).

Even so, He kindly provides some limited insights into the matter of suffering. The question is, do I trust his goodness, love, justice, and promises, even without full explanations? Scripture teaches that we can have a true and personal knowledge of the Creator, but this does not mean we will ever understand him exhaustively.

Our Creator has not lost control. Meditate a while over the reassuring words in Romans 8:28-29, "We know that all things work together for good to those who love God, to those who are the called according to His purpose. For whom He foreknew, He also predestined to be conformed to the image of His Son, that He might be the firstborn among many brethren." (Rom 8:28-29).

"Works together" (sunergeo; derivation of English word 'synergy') - the combination of many elements to produce something brand-new, a positive result, that neither could form separately. Our God of Grace is a God of DIVINE SYNERGY. We can easily lose sight of God's hand weaving together both good and bad strands - including disappointments and disasters - in the lives of those who love Him. Even our darkest moments will ultimately produce a benefit that could not happen any other way (Isa 45:7; Lam 3:37-38). A pharmacist prepares medicine which comprises numerous compounds, some of which if swallowed individually could cause major issues, but collectively ('shake the bottle before taking') work together for the sick persons good. What overall good? God's purpose regarding His sons is not that they enjoy a cosy life, but that they "become transformed into the IMAGE OF HIS SON."

This truth removes fear and anxiety in His "called ones" who love God. They know when life 'goes wrong', it hasn't gone wrong at all! God has not lost control, nor is he indifferent. Only then will suffering make us better, not bitter. God is the master recycler. He recycles our pain and turns it into the fruit of the Spirit for his glory. Nothing is wasted. God is fully engaged in every event in your life.

2. THE CRASH

God created man with *free agency*, free will[88]. There was a possibility for even the perfect man to sin. For God had said, "In the day that you eat of it [the tree] you shall surely die" (Gen 2:17). After the fall, man was not able not to sin. Paul said,

> "For the mind that is set on the flesh[89] is hostile to God, for it does not submit to God's law; indeed, it cannot. Those who are in the flesh **cannot** please God" (Rom 8:7–8 ESV).

> "The natural person does not accept the things of the Spirit of God, for they are folly to him, and he is **not able** to understand them because they are spiritually discerned" (1 Cor 2:14).

---

[88] **Free Will.** There are opposing views of 'free will between Calvinism and Arminianism . Here is the briefest of summaries.

Calvinism: Total Inability or Total Depravity. Because of the fall, man is unable of himself to savingly believe the gospel. The gospel cannot be believed apart from the miracle of divine grace. Why? Because the sinner is dead, blind, and deaf to the things of God; his heart is deceitful and desperately corrupt. His will is not free but in bondage to his evil nature. Therefore, he will not — indeed, he cannot — choose good over evil in the spiritual realm. Consequently, it takes much more than the Spirit's assistance to bring a sinner to Christ - it takes regeneration by which the Spirit makes the sinner alive and gives him a new nature. Faith is not something man contributes to salvation but is itself a part of God's gift of salvation - it is God's gift to the sinner, not the sinner's gift to God (John 1:12-13; 15:16). Armenianism: Free Will or Human Ability. Although human nature was seriously affected by the fall (partial depravity), man has not been left in a state of total spiritual helplessness. God graciously enables every sinner to repent and believe, but He does not interfere with man's freedom. Each sinner possesses free will, and his eternal destiny depends on how he uses it. Man's freedom consists of his ability to choose good over evil in spiritual matters; his will is not enslaved to his sinful nature. The sinner has the power to either cooperate with God's Spirit and be regenerated or resist God's grace and perish. The lost sinner needs the Spirit's assistance, but he does not have to be regenerated by the Spirit before he can believe, for faith is man's act and precedes the new birth. Faith is the sinner's gift to God; it is man's contribution to salvation. (Eph 1:13; James 4:8).

[89] **Flesh.** See footnote 80 on page 107.

This is the nature of all human beings from birth — what Paul calls the "natural person," and what Jesus calls "born of the flesh".

All suffering, all pain, and every tear that has been shed on earth is either a direct or an indirect result of the crash into sin. Even natural disasters[90] happen because the world was cursed (Rom 8:20-21). God is not the creator of suffering - we are. It's not by God's design; it's by our sin. God allows for suffering, but He did not create it. He allows us to exercise our free will, which can lead to bad choices with consequent suffering.

> A man went to a barber's shop to have his hair cut and his beard trimmed. They enjoyed a good conversation on various subjects. When they eventually touched on the subject of God, the barber said to his customer: "I don't believe that God exists".

---

[90] **Natural disasters**. Here are seven factors to consider:
1. **We don't know** all the reasons God brings or permits specific calamities or why particular people are made to suffer by them, but we should trust that in God's omniscience and ultimate wisdom, He knows how to work out what is best for everyone in the end (Job 42:1-6; Isa 55:8-9).
2. **He is not the cause** of such disasters. He is love and is working out a great plan for all humanity (2 Pet 3:9; Rom 8:28; 1 Cor 15:22-24). He also permits Satan, demons, and mankind to exercise their limited will to commit acts of sin, evil, and wickedness.
3. **Humans** bear a heavy responsibility. Some natural disasters are made worse by man's poor judgments (Prov 14:12; 22: 3) and age-long rejection of God and His laws resulting in worsening environmental and climatic conditions. By forfeiting God's oversight, they have lost His protection.
4. **Time and chance** In His design for the world, God allows many events to run their course, "timing and circumstances meet them all". (Eccles 9:11 ISV).
5. **Not penalty for personal sin.** Those dying in accidents or natural disasters are not greater sinners than those who survive (Luke 13:1-5; John 9:2-2).
6. **Future Kingdom**. Those in Christ who die in natural disasters will be resurrected at the return of Jesus Christ (1 Cor 15:51-52; 2 Cor 4:17-18; 1 Thess 4:16; Rev 20:4-6). Others, who never had a genuine understanding of God or real opportunity for eternal salvation, will be raised in the general resurrection under the Kingdom (John 5:28-29; Rev 20:5). Jesus Christ – the one who can control nature - will eventually return to usher in his reign under which natural disasters will no longer plague humankind (Matt 8:25-17; Rev 21:1-5).
7. **We learn** much about God and our dependence upon him during and in the aftermath of a natural disaster. We are often reminded of His fearsome power, our mortality, and finite abilities. We are awakened to the plight of others and are humbled to serve our great and loving God by serving others.

"Why do you say that?" asked the customer.

"Well, you just have to go out in the street to realise that God doesn't exist. Tell me, if God exists, would there be so many sick people? Would there be abandoned children? If God existed, there would be neither suffering nor pain. I can't imagine a loving God allowing all of these things". The customer thought for a moment but didn't respond because he didn't want to start an argument. The barber finished his job, and the customer left the shop. Just after he left the barber's shop, he saw a man on the street with long stringy, dirty hair and an untrimmed beard; he looked dirty and unkempt. The customer turned back and entered the barber's shop again, and he said to the barber, "You know what? Barbers don't exist".

"How can you say that?" asked the barber. "I am here, and I am a barber. And I just worked on you".

"NO!" the customer exclaimed. "Barbers don't exist because if they did, there would be no people with dirty long hair and untrimmed beards, like that man outside".

"Ah, but barbers DO exist. That is what happens when people do not come to me".

"Exactly," affirmed the customer. "That's the point! God DOES exist! That is why there is so much pain and suffering in the world. That is what happens when people do not go to Him and don't look to Him for help".

Another factor is *chance*, or as stated in scripture, "The fastest runner doesn't always win the race, and the strongest warrior doesn't always win the battle. The wise sometimes go hungry, and the skilful are not necessarily wealthy. And those who are educated don't always lead successful lives. It is all decided by **chance**, by being in the right place at the right time" (Eccl 9:11, NLT).

3. THE CROSS[91]

A father whose son was killed in a terrible accident came to his pastor and said in great anger: "Where was God when my son died?" The pastor kindly replied, "The same place he was when His Son died."

God didn't cause the problem of evil but has taken it upon Himself to solve it. Jesus suffered in order to save his people from their sins. His very name, "Jesus" — the Greek form of "Joshua" — identified him as the one who would bring about God's long-awaited salvation for sinners. Jesus' own summary of his mission in Mark

---

[91] **Cross**. See <u>footnote 8</u>.

10:45 - "to serve, and to give his life as a ransom[92] for many" - closely mirrors Isaiah's prophecy of the suffering Servant who would pour out his life to death to bear sins, to bring us healing and wholeness, and "justify many" (Isaiah 53)[93]. Peter makes this explicit when he alludes to this Messianic chapter, writing,

"He himself bore our sins in his body on the tree, that we might die to sin and live to righteousness. **By his wounds you have been healed**" (1 Peter 2:24).

Isaiah's great prophecy about the Servant concludes with his life beyond death: the Servant "shall see his offspring" and "prolong his days;" he shall "divide the spoil with the strong" in victory (Isa 53:10–12). Isaiah does not use the word 'resurrection,' but these verses display the Servant alive after his suffering.

The resurrection of Christ[94] shows not only that God's people will be raised but that God will usher in a new heaven and a new earth. Therefore, the labours we do in the Lord are not defeated by death but have eternal significance (1 Cor 15:53-58).

Trying to unravel just a few of the endless knotted strands of suffering we face daily - personally or internationally - naturally draws our attention. For example, in 1911 there was a dreadful mining disaster in Durham. In the Memorial Service in the packed cathedral, the then-bishop used a tapestry to illustrate his message. Showing the underneath, he revealed a tangled mess of embroidery thread that seemed meaningless. Then Bishop Moule turned over the tapestry to reveal,

---

[92] **Ransom**. See footnote 60.

[93] **Isaiah 53.** The 17th-century Jewish historian, Raphael Levi, admitted that long ago, the rabbis used to read Isaiah 53 in synagogues, but after the chapter caused "arguments and great confusion," the rabbis decided that the simplest thing would be to take that prophecy out of the Haftarah readings in synagogues. That's why today, when they read Isaiah 52, they stop in the middle of the chapter and, the week after, jump straight to Isaiah 54. Here is an outline of this Messianic chapter:

Vs 2	… humble beginnings
Vs 3	… not worthy of attention
Vs 4	… mistaken concept of his death
Vs 5	… pierced as our substitution – vs 6, 10, 11, 12
Vs 6	… sin-bearer of us all
Vs 7	… humility in suffering
Vs 8	… cut off in violent death
Vs 9	… buried like a criminal but in a rich man's grave
Vs 10	… resurrected
vs 11	… many to be counted righteous
vs 12	… a victorious volunteer

[94] **Resurrection of Christ.** See Q12 on page 83.

intricately woven, the words, 'GOD IS LOVE.' From our position, life can seem deeply confusing, but God always works in love. He can bring good from even the worst situations of life.

What does this mean for us today?

The Creator, the crash, and the cross. Or, if you prefer, the Sovereign, the sin, and

| The Creator | The Crash | The Cross |

the Saviour. We may yet have many unanswered questions over this issue of evil and suffering. In likely the oldest book of the Bible, the book of JOB, we read of this faithful but perplexed man who faced the profound loss – of his home, family, and health. Imagine him not only attending the funerals of all his ten children (and possibly their spouses) within about one week but also the funerals of all but a few of his hundreds of servants (Job 1:3, 15-17). He did not endure his trials due to an innate toughness. In fact, his suffering brought forth bitterness, *self-pity*, and a desire for death. He said, "I hate this life! Who needs any more of this? Let me alone! There's nothing to my life - it's nothing but smoke". ... "God alienated my family from me; everyone who knows me avoids me. My relatives and friends have all left". ... "Where's the strength to keep my hopes up? What future do I have to keep me going? Do you think I have nerves of steel? Do you think I'm made of iron? Do you think I can pull myself up by my bootstraps? Why, I don't even have any boots!" (Job 3:24-26; 6:8-13; 17:11-16; 19:13-22, Message Bible). He candidly admitted his feelings, as Paul did when he felt overwhelmed to the point of despair (2 Cor 1:8).

The book of Job has about 300 questions and most of them Job's. Eventually, God spoke to Job, and guess what? God plied him with questions of His own! This set of questions related to God Almighty being in total control of all creation. Job was faced with the proposition – 'was he more eager to know the *reasons* for suffering or to deepen his *relationship* with the Sovereign Creator?' The bottom line: was he prepared to place his confidence, his trust in God – His promises and presence? In the final chapter of the Book, Job exclaims:

> "I know that you can do anything and that no one can stop you. You ask who it is who has so foolishly denied your providence. It is I. I was talking about things I knew nothing about and did not understand,

things far too wonderful for me. "You said, 'Listen and I will speak! Let me put the questions to you! See if you can answer them!' "But now I say, 'I had heard about you before, but now I have seen you, and I loathe myself and repent in dust and ashes.'" (Job 42:1-5, Living Bible).

Yes, trials taught Job to place his confidence in God and draw near to Him. God didn't give him a lecture on why suffering exists; rather, He, in effect, said I'm with you, and I will not leave you. Job's endurance, and ours, do not originate from personal strength or a test of tenacity. It emerges from God's mercy and compassion for flawed individuals who lack unwavering faith. It is the Holy Spirit's work in a believer's life. While Job was speaking negatively, God, who sees all things from the perspective of eternity, was calling him blameless and upright (Job 1:8). God rewrote the story of Job's miserable life, and the ending was far better than anything Job could have imagined.

We need an *eternal perspective*. One day it will all make sense. But in the meantime, we do not suffer alone. We must recognise that God sees the larger picture and how He orchestrates everything for His glory, which is to our eternal benefit. You and I are not the centre. There's a larger story unfolding that you and I are not fully privy to. "Our present troubles are small and won't last very long. Yet they produce for us a glory that vastly outweighs them and will last forever!" (2 Cor 4:16-18, NLT). We have to ask ourselves if we trust that God's plan is good, even if it doesn't seem good at the moment. That's what faith demands, believing in advance what will only make sense in reverse. Trust His grace! Succinctly, C. S. Lewis wrote: "They say of some temporal suffering, 'No future bliss can make up for it,' not knowing that Heaven, once attained, will work backwards and turn even that agony into a glory".

We endure and find rest by abiding in Christ and holding fast to His name (Rev 2:13; 2 Pet 1:2-3). The Lord empathizes with our pain and comes flying to our aid (Deut 33:26). The abundance of endurance-related verses in the Bible does not seek to instil fear or uncertainty in believers but rather to inspire trust in the One who empowers us to remain steadfast until the end.

Many choose to ESCAPE trials by compromising or blaming others (Jer 5:3); yet others may ENDURE trials, gritting their teeth and hanging on; but Christians will ENLIST trials, allowing adverse circumstances to *refine their faith* in God and deepen their sympathy and care for their fellow man (1 Pet 1:6-7). Christian author Kay Arthur said, "The disappointment has come - not because God desires to hurt you or make you miserable or to demoralize you or ruin your life or keep you from ever knowing happiness. He wants you to be perfect and complete in every aspect, lacking nothing. It's not the easy times that make you more like

Jesus, but the hard times". As the saying goes, "Today's mighty oak is just yesterday's little nut that held its ground".

It's true that we may not fully comprehend the reasons why God allows the suffering, but we can say with conviction that He is not to blame. Psalm 147:3-4 says, "He binds their wounds, heals the sorrows of their hearts. He counts all the stars within His hands, carefully fixing their number and giving them names". Think of that! The God of the galaxies is the God who knows when your heart is broken – and can heal it! He can number and name all the stars, yet He watches over His people personally and individually! No wonder the psalmist continues, "Our Lord is great. Nothing is impossible with His overwhelming power. He is loving, compassionate, and wise beyond all measure" (Ps 147:5 The Voice). May we continue to draw ever closer to our God of all grace.

> *"We must learn to regard people*
> *less in light of what they do or omit to do,*
> *and more in the light of what they suffer".*
> *- Dietrich Bonhoeffer*

Unit 6: Sin

Digging Deeper - Why do we Suffer?

Scan the QR code for informative links to each of these questions.

1. What key **factors,** do you think, will help in understanding the matter of evil and suffering?

2. Read **Ps 139:17**. Is this verse describing David's amazement at the extent of God's thinking processes in general or at the incomprehensible knowledge of God for him personally?

3. Why does God allow **Satan** to live?

4. Read Job 4:8 and Gal 6:7. Is reaping what you sow just **karma**?

5. Can you begin a list of seven **promises** in scripture that gives you personal hope? Now, how about considering *one each day* as you pray over the next week?

See Suggested Answers at the end of this book.

Action Point

Read through 2 Corinthians 4. What is the enlightening message everyone needs? How do verses 7-12, and 16-18, help you cope with your present anxieties?

Prayer

> Father, God of all comfort, how I praise and thank you for being with me in this deep, dark valley. Your rod and staff sustain and keep me during this time of suffering, sadness, and loss. I pray also for others who are walking through dark times; may your promised grace be sufficient to carry them through. I pray this in the name of Jesus, my good Shepherd, the One who endured so much suffering for my sake. Amen.

Q18. WHAT HAPPENS AT DEATH?

Grief tears life to shreds; it shakes one from top to bottom; it pulls apart at the seams. Grief is truly nothing less than a life-shattering loss. You may know this experience all too well. Jesus, "a man of sorrows and acquainted with grief" wept over his friend Lazarus (Isa 53:3).

All cultures have shown interest in life after death. Egyptians dedicated pyramids to their dead. Chinese built monumental emperor tombs with ceramic armies to protect them in the afterlife. Vikings dressed fallen warriors and released them to the wind in burning ships. American Indians buried weapons and tools with their dead for use in the Happy Hunting Ground. Hence the question: What happens when we die?

There are various takes on this question among Christians, but mainstream churches certainly adhere to the belief in an afterlife in some form. However, the LDS[95] church extends its belief in an afterlife to include prayers and vicarious baptism for the dead. On the other hand, some denominations, like Christadelphians, Jehovah's Witnesses, Seventh-day Adventists, and some Lutherans, teach Christian mortalism[96] - what has been called "soul sleep". This

---

[95] **LDS**: The Church of Jesus Christ of Latter-day Saints (Mormons). The LDS scripture states that at death, "the spirits of all men, whether they be good or evil, are taken home to that God who gave them life" (Alma 40:11). They are then assigned to a state of paradise or hell in the spirit world until the final judgment when they will either be received into a state of glory in the Kingdom of God or be cast off into Outer Darkness. Like many Eastern Orthodox and Catholics, the LDS Church teaches that the prayers of the righteous living may be of help to the dead. Still, the LDS Church takes this further in practising vicarious baptism of the living for the dead, based on their interpretation of 1 Corinthians 15:29.

[96] **Mortalism** is the avowed belief of some Christians that the human soul is not naturally immortal and includes the belief that the soul is "sleeping" after death until the Resurrection of the Dead and the Last Judgment, a time known as the intermediate state or thnetopsychism. The earliest clear instance of soul sleep is found in Tatian, a Christian theologian from the late second century. He writes in Oratio ad Graecos: "The soul is not in itself immortal... If, indeed, it knows not the truth, it dies, and is dissolved with the body, but rises again at last at the end of the world with the body, receiving death by punishment in immortality. But, again, if it acquires the knowledge of God, it dies not, although for a time

is the teaching that when people die, their physical body ceases to function, and the life force of the spirit is removed. This would mean that their conscious existence completely ends while they wait in the grave for a resurrected body restored by God at the end times. "When you're dead, you are really dead!" – they maintain. This concept of soul sleep became popular among some Christians in the 1830s. Men like Methodist preacher George Storrs, Baptist deacon Henry Grew, and about the same time, William Miller, all promoted this mortalist view known as "soul-sleep".

They leaned heavily on a few OT passages, especially in Ecclesiastes, to buttress this position, along with NT passages where dead people are referred to as "sleeping" or "asleep," as proof that the dead are now in a sort of unconscious state of non-being.

Let's examine two of their 'proof texts', starting with **Ecclesiastes 9:5-6, 10**

> "For the living know that they will die, but the dead know nothing at all, nor do they have any more reward, because all memory of them is forgotten. Also, their love and their hate and their jealousy have already perished, and they no longer have any share in what is done

---

it be dissolved". In later times, William Tyndale, John Wycliffe, Martin Luther, and William Miller, were exponents of the idea. Soul sleep stands in contrast with the traditional Christian belief that immortal souls immediately go to heaven or hell after death.
Examples of religions teaching 'soul-sleep'.

Jehovah's Witnesses:
> "The Bible teaches that the soul is not immortal, but that it dies when the body dies. The dead are in a state of unconsciousness, similar to sleep, and they do not have any thoughts, feelings, or awareness".
> 'What Does the Bible Really Teach?'

Seventh-day Adventist:
> "The Bible teaches that the dead are unconscious in death and do not have any thoughts, feelings, or awareness until the resurrection".
> 'Fundamental Beliefs of Seventh-day Adventists, published by the General Conference of Seventh-day Adventists.'

Christadelphian:
> "We believe that death is the cessation of life, and that the dead have no conscious existence until the resurrection". 'Statement of Faith of the Christadelphians.

The Church of Scientology:
> "Reincarnation is a fact of existence. It means the thetan [the spirit] leaves the body and goes to a new one after death. The being retains its identity and awareness from one life to the next". - L. Ron Hubbard, "The Fundamentals of Thought".

under the sun. ... Whatever your hand finds to do, do it with all your might; for there is no activity or planning or knowledge or wisdom in Sheol where you are going".

These verses do indeed appear to support the concept of "soul-sleep". Is this how you have always viewed this proof text? However, have you considered an alternative take on this passage? Here are three questions to ponder:

Question: If the dead "no longer have 'any share' in what is done under the sun," what does this mean regarding their resurrection? Who only can give a dead person any share in life again? Not a human but only God. So according to this reading and interpretation of the verse – Jehovah will not resurrect the dead!

Question: Are these verses the author's final conclusions? Or do they represent a stage in his fluctuating reasonings on how things appear from a human viewpoint? For example, Solomon argues back and forth on other questions: is it better to be dead or alive? (Eccl 4:2-3; cf. Eccl 9:4); what happens to man's spirit? (Eccl 3:19-21; cf. Eccl 12:7); what is the fate of the righteous? (Eccl 9:2-3; cf. Eccl 12:13-14).

Question: If Solomon believed in soul sleep, why did he write at the end of the same book, in Ecclesiastes 12:7, "Then the dust returns to the earth as it was; and the spirit returns to true God who gave it"? That would indicate some sort of afterlife.

Shortly, we will consider other scriptures that those in mainstream Christianity perceive to support the teaching of the soul/spirit surviving the death of the body, but first, we must make an observation about the other key scripture used by other religious groups, namely **Ezekiel 18:4**.

"Look! All the souls – to me they belong. As the soul of the father so also the soul of the son – to me they belong. The soul **who sins is the one who will die**" (NWT).

What is the context? Ezekiel was correcting a false teaching that Israelite children were punished for what their fathers did. So, here in verse 4, he gave God's reply, which reads, according to the Contemporary English Version, "The lives [nephesh] of all people belong to me – parents as well as children. However, only those who sin will be put to death" (CEV). The prophet was not speaking here about the condition of the dead but rather about individual rebellious Israelites being cut off from God's living presence and ending up dead physically.

The word "die" (מוּת mooth) used here in Ezekiel 18:4, occurs 842 times in the OT, mostly relating to the physical death of people, but never to extinction or annihilation.

But what does the word soul[97] mean?

The word "soul" (נֶפֶשׁ nephesh) occurs 754 times in the OT, mostly referring to:

(1) a person or his life, which, in this sense of the word, is mortal, as here in Ezekiel 18:4. Joshua 11:11 is another example, where most translations use the wording "anyone who breathed," or similar.

(2) Soul can also refer to the inner part, the immaterial nature of man (ψυχή psyche in NT) that lives on after death. The soul - the inner person - combines the mind, will, and emotions. The graphic depicts how many Christians like to depict the trichotomy of body, soul and spirit.

Now, let's turn our attention to scriptures that reassure many Christians of an afterlife – that the soul/spirit lives on.

---

[97] **Soul.** Vine's Expository Dictionary of New Testament Words, after noting that "the word soul [1. G5590, psuche] denotes the breath, the breath of life," then "the soul," in its various meanings". Vines then proceeds to analyse the word with ten shades of meaning. Notice the first two are listed as:
(a) the natural life of the body, Matthew 2:20; Luke 12:22; Acts 20:10; Revelation 8:9; Revelation 12:11; cp. Leviticus 17:11; 2 Samuel 14:7; Esther 8:11.
(b) the immaterial, invisible part of man, Matthew 10:28; Acts 2:27; cp. 1 Kings 17:21.
After his full listing, Vine adds this comment about the soul and the spirit:
"The language of Hebrews 4:12 suggests the extreme difficulty of distinguishing between the soul and the spirit, alike in their nature and in their activities. Generally speaking, the spirit is the higher, the soul the lower element. The spirit may be recognised as the life principle bestowed on man by God, the soul as the resulting life constituted in the individual, the body being the material organism animated by soul and spirit".
For a deeper consideration of the workings of the human spirit, soul, and body, the book "The Spiritual Man" by Watchman Nee, may prove helpful (1968 by Christian Fellowship Publishers).

Is there any scriptural evidence of an afterlife?

a) **John 11:11, 25-26**. Jesus speaking kindly to Martha upon the death of her brother Lazarus, said, "Our friend Lazarus has fallen asleep, but I go to awaken him". ... "I am the resurrection and the life. Anyone who believes in me will live, even after dying. Everyone who lives in me and believes in me **will never ever die.** Do you believe this, Martha?" (NLT). The sleep referred to is always identified with the body. Never once does the Bible refer to the *soul* sleeping. Yes, someday you'll pass through the curtain of death, but beyond it is a person who already dwells within you. It's Jesus, the very definition of resurrection and life, as He says here in John 11. Physical death happens to everyone - but if you believe in Jesus, His resurrection life already dwells inside you.

b) **Luke 20:38**. Jesus said previously, "He is not the God of the dead but of the living; for they *all live* to Him". Not just alive in God's memory as some theologies state, but they are alive!

c) **Acts 7:59.** Or, what about the account of the death of Stephen here in Acts 7? Doesn't Stephen pray to Jesus to "*receive my spirit*" just before he dies? Doesn't this indicate that Stephen believed his spirit or soul would live on beyond his bodily existence? If Stephen's soul or spirit was about to cease to exist when his body died, how could Jesus, who was in heaven, receive Stephen's spirit?

d) **Philippians 1:23** "I am hard pressed between the two. My desire is to *depart and be with Christ*, for that is far better". Did he have to wait 2000 years to be finally with Christ?

e) **2 Corinthians 5:1-8** "Yes, we are of good courage, and we would rather be *away from the body and at home with the Lord".* Doesn't that indicate Paul believed in the existence of the soul or spirit after bodily death?

f) **2 Timothy 4:6** "For I am already being poured out as a drink offering, and the time of my *departure* has come". Paul used an interesting word for death; he called it "departure". The Greek word is a military term: "taking down a tent and relocating".

g) **Revelation 6:9-11,** "When he opened the fifth seal, I saw under the altar the *souls* of those who had been slain for the word of God and for the witness they had borne. They *cried out with a loud voice,* "O Sovereign Lord, holy and true, how long before you will judge and avenge our blood on those who dwell on the earth?" Then they were each given a white robe and told to rest a little longer, until the number of their fellow servants and their brothers should be complete, who were to be killed as they themselves had been".

As stated in the introduction, there are various views of the exact state of the soul in the present afterlife before Jesus returns and reunites the soul with its physical body in the resurrection[98]. It may take some time to absorb the scriptures above if we have been associated with a group that promoted mortalist views.

Consider Jesus' reassuring words, "Do not let your heart be troubled; believe in God, believe also in Me. In My Father's house are many rooms; if that were not so, I would have told you, because I am going there to prepare a place for you. And if I go and prepare a place for you, I am coming again and will take you **to Myself,** so that **where I am, there you also will be**" (John 14:1-3). Death for the follower of Jesus Christ is an ramp, not an exit. However we understand these words, we see the shift from a place to a person. We are not so consumed with identifying our state or location but with the joy of being entrance with Jesus eternally!

Why can a Christian have such a sure hope? Because death has been defeated. We read in 1 Corinthians 15:55-57, "'O death, where is thy victory? O death, where is thy sting?' The *sting* of death is sin, and the power of sin is the law. But thanks be to God, who gives us the victory through our Lord Jesus Christ". For the Christian, death's sting is drawn. Imagine an angry wasp attacking your child and you placing yourself between the youngster and the irritated insect to 'draw' the sting. So, Jesus, through his work on the cross, has dealt with the penalty of our sin. Christ's victory is our victory; death has been defeated. We shall still experience death, but we shall pass through it. It shall not claim us. That is how

---

[98] **Resurrection.** Anastasis (from ana = up, again + histemi = to cause to stand) denotes "to stand again" or "to cause to stand again," and most NT uses refer to a physical body rising from the dead or coming back to life after having once died. The resurrection from the dead to eternal life is the hope and assurance of all believers in Christ. This hope is based on the fact of Christ's own resurrection from the dead and his ascension to heaven, where he lives forever (see Question 12). It is also assured by the guarantee and seal God has given us, namely the gift of his Holy Spirit (Eph 1:13-14). The resurrection is of both body and soul (the body from the corruption of the grave and the soul from Hades). However, the body raised will no longer be flesh and blood but a glorified body, heavenly and immortal. The mortal body that dies is like a seed. Though a seed dies in the ground, a plant arises from it (1 Cor 15:35-58). The resurrection is distinguished from belief in reincarnation, which usually involves a series of rebirths from which the soul may seek release. Resurrection has primary reference to the body. The resurrection is the central, defining doctrine and claim of the gospel, for as Paul wrote, "If Christ has not been raised, then our preaching is vain, your faith also is vain". (1 Cor 15:14)

we look at death: we look *through* it. And once we are able to die without fear, we are able to live without it too.

A poem: "**God's Eternal Love**" by Betty Ferguson

When our time to pass is upon us
And our eyes are growing dim
God's gentle arms are waiting
To unfurl and guide us in
A sense of peace awakens
We have a smile on our face
And we know that he is waiting
To share his amazing grace
Our life appears before us
And although it's surely passed
Each memory remembered
More precious than the last
We think about the good times
And we think about the bad
And we're glad that God's been with us
Though many times we have been sad
With his presence always with us
We're strong enough to carry on
But over time we do grow weary
Then quietly our life is gone
When we see God's face before us
Our new home awaiting too
Our eyes close, we hear him whisper
Amazing grace is here for you

When John Owen, the great Puritan, lay on his deathbed his secretary wrote (in his name) to a friend,
"I am still in the land of the living".
"Stop," said Owen.
"Change that and say, I am yet in the land of the dying, but I hope soon to be in the land of the living".

Digging Deeper - What Happens at Death?

Scan the QR code for informative links to each of these questions.

1. How do many Christians explain the **three-part** (trichotomy) nature of man? Do you agree?

2. **a**. What is the **soul**? Is it the same as the spirit? What happens to the spirit at death? (Ps 146:3-4; Eccl 3:21; 12:7)

3. How can you overcome **fear of death** and fear of **dying**? (Heb 2:14-15)

4. Does the Bible point to a **resurrection of the body**?

5. Are our loved ones **looking down** on us from heaven?

See Suggested Answers at the end of this book.

Action Point
How could you help someone recently bereaved?

Prayer

Jesus, You know what it is like to feel abandoned. You know pain and loss better than anyone else. We know that you are close to the broken-hearted and comfort those who mourn. Help us to let you into our doubts and grief. Amen.

THE TRUTH
Everyone who believes that Jesus is the Christ
has been born of God - 1 John 5:1

Q19. WHAT DOES IT MEAN TO BE BORN AGAIN?

The word salvation is frequently on the lips of Christians. It has been well said, "Salvation[99] is not the reward for the righteous; it is, through the Grace of God, a gift for the guilty".

Here's the question, though, saved from what, to what? In just a few words, we are saved from God, by God, for God. Isn't this what Paul is saying in 1 Thessalonians 1:9-10? "You turned *to God* from idols to serve the *living and true God,* and to wait for his Son from heaven, whom he raised from the dead, Jesus who delivers us from the *wrath* to come".

Yes, you are saved from wrath, judgment and condemnation, not just for forgiveness[100] but into His presence and service. "You make known to me the path of life; in your *presence* there is fullness of joy; at your right hand are pleasures forevermore" (Ps 16:11).

Entering into salvation involves being born again. What does this mean? What are a few misconceptions about being born again? Some may regard 'born again' individuals as usually overly emotional Christians, like Pentecostals, who are very vocal about Jesus. Some Christians may mistakenly consider themselves as 'born again,' based on an emotional experience, reciting a 'salvation prayer,' drastically reforming their life, their church membership, partaking of communion, water baptism, or simply because of their good works. Perhaps you

---

[99] **Salvation**. The original word for salvation (soteria) means deliverance in the sense of being rescued. Jesus is the Deliverer who rescues us from our enemies, saves us from our sins, delivers us from the evils of this present age, and saves our souls from death (Matt 1:21; Luke 1:71; Gal 1:4). Salvation looks like Jesus - (Luke 2:30). Manmade religion says we can save ourselves, but salvation is entirely of God (Php 1:28; Rev 19:1). Noah's ark provides a picture of your salvation (Heb 11:7). When the flood comes, it does not matter how good a swimmer you are; it only matters how good your ark is, and Jesus is our unsinkable ark. It is only on account of his grace that we may be saved (Acts 15:11; Eph 2:5; Titus 3:5). Some say that the whole world is saved. But if that were true, why would Jesus say, "If anyone enters through me, he will be saved" (John 10:9), or why command people everywhere to repent and believe in the name of his Son to be saved (Acts 17:30; Rom. 10:9; 1 John 3:23)?

[100] **Forgiveness**. See footnote 82 on page 108.

Unit 7: Salvation

are, or once were, a Jehovah's Witness. Their theology asserts that the idea of being 'born again' is reserved just for a select few, the remaining thousands ("remnant") of the 144,000 yet alive on earth, who partake of the bread and wine once a year at the Memorial[101], hoping to go to heaven when they die.

We can start by looking at the only place in the Gospels that uses this term, namely, John 3:3-5. We read about Nicodemus' night-time conversation with the Lord. He was a religious leader in Israel who had no doubt scrupulously obeyed traditional Jewish codes of upright conduct. He recognised Jesus' role as a genuine Teacher, but Jesus knew this leader was missing the point - he needed a Saviour (vs 14-16).

> "Jesus answered him, I assure you, most solemnly I tell you, that unless a person is born again (anew, from above), he cannot ever see (know, be acquainted with, and experience) the kingdom of God" (John 3:3, Amplified Bible).

Just knowing doctrines about Jesus, improving our morality, or having a strict religious routine of study, prayer, church attendance, and good works, is no guarantee of oneness with the Father and Son. Our religion, morality, and works will not save us. Rather, we need a new birth to enter a new life with an intimate relationship with Jesus at its core. Why? Because of our sinful nature, we are not members of God's family, and have no right to inherit eternal life. The Bible says we were "alienated from the life of God ... due to the hardness of [our] heart" (Eph 2:1-3; 4:18).

We may not see ourselves as bad people, but in God's eyes, even one sin is enough to keep us out of heaven. But interestingly, not once does the Bible say 'repent of your sins' like drunkenness, drugs, immorality, or turn over a new leaf in order to be saved. No – this would be working for your salvation, accumulating "dead

---

[101] **Memorial**. Annually on Nisan 14th - the first full moon after the spring equinox –, JWs have their most attended sombre gathering to 'observe' the anniversary of the death of Jesus. We note, though, that as the Bible does not give us specific instruction on frequency, there is some latitude in how often a church should observe the Lord's Supper or communion, whether annually, monthly, or more often. At their Memorial, JWs pass the emblems of bread and wine, but only about 1% (mostly elderly) partake. This is because they believe the New Covenant is reserved only for a special group of 144,000 people, of which only a few thousand, exclusively JWs, remain alive on earth. They teach that the earthbound "great crowd" of Christians are not included in the New Covenant. But note from verses in Revelation the similar descriptions: the 144,000 are redeemed from every nation and stand before the throne (5:8-9; 14:3), and so are the great crowd (7:9,14). Their Memorial consists of a talk, though acknowledging Jesus' death, emphasises qualifying for paradise by loyalty to their organisation.

Unit 7: Salvation

works"- yet we know salvation is a free gift, not one iota dependant on our works (Eph 2:8-10; Heb 6:1). But the one crucial sin (not sins) is unbelief in His Son (James 2:10; John 3:18,36). A born-again Christian is someone who has, **repented**[102] **of the one sin of unbelief in Christ and turns to him for their salvation**, and as a result, has become part of God's family forever. Any clean-up restoration work thereafter will be led and empowered by the Holy Spirit.

Why would Jesus use the idea of birth? Obviously, a person cannot get themselves born! A mother bears a child, has labour pains, sheds blood, and the baby does nothing. Similarly, we see the hand of divine activity in that God gifts us with repentance, faith[103], and the Spirit – all is of grace. The Lord bears everything for our rebirth. Read John 1:12-13, where Jesus explained:

> "But to all who received him, he gave the right to become children of God. All they needed to do was to trust him to save them. All those who

---

[102] **Repent**. See footnote 10 on page 27.

[103] **Faith**. The well-known Bible definition is found in Hebrews 11:1, "Now faith means putting our full confidence in the things we hope for, it means being certain of things we cannot see". (Phillips NT) It could be said that faith contains two aspects: (i) Intellectual - being convinced that something is true; in this case, "hearing the word of Christ" – who he is and what he accomplished (Rom 10: 17), and (ii) Trust - actually relying on the fact that the something is true. Some would go further and include the connotation of allegiance or loyalty, rendering it as a vow (or pledge, as in a covenant of allegiance) to a faithful relationship as the truer understanding of the word in the early church. This change of allegiance from your "gods" to the one true God and His anointed king may result in excommunication from family, friends and society, as in the case of Muslims becoming Christians.

Many of us have been accustomed to the idea that faith is something you manufacture through sheer dogged determination. Yet, we come to realise that it is not a work of the flesh but a fruit of the Spirit (Gal 5:22) and a gift from God (Eph 2:8). God commands us to believe in the name of his Son Jesus Christ (1 John 3:23), and John wrote his gospel "so that you may believe that Jesus is the Christ, the Son of God; and that by believing you may have life in his name" - the verb 'believe' appears more than 90 times in John's Gospel (John 20:31). If faith is the noun – the state of being persuaded that God loves you – then believing is the verb or activity that flows from that conviction. We do not believe to create faith. Rather, believing is the action that reveals our faith. "Having the same spirit of faith... we also believe" (2 Cor 4:13). Many conclude, therefore, that we can only believe as a Christian because we are first gifted with faith that came from God (2 Pet 1:1; Phil 1:29; Acts 3:16). Faith is the cause and belief is the effect. A great definition of faith is the empowerment of God. His gift of faith empowers us to believe and hope.

Faith is like the clutch that a car driver uses to engage the engine. So Jesus, our driver, engages the engine of salvation by imparting his faith to us as his passenger sat in this vehicle called Grace.

164   Unit 7: Salvation

believe this are reborn! —not a physical rebirth resulting from human passion or plan—but from the will of God" (Living Bible).

Jesus did not say, "Nicodemus, you are halfway to the kingdom already, keep trying hard, and I will help you to the finishing line". No - he said all your works and morality so far are of no use - scrap the record – start all over! Go back to the beginning. Become "born from above". Not a renewed life but a new life. Not a heart bypass but a heart transplant. Not reformation, but transformation. A new creation (2 Cor 5:17). New birth is an act of God whereby eternal life is imparted to the person who believes, and he becomes a forgiven child of God (Titus 3:5-7; 1 Pet 1:3; 1 John 5:1-4,18).

Now, physical birth is certainly a process made up of a series of events, from the first contractions of the uterus, through the emergence of the newly born baby and the cutting of the umbilical cord, to the first breath and cry. We could add that the foetus had already existed in darkness for some nine months. Similarly, we could say that although the new believer may well vividly remember the impact of being born again, from another viewpoint, we could draw some apparent parallels: the first pains of 'conviction,' the cutting of the umbilical cord in 'repentance' of unbelief, and the crying out in the Spirit of 'Abba.' In this sense, being born again is our transition to a spiritually resurrected new life after dying to self. The funeral is over, and now we can begin to really live! This is not just a new start in life; it is a new life to start with.

What does being born of "water *and* spirit" mean?

Jesus said a person needed to be born of "*water and spirit*". Nicodemus would be well aware of the prophecy in Ezekiel 36. God spoke through Ezekiel,

"For I will take you from the nations, gather you from all the lands and bring you into your own land. Then I will sprinkle clean water on you, and you will be clean; I will cleanse you from all your filthiness and from all your idols. Moreover, I will give you a new heart and put a new spirit within you; and I will remove the heart of stone from your flesh and give you a heart of flesh. I will put My Spirit within you and cause you to walk in My statutes, and you will be careful to observe My ordinances" (Ezek 36:24–27).

There are several views as to what the water represents. You may wish to refer to the link under 'additional information' on the Question page. Here are a few popular understandings:

a. Some assert that Jesus was referring to *natural* (flesh, physical) birth from mum, which involved water (semen of man or waters in the womb) contrasted to the work of the Holy Spirit in the new birth of regeneration

(John 3:4,6). This view is credibly based on Jesus' apparent paralleling of the phrases "in his mother's womb" (vs 4), "born of water" (vs 5), and "born of flesh is flesh" (vs 6).

b. Others see here a reference to the cleansing *Word of God* (Eph 5:26; 1 Pet 1:23).

c. *Water baptism* is also suggested as Nicodemus was aware of John the Baptist's activities (John 1:26,33). Literal water, in this case, would be a sign of cleansing renewal, while "spirit" would refer to the Holy Spirit's work of regeneration.

d. Could this be a *double metaphor*? This would mean that being "born of the water and of the spirit" are two ways to say the same thing (hendiadys). Jesus said that you must be "born again" in previous verses and then "born of water and the spirit" in later verses. This view, which sounds more plausible, would follow the description in Isaiah 44:3 and be implied in Ezekiel 36:24-27 (quoted above).

Nicodemus undoubtedly meditated on this conversation for a long time, likely trying to figure out the meaning of Jesus' further words in John 3:14, "Just as Moses lifted up the serpent in the wilderness, so the Son of man must be lifted up". Then one day, he actually saw Jesus raised up on the pole as his sin-bearer, and he then believed and cared for his Lord's body. It took a long time for the Spirit to awaken his spirit. The Father is very patient with us.

Turning to the Lord.
Is this your day for turning to the Lord for Salvation? This chart below is not intended to follow a strict sequence. Instead, I hope it serves as a mnemonic of numerous aspects of the new birth.

B	Believe	By the gift of faith, accept Jesus as your personal saviour and Lord.	Rom 10:9-10; 1 John 1:12-13; 5:1
O	Obey	Trust in Jesus' perfect obedience; let His spirit produce fruitage in your life.	Rom 1:5; 5:19
R	Repent	Repent of your former life of unbelief in Jesus which led to many sins; receive forgiveness.	Acts 3:19; 11:18; 20:21
N	New Heart	Receive a brand new heart, a transplanted, not a reformed heart. By His grace live an abundant life.	Ezek 11:19; 36:24-27; 2 Cor 3:3

A	Adore	Honour, love and adore our Lord Jesus. Find joy in your relationship with Him.	Eph 6:24; Rev 5:13-14
G	Grow	Grow in Christlikeness as you progress in knowledge, faith and love through prayer.	2 Cor 3:18; Eph 4:15-16
A	All	All true Christians are born again. We need fellowship with each other.	John 3:3-5; 1 Pet 1:3, 22-23
I	Indwelling	Indwelt by the Holy Spirit; all believers have been baptised by the Spirit.	Rom 8:9; 1 Cor 6:19; 12:12-13
N	Not sin	Not to continue in patterns of sin; pursue sanctification.	1 Cor 6:11; Heb 12:14; 1 John 3:6; 5:18

- See God's Love. Jesus told Nicodemus, "For God so loved the world that He gave His only begotten Son that whosoever believes in Him should not perish but have eternal life" (John 3:16). Only through God's love and grace do we receive eternal life and not perish.

- See your Separation. God created man to fellowship with Himself. Adam, not trusting in God's love and seeking independence, rebelled and thereby separated himself from God. The result was spiritual and, eventually physical death. He could no longer walk with God, and all mankind inherited this same separation. "For all have sinned and fallen short of the glory of God" (Rom 3:23; 6:23).

- See Jesus as the Answer. "But God shows His love for us, in that whilst we were still sinners, Christ died for us" (Rom 5:8). There is no one that Jesus cannot help. Jesus is the only way to be saved (John 14:6). We are saved "by grace, through faith, and that not of ourselves, it is the gift of God" (Eph 2:8). This involves receiving the gift of repentance and turning to God by faith, and asking Jesus to be the Lord and Saviour of your life – no longer living for yourself (Rom 10:9; 2 Cor 5:14-15). We receive total forgiveness and become his sons with a new heart, a new life – abundant life, eternal life (John 1:12-13; 10:10). "Therefore, as you received Christ Jesus the Lord, so walk in Him" (Col 2:6). Late evangelist, Major Ian Thomas, made this comment about eternal life, "Eternal life is not a peculiar feeling inside! It is not your ultimate destination to which you will go when you are dead. If you are born again, eternal life is that quality of life you possess right now".

Summary

- **All** true Christians have been born again. No one can see God's Kingdom, nor enter it, without being born again.

- When a person is faced with the "gospel of the glory of Christ" (2 Cor 4:4-6) and accepts Him as his/her **personal Saviour**, the Spirit of God graciously bestows the miracle of the new birth. Everyone who believes that Jesus is the Christ has been born of God (1 John 5:1). At the same time, the individual repents of his disobedience in living a life of unbelief.

- The **gifts of faith and repentance** (not personal reformation) can be described as the two sides of the same coin, as they are inseparable; repentance is the turning from unbelief, reliance on any or all dead works of religious righteousness, to believe in Jesus Christ for salvation (Acts 20:21). Repentance is part of saving faith; it is the effective agent for forgiveness and remission of sins (Mark 1:14-15; Luke 24:47; Acts 2:38; 3:19; 11:18; 17:30-31).

- One who has been 'born from above' has been cleansed from his sin, has a new, living relationship with God, and is **enabled by the Holy Spirit** to live an obedient[104], sanctified life. Köstenberger in a comment regarding 1 John 3:9 states, "In all this, John makes clear that it is not spiritual perfection that is expected; such perfection awaits the second coming of Christ. Yet regeneration will inexorably produce a heart that

---

[104] **Obedient**. Romans 1:5 says, "[Christ] through whom we have received grace and apostleship to bring about the *obedience of faith* among all the Gentiles in behalf of His name". Our obedience is "of faith," or belonging to faith; that is, we have implicit trust in Christ's perfect obedience (Rom 5:19). This verse is not teaching that faith must produce obedience, though that is normally its effect. Instead, Paul is saying here that faith is obedience to God in that God commands everyone to believe in Christ. Ironically, it is when we live from that truth, we find our lives conforming to what the Bible says about godly living. Obedience is *a fruit, not a root*. This is not a works righteousness but a works confirmation, in that eternal life has observable characteristics (John 15:1-8). Beware of manufacturing cold obedience prompted by a desire to please others, a fear of men, or to attain salvation. Avoid being controlled by any religious body that demands absolute conformity to them or their detailed requirements for salvation. Paul asked why "do you take the slightest notice of these purely human prohibitions .... in actual practice, they are of no moral value, but simply pamper the flesh". (Col 2:21-23 Phillips) Salvation is not a ladder of obedience to climb – it was Christ who came down to us - but a call to rest in the Son's arms as he carries us to Father (Luke 10:34; 15:5). The truth is, disobedience happens not when we think *too much* of grace, but when we think *too little* of it. Almost counterintuitively, progress in obedience happens only when our hearts realise that God's love for us does not depend on our progress in our obedience,

confesses sin and continues in righteousness. Continuing in sin is an impossibility for those who are truly God's children." (Theology of John's Gospel and Letters, p.268)

- Many hold the view that the new believer celebrates his salvation by **water baptism**.[105]

---

[105] **Baptism**. While the views of Mormons, Jehovah's Witnesses, Plymouth Brethren, and Moonies may differ over the significance of baptism, they all consider water baptism by immersion an important step for membership in their respective religious groups.

The scriptures mention several types of baptism, including John's baptism of repentance; water baptism done in Jesus' name (Acts 19:3-5); Holy Spirit baptism (Acts 11:16); Jesus' baptism of suffering (Luke 12:50); and baptism for the dead (1 Cor 15:29). Paul said there was only one baptism (Eph 4:5), while Peter referred to the "baptism that saves" (1 Pet 3:21). Both were referring to the baptism done to every believer by the Holy Spirit when they first turn to the Lord in faith. The moment you came to Jesus, you were baptised or placed into his body by the Holy Spirit (1 Cor 12:12–13; Gal 3:27).

Two NT words are commonly translated as baptism and baptise. They relate to dipping, submerging, or immersing. This did not happen when you were water baptised; it was done to you by the Holy Spirit the moment you said yes to Jesus. "For by one Spirit we were all baptised into one body" (1 Cor 12:13).

To be baptised into Jesus' death means your old self is history. He's done and dusted, dead and buried. But that is only half the story. "We have been buried with him through baptism into death, so that as Christ was raised from the dead through the glory of the Father, so we too might walk in newness of life" (Rom 6:4). The Holy Spirit didn't leave you in the grave. Just as he raised Jesus, he raised you (Col 2:12). Because of the baptism done to you by the Holy Spirit, the old has gone, and the new has come. The life you live, you live by faith in the risen Son of God. This revelation will free you from the curse of trying to rehabilitate the old self (he's dead) and liberate you from your struggle with sin (reckon yourself dead to it). When you know you have been baptised and raised by the Holy Spirit, you will truly live.

"Is water baptism essential for salvation?" You are saved by grace through faith (Eph. 2:8). You are not made right with God by water; only the blood of Jesus makes us clean. If water baptism were a mandatory requirement for entry into the kingdom, Paul would not have said, "For Christ did not send me to baptise, but to preach the gospel" (1 Cor 1:17). So why get water baptised? (1) Jesus did it (Matt 3:13); (2) he said his followers would do it (Matt 28:19); and (3) because water baptism is a public demonstration of our already being saved. Salvation is a faith issue that is settled in your heart, not in water. The one who has called on the Name of the Lord is well and truly saved (Rom 10:13). But not getting water baptised is like not getting married when you've found your soul mate. In the words of the Ethiopian, "Here's water. Why can't I be baptised?" (Acts 8:36).

What are the requirements for water baptism? There is only one: Believe in Jesus (see Acts 2:41; 8:13; 16:14–15; 18:8; 19:4–5). After baptism, a number of groups practice the laying on of hands when prayers are made to God that he (if it is His will) grant the baptised person the gift of his Holy Spirit (Acts 8:14-17; 19:4-6; Heb 6:2).

Unit 7: Salvation

- We will know when we are born again. We will have a free conscience, a desire to do right, and **an assurance** of a home in heaven. At least to some degree, we will genuinely display the fruitage of the Spirit (Gal 5:22-26).

- Some strongly believe that being born again is a one-time event, yet others think it's a life-long process. But maybe that's not so important as the fact that it happens at all. And once it does, you can't stop there. You need to continue to **follow Jesus in your everyday life**. A sunrise takes just a few minutes, but once the sun pops above the horizon, it doesn't just sit there the rest of the day. It continues its journey across the sky until it sets.

- **Pray** in sincerity and heartfelt repentance that you may enter into the life of God and Christ through His Spirit.

This new birth is just the beginning of our eternal Christian life.

J C Ryle comments, "To be born again is, as it were, to enter upon a new existence, to have a new mind, a new heart, new views, new principles, new tastes, new affections, new likings, new dislikings, new fears, new joys, new sorrows, new love to things once hated, new hatred to things once loved, new thoughts of God, and ourselves, and the world, and the life to come, and salvation."

It is crucial to be born again, but then we must continue to grow to maturity in Christlikeness. In conclusion, the words of C S Lewis, "It may be hard for an egg to turn into a bird; but it would be a jolly sight harder for it to fly while remaining an egg. We are like eggs at present. And you cannot go on indefinitely being just an ordinary, decent egg. We must be hatched or go bad".

> *"Because your rebirth was an act of God,*
> *you cannot undo what the Lord has done.*
> *Because you have been born of imperishable seed,*
> *you are eternally saved and secure" - Paul Ellis*

Unit 7: Salvation

DIGGING DEEPER -
WHAT DOES IT MEAN TO BE BORN AGAIN?

Scan the QR code for informative links to each of these questions.

1. Enjoy watching this 3-mins clip based on **John 3** then consider the following questions:

    a. What did Jesus mean by the wind blowing?

    b. Why did Jesus refer to the serpent on the pole in the wilderness?

    c. What decision faced Nicodemus and also faces us today?

2. Do our **morality and good works** contribute to our being born again? Scriptural support?

3. What do you think? Must **all** Christians be born again? (John 1:12-13; 3:3-5; Rom 8:8-9; 1 John 5:1,12)

4. What comes first, putting on the **new personality,** or being born again? (John 15:4-5; 2 Cor 5:17; 1 John 5:18)

5. Can you list some of the **blessings** received at regeneration? (1 Cor. 6:19; 12:13; Titus 3:5,6; Rom 5:5; Eph 4:30; 1 John 2:27)

See Suggested Answers at the end of this book.

Action Point

(Have you received Christ? Here is the QR is a 1 hr 28 min **film:** "Hudson Taylor" - 1981) (Here are listings in the same QR of over 700 inspiring biographies on **podcasts**!)

Prayer

O God, be merciful to me. I am a sinner. I have tried to reform my life. I have even tried to be religious. But I know all this will not save me - only faith in your Son, who died for me, will save me eternally. I confess and repent of my unbelief in Him. Let His blood cleanse me today.

Q20. IS OUR SALVATION SECURE?

The debate between two main opposing theological viewpoints continues: One is called Arminianism.[106]

---

[106] **Arminianism**. While Calvinism emphasises God's sovereignty, Arminianism places the emphasis on man's responsibility and claims that he has a completely free will. Jacob Arminius was a Dutch theologian of the 16th century. What are the Five Points of Arminianism?

a. Human Free Will. Arminians claim that though people are fallen, they are still able to make a spiritually good decision to follow Christ based on the grace that God bestows to all people. Compare Rom 3:10-12.

b. Conditional Election. This belief says that God looks down the long hallway of time into the future to see who is going to choose Him. Compare Rom 8:29-30; 9:16.

c. Universal (unlimited) Atonement. This belief states that Christ's redeeming work made it possible for everyone to be saved but that it did not actually secure salvation for anyone. Compare 1 Pet 1:2.

d. Resistible Grace. This teaches that the grace of God can be resisted until it is quenched; that you can say no to the Holy Spirit when He calls you to salvation. Compare John 6:37.

e. Fall from Grace. The Arminian teaching claims that a person can become saved, and then lose his salvation. This happens when a person fails to keep up their faith or commits a grievous sin. Compare 1 Thess 5:23-24; 1 John 2:19.

Here follows a short list of some of the major Christian religions that explicitly identify as Arminian:

Methodist Church (including United Methodist Church, Free Methodist Church, Wesleyan Church); Salvation Army; Free Will Baptist Church; Pentecostalism (including Assemblies of God, Church of God, and the Foursquare Church); Nazarene Church; Church of the Nazarene; Seventh-day Adventist Church; Anabaptist Churches (including Mennonite, Amish, and Hutterite Churches); Church of God in Christ.

It is important to note that some denominations and churches may not explicitly identify as Arminian but still hold to some or all of the tenets of Arminianism. Additionally, there are variations within the Arminian tradition itself, such as differences between the Methodist Church and the Church of God in Christ.

Another is Calvinism[107]. The difference between Calvinism and Arminianism hinges on how much responsibility we have for our own salvation as opposed to God's ultimate sovereignty. For example, Arminians believe that they owe their election to their faith, whereas Calvinists believe that they owe their faith to their election. Arminians believe that future salvation and eternal life are secured but is conditional on remaining in Christ and can be lost through apostasy. Calvinists believe that because God chose some for salvation and actually paid for their particular sins He keeps them from apostasy and that those who do apostatise were never truly regenerated, that is, born again.

These couple of points are a vast oversimplification. Time doesn't allow for debate here. Nor does one's stance on this issue determine a person's initial salvation through faith in Christ – his blood, his resurrection. Because of my religious background – being grounded in a form of Arminianism, coloured by a unique two hope soteriology - I found great difficulty with the idea that our

---

[107] **Calvinism**. John Calvin did not originate this belief. He followed the soteriological understanding of Augustine, which, it is claimed, was the view of the church all the way back to the apostles. What are the Five Points of Calvinism? - TULIP

   a.   Total depravity. Man's entire being is corrupted by sin: his heart, his mind, his will, his physical body. Because we are so corrupt, we cannot do anything that is completely good, including seeking God. See Rom 3:10-12; Col 2:13.

   b.   Unconditional election. God has not and will not base His election on anything that He sees in us. There is nothing we do to earn our salvation. God chooses to whom He will be merciful. See Rom 9:11,15-16; Eph 1:4-5.

   c.   Limited atonement. Christ's death was sufficient for the salvation of all mankind, but it was not effectual for the salvation of each and every person. He died for all. See John 10:14,26; 17:6,9.

   d.   Irresistible grace. When God calls someone to salvation, they cannot ultimately turn away from His calling. The Holy Spirit draws and seals the person who has been chosen by God. See John 6:37,44; 2 Tim 1:9.

   e.   Perseverance of the saints. Since we did nothing to earn our salvation, we can do nothing to lose salvation. It is not ours to lose. What God has started in us He will not allow it to go incomplete. See Rom 8:30-31; 1 John 2:19; Heb 7:25.

Here follows a short list of some of the major Christian religions that explicitly identify as Calvinist:

    Presbyterian Church (USA); Reformed Church in America; Christian Reformed Church in North America; United Church of Christ; Free Reformed Churches of North America; Dutch Reformed Church; Associate Reformed Presbyterian Church; Heritage Reformed Congregations; Orthodox Presbyterian Church; Continental Reformed Churches. Other Christians, such as William Lane Craig and Alvin Plantinga, are proponents of an in-between view of **Molinism**, where God has 'middle knowledge'. (See Additional Information in the QR below)

salvation could be eternally secure; that is, once we are saved at the moment of believing in Christ as our personal Lord, we possess the assurance of eternal salvation. I was taught that such a Calvinistic teaching was both unscriptural and the height of arrogance! After all, doesn't the Bible say only those who "*endure to the end* will be saved"? And somewhere in Philippians, that you must "work out your own salvation"? We hope to come to those verses, and others, eventually. But are you agreeable to at least considering an opposing view for today's discussion? For this experiment, I will take on the role of someone believing in Calvinism in explaining a short list of Scriptures that appear to support eternal security. Of course, you are free to choose which view, if either, in your estimation, follows the true scriptural meaning. You may well find yourself protesting out loud at certain points presented below. Enjoy the grace ride. May the Spirit move us to love our Lord even more.

What Scriptures appear to support eternal security?

Amazingly we don't find one scripture that directly says that we can lose our salvation or become un-'born-again' for that matter. Yet, we are so used to looking at scriptures through the glasses of religion, with just one lens, either that of "*obedience*," or alternatively, "*guilt*," that we easily misconstrue, or even invert, the meaning of many verses. Yes, there are bad consequences to straying or falling from grace, but having your Father abandon you as His child is not one of them. Imagine a judge asking a witness in his courtroom, "Are you the son of So-and-so?" and receiving the reply, "I was last year, and I may be again in the future, but I am not so at present". The court would likely laugh because such a condition is possible of service; it is quite impossible of sonship.

What, then does it mean to fall from grace as stated at Galatians 5:4? We fall from the high place of grace when we start temporarily walking after the flesh: for example, making sacrifices to impress God, worrying about our life, nurturing our reputation, relying on our own efforts, etc. But falling from grace does not mean you who are "in Christ" have lost your salvation. You may let go of Christ, but he will never let go of you. Even when you are faithless, he remains faithful (2 Tim 2:13). Fall from grace and we will lose our freedom and not benefit ourselves (Gal 5:1-2), but Paul never tells the Galatians, "You are losing your salvation". Instead, he says, "You are indulging the flesh" (Gal 5:13; 3:3). In one sense, when you sin (as we will; 1 John 1:7-9) you don't fall from grace but into grace. It's not possible to sin yourself beyond the reach of God's love (Rom 5:20). To be justified means that you're forever right with God, eternally in. Suppose you go out to lunch with a friend and while you're in the restroom, your friend pays the bill. When you return, your friend says, "We're good". It means your debt has been paid, your obligation taken care of; "It is finished!"

Check out the following eleven scriptures.

SCRIPTURE	QUOTATION	COMMENT
John 5:24	"Truly, truly, I say to you, he who hears My word, and believes Him who sent Me, has eternal life, and does not come into judgment, but has passed out of death into life".	Jesus says nothing about a reverse procedure of crossing from life to death if you falter. It is a one-way trip; you crossed from death to eternal life[108]. The old life has gone, and the new life has come.
John 6:37,39	"All those the Father gives me will come to me, and whoever comes to me I will never cast out".	Why are we never cast out? Because of coming to Jesus. That's it. There is no, "if you wobble off course (as Jesus knew we would at times) - you will be booted out.
John 10:27,30	"My sheep listen to my voice; I know them, and they follow me. I give them eternal life, and they shall never perish; no one will snatch them out of my hand ... No one can snatch them out of my Father's hand".	You listened to Jesus' voice in initially calling you to salvation. The moment you put your faith in Him, you crossed over from death to life (John 5:24). Notice that there is a double guarantee of your secure position: Jesus holds you, and so does the Father. What about the sheep that wanders off? He doesn't turn into a goat[109]; he remains a sheep. And Jesus will find him, for the Good Shepherd knows and keeps his sheep.
Rom 8:1	"Therefore, there is now no condemnation for those in Christ [110]Jesus".	The gift of no condemnation[111] is irrevocable. "God doesn't take back the gifts he has given or disown the people he

---

[108] **Eternal life**. See footnote 69 on page 96.

[109] **Goat**. The sheep are those who believe in Jesus, those born of the Spirit. "If anyone does not have the Spirit of Christ, he does not belong to him" (Rom 8:9; John 10:26). The ensuing works, mentioned in Matthew 25:34-46, of serving fellow Christians, Christ's brothers, are the evidence of salvation, not the means to salvation; the fruit, not the root. So, they inherit a kingdom; they don't earn it. Good works do not make a sheep, and bad works do not make a goat. They are not separated based on works but identity. A sheep is someone who believes in Jesus, while a goat is someone who rejects Him and is consigned to the place of dishonour and rejection (Matt 7:23).

[110] **In Christ**. See footnote 135 on page 159.

[111] **Condemnation**. Paul says in Romans 8:1 that God's judgment is not going to come down upon you (katakrima), not now, not ever! From the valley of despair and defeat of living

		has chosen" (Rom 11:29 CEV). Old covenant thinking is, "maybe I'll have no condemnation when I stop sinning." In the new covenant, we start from a place of no condemnation and the result is we are empowered to stop sinning. "Neither do I condemn you; go and sin no more" (John 8:11).
Rom 8:38-39	"For I am convinced that neither death nor life, ... nor anything else in all creation, will be able to separate us from the love of God that is in Christ Jesus our Lord".	Truly nothing can separate us from the eternal grip of our Father's love[112]. We were not saved because we were holy. We cannot sin our salvation away because Jesus dealt with the sin issue, full stop! If we can lose our salvation through sinning, as some dogmatically claim, there is no hope for anyone, including those preachers who proclaim that message!
1 Cor 1:8-9	"He will also keep you firm to the end, so that you will be blameless on the day of our Lord Jesus Christ. God is faithful, who has called you into	We may not be a model of faithfulness, but he who called us is always faithful. The Amplified Bible reads, "God is faithful (reliable, trustworthy, and therefore ever true to His promise, and He can be depended on)". Therefore, we can be

under the Law in Romans 7, the apostle now climbs the heights with the triumphant shout, "No condemnation," because of the believer's justification by faith. Those in Christ are not condemned because Christ was condemned in their stead. There is no punishment for them because Christ bore their punishment. Charles Hodge calls Romans 8 "a rhapsody on assurance".

The word "condemnation," is not to be confused with the word judgment. It is the stronger word and refers to final judgment, that of eternal judgment. They are freed from condemnation, the condemnation of the Law of God, because their penalty has been paid by a substitute, the Lord Jesus Christ. They are also freed from bondage to sin by the Holy Spirit, a product of Christ's payment of the penalty. Paul does not base his assertion of no condemnation of the saint upon the saint's conduct but upon the saint's position, that of being in Christ.

Matthew Henry wrote: "He does not say, "There is no *accusation* against them," for this there is; but the accusation is thrown out, and the indictment quashed. He does not say, "There is nothing in them that *deserves* condemnation," for this there is, and they see it, and own it, and mourn over it, and condemn themselves for it; but it shall not be their ruin. He does not say, "There is no cross, no *affliction* to them or no displeasure in the affliction," for this there may be; but no condemnation".

[112] **Love.** See Q23 - How do we Grow in Love?

Unit 7: Salvation

	fellowship with his Son, Jesus Christ our Lord".	confident that he will complete the good work he began in us (Php 1:6).
Eph 2:8-9	"For by grace you have been saved through faith. And this is not your own doing; it is the gift of God, not a result of works, so that no one may boast".	If I did not do good works to get saved, then how can I do bad works to be unsaved? Salvation is humbly receiving, not giving. If I gave a friend a gift, would I then say to him, "I'm going to be watching you next year to see if you remain good enough to keep it - if not, I'm taking it back!"? Does God give the gift of eternal life with conditional strings attached? (Rom 6: 23). It is all by His grace[113].
Php 1:6	"And I am sure of this, that he who began a good work in you will bring it to completion at the day of Jesus Christ".	You can trust Jesus to finish what he began. The perfect tense (peitho – I am sure, confident) indicates that Paul had come to the settled persuasion and that he remained confident of God's desire and ability to continue His transforming work in the lives of the Philippian believers. Paul's confidence did not rest ultimately on the Philippians themselves but on God, who would preserve them and enable them to reach the goal.
1 John 3:9	"No one who has been born of God practices sin, because His seed remains in him; and he cannot sin continually, because he has been born of God".	Those who have been born again to new life are no longer sinners by nature because they carry the seed (or DNA) of Jesus, and in him there is no sin (1 John 3:5). Vine comments, "The seed signifies the divine principle of imparted life in the believer, and this, once it is imparted, is unalterable; it remains in the believer. The child of God stands eternally related to Christ. The one who goes on doing sin (in other words, lives in sin), has never become a child of God".
1 John 5:13	"These things I have written to you who believe in the name of the Son of God, so that you may know that you have eternal life".	If you believe in Jesus, you need have no doubts about your salvation. Your salvation is as secure as God's promises and as solid as his word. Eternal life is not merely being cleansed from your sins (which is forgiveness) but is knowing and

---

[113] **Grace.** See Q2 - What is Grace?

Unit 7: Salvation

		living in union with Christ (John 17:3), and it begins the moment you say yes to Jesus.
Rev 3:5	"The one who conquers will be clothed thus in white garments, and I will never blot his name out of the book of life. I will confess his name before my Father and before his angels".	God would have to blot our names out of the book of life when he said he wouldn't. Since the word "not" in the original Greek is emphasised, we can read it as, "I will not ever, ever, under any circumstance, erase your name from the Book of Life". It is an emphatic promise.

Let's go back to just one of the scriptures that seems to create a major problem for the above Calvinistic view: **Matthew 24:13**, which says, "But the one who endures to the end, he will be saved". Jesus used similar wording about "enduring to the end" four times (Matt 10:22; 24:13; Mark 13:13; Luke 21:19). At first glance, Jesus seems to be saying that salvation hinges on our endurance; that if we don't endure, we are not fit for the kingdom. So, the question is, can I lose my salvation if I fail to stand firm or endure to the end? What if I have a bad day, a bad month, or a bad year? What if I stray?

Vines Expository Dictionary gives us nine meanings of the word sōzō (salvation), the first of which is "preserving life" physically. The above four scriptures in the Gospels of Matthew, Mark, and Luke were written in the context of the first century Christians facing physical persecution up to 70 AD. Luke 21:19, the parallel account reads, "By your endurance you will **protect your lives**" (ISV, also Expanded Bible). What was the context of these scriptures? The surrounding verses (12-20) refer to the need of believers to act prudently during those years to protect their lives. Many survived the destruction of Jerusalem in 70 AD by following the safety advice from Jesus. By fleeing from persecution to another city, they lived to preach another day. They couldn't fulfill the Great Commission if they were dead! If this is the case, then Matthew 24:13, "endure to the end and be saved," according to context, is not the bad news of conditional salvation. There is no condemnation, no judgment, for those now in Christ (John 5:24). From start to finish, our Christian course is centred on *God's* faithfulness, *not our* wavering faithfulness - and God is faithful (Rom 8:29-30; 1 Cor 1:8-9; Jude 24).

In summary, says the Calvinist, the fact that we are enabled to endure with joy gives evidence to others that we have already been genuinely saved, just as the fruitage of the Spirit is external evidence to onlookers of having been internally changed in heart by Christ's Spirit dwelling in us. Salvation is not about you but Him. Our friend, the Calvinist, would assert that it cannot be arrogant to express our trust in God's ability to save us - entirely by His grace. So from this perspective, those who reject "once saved, always saved" are far from expressing

178

true humility. They are implying that their salvation is ultimately up to what **they do**, reaching some sort of grade. But the Bible says,

> "Then what can we boast about doing to earn our salvation? Nothing at all. Why? Because our acquittal is not based on our good deeds; it is based on what Christ has done and our faith in him. So it is that we are saved by faith in Christ and not by the good things we do" (Rom 3:27-28, Living Bible).

One pastor expressed it this way, "The determining factor in my relationship to God is not my past or my present, but *Christ's* past and *his* present".

In the Question section, you will have opportunity to respond to five scriptures which certainly appear to support the opposing view, that of Arminianism. Have fun! But remember, your salvation doesn't depend on settling theological arguments but in expressing a simple faith in our Lord Jesus Christ. "Whoever believes in the Son has eternal life" (John 3:36).

"Noah's ark provides a picture of your salvation (Heb 11:7).
When the flood comes,
it does not matter how good a swimmer you are;
it only matters how good your ark is,
and Jesus is our unsinkable ark".
– Paul Ellis

Digging Deeper - Is our Salvation Secure?

Scan the QR code for informative links to each of these questions.

Can you see alternative interpretations of the following five scriptures? You may find these Bible commentaries interesting to compare: John Gill's Exposition & Ellicott's Commentary.

1. **Philippians 2:12**, "So then, my beloved, just as you have always obeyed, not as in my presence only, but now much more in my absence, **work out your salvation** with fear and trembling".

2. **Hebrews 3:14**, "For we have become partakers of Christ, **if we hold fast** the beginning of our assurance firm until the end". (NASB)

3. **John 15:1-2**, "I am the true vine, and my Father is the gardener. He **cuts off** every branch in me that bears no fruit". (NIV)

4. **John 14:15**, "**If you love** Me, you will keep My commandments". This sounds like we must prove our love for God by exerting ourselves to do what He commands; what's your take?

5. **James 2:26**, "For just as the body without the spirit is dead, so also **faith without works is dead**". Surely this passage is telling us that works are part of our salvation, or it?

See Suggested Answers at the end of this book.

Action Point

It has been said, "Christ is the ground of our salvation, faith is the instrument of our salvation, and works are the fruit of our salvation". What sort of fruitage gives evidence of *your* salvation? A deepening love of: Christ, prayer, righteousness, scripture, fellow believers, the lost and needy? What animates your obedience? Is it fear of faith? Is it guilt or gratitude?

Prayer

My Lord, my Father, you lavishly pour out Your grace upon us. You crushed your Son for us, a lost, wayward people, to pay the penalty for our sin. Such is your love! You saved us and brought us near to yourself with His blood. We were enemies, but through Christ we have become your beloved children. This is grace! We deserve absolutely nothing, but you, Lord, give us life. Jesus came to make dead men live. We worship you. Amen.

Q21. HOW CAN WE SHARE THE GOSPEL OF GRACE?

Every aspect of society may appear to be broken, every person in need, if not mentally, emotionally, physically, then spiritually. However, there is One who mends and starts again. We are not ashamed to tell others about Him. On the other hand, a Christian should not view their role as being a cold 'preaching machine!' Do you feel under a constant compulsion to dutifully proselytise everyone you encounter?

Remember, Jesus told his disciples, "You are the salt of the earth; ... You are the light of the world" (Matt 5:14-16). Both are silent positive influences. Salt as a preserver and flavour enhancer; light shining as an illuminator. A Christian's lifestyle and simple loving kindnesses provide wordless testimony to God's praise and glory.

Regarding preaching, the starting point is to engage in fervent prayer and preaching the gospel to ourselves daily so that Christ's preciousness becomes real to us. Then we are better positioned to enjoy an interchange of gospel thoughts, at least with fellow Christians. However, the Lord may well provide us with an excellent opportunity to help an unbeliever understand the true gospel message of grace, but if so, what can we say? We certainly do not want to proclaim, "a distorted" false gospel by "preaching another Jesus" (Gal 1:6-8; 2 Cor 11:4).

While claiming a belief in Jesus as redeemer, there are many denominations that also require unquestioning obedience to their central leadership as essential for salvation. Sadly, such religions view salvation as an upward hard slog up a stairway of policies, ordinances, and 'new light' to hopefully and eventually secure God's approval. Roman Catholics, for example, are expected to obey papal infallible utterances spoken ex-cathedra. Another case is that of the LDS, who preach using the name of Jesus and refer to the Holy Bible (along with their other sacred scriptures), yet expect conformity to a list of saving ordinances[114] for

---

[114] **LDS ordinances** - saving ordinances; essential for our salvation: Baptism (to be born again and to enter the celestial kingdom); Confirmation (the laying on of hands for the gift of the Holy Ghost); Receiving the Melchizedek Priesthood (for men); The temple endowment and initiatory ordinances; Marriage sealing (temple marriage).

exaltation. A further example is the Jehovah's Witnesses. They may pride themselves in preaching worldwide (their interpretation of God's Kingdom; Matt 24:14) but promote loyal obedience to their 'Governing Body' as necessary to eventually become saved for everlasting life. Rather than judge people, we pray compassionately for such ones individually that the Holy Spirit prepares them to hear the true gospel (John 3:17; 12:47-48).

As mentioned in Question 12, the core of the gospel is **Jesus,** who through his death and resurrection, imparts to those believing in him, forgiveness, justification, salvation, reconciliation, life, transferral into his Kingdom (from 33 AD) as sons, and finally, glorification. The cross and being reconciled to God are always at the centre of the message. Evangelism is showing people the door ... to the Kingdom (John 10:7), or one hungry soul telling another where to find bread (John 6:33-35). It involves preaching persuasively, from a heart full of love for the person, for a response, a verdict. The listener should understand the need of repentance and turning to Christ, otherwise they will die in their sins, eternally estranged from God (note: Luke 24;45-48 and John 3:16-18,36).

Beware false Gospels. Christians recognise that the Kingdom has a number of progressive stages, climaxing with the future 1000-year Kingdom[115]. However, in the case of Jehovah's Witnesses, their good news stresses the year 1914, when they assert, Jesus started to reign invisibly, and will soon annihilate every person who is not loyal to their Governing Body[116] as an active, baptised JW. The real

---

[115] **Kingdom**. See Q12 – the heading "Kingdom" on page 87.

[116] **Governing Body**. Presently in 2023, there are a group of nine men in Warwick, New York, who profess to be the exclusive "faithful and discreet slave" over the eight million JWs (Matt 24:45).

- "That faithful slave is the channel through which Jesus is feeding his true followers in this time of the end. It is vital that we recognise the faithful slave. Our spiritual health and our *relationship with God* depend on this channel". (Watchtower 2013 July 15 p.20).
- "Jehovah's servants already belong to the only organisation that will *survive the end* of this wicked system of things" (Watchtower 2007, December 15, p.14).
- "Bible students need to get acquainted with the organisation of the "one flock" Jesus spoke about at John 10:16. They must appreciate that identifying themselves with Jehovah's organisation is *essential to their salvation*.'(Rev. 7:9, 10, 15) Therefore, we should start directing our Bible students to the organisation as soon as a Bible study is established". (Kingdom Ministry, Nov 1990).

Unit 7: Salvation

"gospel of the glory of Christ" as Lord, and being saved when you put faith in him alone, remains hidden (See, Rom 5:1-2; 2 Cor 4:3-6). Here we have a 'salvation' which could easily be erased by failure to obey implicitly over the next thousand and more years! Many sectarian groups follow a similar step by step progression but with modified labelling. (Scan the QR attached to Question 1 section and check out "Progressive Christianity" under Additional Information.)

This is not *receiving* God's grace but *achieving* God's approval by one's own works. It is putting sanctification[117] ahead of justification[118].

On a side note: The Kingdom hope of a New Heavens and New Earth[119] after Christ returns in his second coming[120] is real - a repeated promise from God and

---

- "And while now the witness yet includes the invitation to come to Jehovah's *organisation for salvation*, the time no doubt will come when the message takes on a harder tone, like a "great war cry". – WT 1981, Nov 15th p.16-21
- "Let the honest-hearted person compare the kind of preaching of the gospel done by the religious systems of Christendom during all the centuries with that done by Jehovah's Witnesses since the end of World War I in 1918. They are not one and the same kind. That of Jehovah's Witnesses is really "gospel" or "good news," as of God's heavenly kingdom that was established by the enthronement of his Son Jesus Christ at the end of the Gentile Times in 1914". (Watchtower 1981 May 1, p. 17)

[117] **Sanctification**. See footnote 14 on page 32.

[118] **Justification.** See footnote 14 on page 32.

[119] **New Heavens and New Earth**. This event comes after the tribulation and after the following events: the Lord's second coming, the millennial kingdom, the final rebellion, the final judgment of Satan, and the Great White Throne Judgment. "The heavens will vanish with a [mighty and thunderous] roar, and the [material] elements will be destroyed with intense heat, and the earth and the works that are on it will be burned up.... For on this day the heavens will be destroyed by burning, and the [material] elements will melt with intense heat!" (2 Pet 3:10, 12, AMP). In the Millennium Kingdom, Jesus will be ruling this entire earth from the city of Jerusalem. It will be God's capital. However, in the New Heaven and New Earth, we will be getting a New Jerusalem. In Revelation 21:1, God does a complete make-over of heaven and earth (Isa 65:17; 2 Pet 3:12–13). Many Christians take this to apply to the physical, atmospheric heavens – not to a heavenly government - along with a new earth. The new heaven and new earth will be the setting for the eternal state "where righteousness dwells" (2 Pet 3:13).

[120] **Second Coming**. After Jesus ascended into heaven, the angels declared to the apostles, "'Men of Galilee,' they said, 'why do you stand here looking into the sky? This same Jesus, who has been taken from you into heaven, will come back in the same way you have seen him go into heaven'" (Acts 1:11). Zechariah 14:4 identifies the location of the second coming as the Mount of Olives. Matthew 24:30 declares, "At that time the sign of the Son of Man will appear in the sky, and all the nations of the earth will mourn. They will see the Son of Man

should be kept in mind. All traditional churches teach this too, but realize that Jesus severely warned about false teachers, "Many people will come claiming to have My authority. They'll shout, "I'm the One!" or "The time is now!" Don't take a step in their direction". (Luke 21:8, The Voice). It is working against Jesus to keep people in a state of fear and hyper-excitement of an imminent Armageddon and a New World (Acts 1:6-8). Yes, these events will arrive, but "when it is *least* expected". That's why we live, not just for the future hope, but in the present, enjoying a relationship with Jesus, knowing he knows and loves us right now. Have you ever thought that the first Christians never preached about "the end" coming as the focus of their message - if they mentioned it at all? The cross and being reconciled to God were always the centre. They preached with urgency: 'come to Christ today - don't delay in becoming one of God's sons!' (Acts 3:26; 5:42; 8:12,35; 10:42-43; 28:30-31; 2 Cor 5:19-21; also, Col 2:11-12, NWT).

What is our fundamental need? To become more religious? To do more? No. Colossians 2:19 explains, "**They are not connected to Christ**, the head of the body" (NLT). Yes, all men need to repent of not exalting Christ as Lord in their life. Dethrone self and enthrone him – if one is to enjoy a personal living relationship with him. We shouldn't hold back from speaking plainly and tactfully. Scripture says men are alienated from God, dead in their sins, having a deceitful heart of stone. But through the mercy and grace of God, he offers a brand-new heart! A heart indwelt by the Holy Spirit.

This was promised in Ezekiel 36:26, "And I will give you a new heart, and I will put a new spirit in you. I will take out your stony, stubborn heart and give you a tender, responsive heart".

---

coming on the clouds of the sky, with power and great glory". Titus 2:13 describes the second coming as a "glorious appearing".

In His first coming, Jesus was the suffering Servant. In His second coming, Jesus will be the conquering King (Rev 19:11-16). In His first coming, Jesus arrived in the humblest of circumstances. In His second coming, Jesus will arrive with the armies of heaven at His side.

1 Cor 1:7 "...awaiting eagerly the revelation of our Lord Jesus Christ".

2 Thess 1:7 "The Lord Jesus shall be revealed from heaven with his mighty angels".

1 Pet 1:5-7,13 "...glory and honour at the revelation of Jesus Christ".

1 Pet 4:13, 5:1 "...so that also, at the revelation of his glory, you may rejoice with exultation".

Luke 17:30 "...on the day that the Son of Man is revealed".

Although opinions vary, it is often asserted that the rapture is the return of Christ in the clouds to remove all believers from the earth before the time of God's wrath. The second coming is the return of Christ to the earth to bring the tribulation to an end and to defeat the Antichrist and his evil world empire (1 Thess 4:17; .Rev 19:14).

Unit 7: Salvation

So, suppose you encounter someone and feel prompted to share the real gospel with them; where do you start? As we have been talking about our hearts, we can use an acronym - **CPR**. First, it is important to approach with:

C – **COMPASSION**. Paul said regarding his fellow countrymen, the Jews, who were stuck in a religious system claiming still to be "God's people,"

> "I am in Christ and am telling you the truth. I am not lying. And my conscience, ruled by the Holy Spirit, agrees that what I say is true. I have **great sorrow** and always feel much sadness for my own people. They are my brothers and sisters, my earthly family. I wish I could help them. I would even have a curse on me and cut myself off from Christ if that would help them" (Rom 9:1-3, ERV).

So preceding any conversation, we need an attitude of compassion. Prayerfully approach in a spirit of love. In this regard, it is worthwhile spending time to establish a friendly relationship, a two-way conversation, and thereby begin to understand their present viewpoints. Any explanation of the gospel should start where they are, in a non-pushy, kind, and tactful[121] manner. Compassion will

---

[121] **Tactful.** On a personal note. In the Spring of 2023, I joined two evangelists in a different area, one where my background was unknown, to set up a book table. As we turned a corner with boxes, a foldable table etc, I saw two quite elderly Jehovah's Witnesses standing at their book cart, so I prayerfully approached them. I simply asked how they were doing and how long they had been JWs. They said over 50 years and were only doing an hour on the cart because they felt frozen. I smiled and said I don't blame them because we were from a Christian mission and were about to set up 100 yards away and felt cold already! The man (Bill) asked if I'd heard about an incident that had faced JWs in Hamburg (March 2023). I said yes, and what a sad tragedy it was and how I had been praying for their families. I asked if they agreed we need Jesus to come in his Kingdom when faced with such a violent world. They readily agreed, of course! Quickly they showed me Revelation 21:1-4 from their tablet, saying that God's tent will come one day soon. "We will not see God or Jesus actually coming to earth, of course!" added Bill's wife, Christine. I said what a wonderful scripture that is, and look forward to seeing new heavens and new earth. I also said that I had been thinking about Jesus coming recently and had concluded that we need Him and his kingdom to come into our individual hearts and lives right now - do you both agree? They were silent. I asked if they could check out Gal 2:20-21 on their tablet. This gave me an opportunity to clarify IN Christ, GRACE, and LAW - explaining this was far more than just 'union' (harmony) with Christ as in their New World Translation. But as Rom 10:9 says, if we declare Jesus as Lord and believe in our heart that he is resurrected, we are saved ... what did they think about this verse. They hemmed and hawed ... and then the lady jumped to John 17:3. I listened to her explanation, then, after a few minutes, showed them John 5:24 from my own NASB pocket Bible. Look - I said, it says we HAVE everlasting life; what is this everlasting life a believer presently possesses? They didn't answer. So, I explained that most Christians hold to the

also help us avoid any superior attitudes, jumping critically on everything they say to correct them (Matt 12:18-21, Message).

P - PERSONAL TESTIMONY. It is often a good idea to ask what attracted them to their present religion. It may be tempting to raise controversial issues of doctrine or policy – for example, false predictions, afterlife, baptism for the dead, communion, central control, CSA, shunning, and so on - but usually, this proves to be counterproductive, resulting in them shutting down and reinforcing their persecution complex. After listening them out, it would be appropriate to share your personal testimony of joy in accepting Christ as your saviour.

R – READ. Simply suggest that they read the Bible itself without reference to any other books. For example, they could prayerfully read the gospel of John, one chapter a day, or the book of Romans from a different translation to the one they regularly use. You could offer a tract which highlights key scriptures (see Question page below), or some have found it effective to write down a couple of references for them, e.g. John 5:22-25; Rom 4:1-8; Eph 2:1-10; 1 John 5:10-13.

There we have it, CPR! Compassion + Personal testimony + Read the Bible.

Now, though, imagine that they are either willing to continue the conversation or even meet with you again; what then? How can you explain the true gospel? Here are a few easy ideas:

a) Conduct them down the "**Romans Road**." Watch the two-minutes animation linked on the Question page. Note down the verses used. How about writing the Roman Road in your Bible? Go to Romans 3:23, underline it, write Romans 6:23 next to it, and so on. That way, all you need to do is memorise where you start, Romans 3:23.

Bible's view that it is not just the duration (longevity) of life but the very life of God in Christ dwelling in us by the Holy Spirit! An abundant joyful life. This life is for those acknowledging their sins in the face of such love, repenting, and turning to Christ. Then we have no condemnation or fear of judgment (Rom 8:1) - isn't this wonderful, true grace, because we cannot earn this whatever we do! At that point, I thanked them for the 20 min conversation. They asked where I was from. I said Jim from the local area, working alongside this Christian Mission. I didn't feel it necessary in this case to explain my backstory but to plainly point to Christ crucified and risen - our Lord Jesus. At that point I halted the chat, thanking them again by saying that I must catch up with my two brothers further down the street because we had come to simply preach Christ. I thank the Holy Spirit for this encounter and the fact that we all listened respectfully to each other and avoided any mention of Watchtower Organisation's major doctrinal errors or malpractices. I continue to pray for them both.

We could make a couple of observations regarding the helpful Romans Road method:

i) Some may feel it more appropriate to begin with *Romans 1:20,* where the character of God is expressed through creation. We see evidence of His "common grace" to all men regardless of belief. This loving God is reaching out to men to save them from the miserable consequences of sin!

ii) Note that the scriptures selected from the book of Romans are only certain highlights, so we would want to encourage them to read the whole of Romans for themselves.

iii) The "Romans Road" method doesn't mention the "wrath of God" against sin, or indeed, the turning away from sin in repentance nor justification.

iv) If a 'sinners' prayer' is included at the end, we must make it plain that these words in themselves do not magically secure salvation; otherwise they would be relying on works or words rather than grace for their salvation.

b) Some people who enjoy visual images may like the three-minutes video, the "**Chair Gospel**".

c) A simple way to present the gospel is in **three steps** (*problem* of sin → *solution* of the cross → *response* of repentance and faith). Also see Q19: heading, 'Turning to the Lord'.

d) Finally, we could follow the acronym **GRACE**:

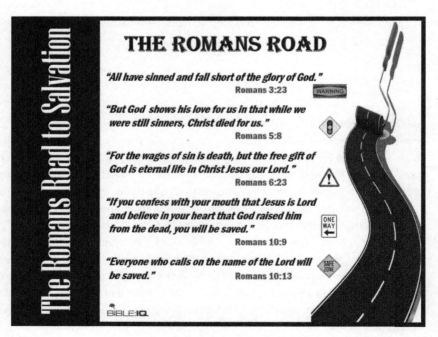

G – GOD is Holy, so hates sin; it is the barrier to your relationship with Him as a loving Father.

R – REPENT of sins - especially unbelief in Christ as saviour. Repentance is a grace gift of God.

A – ACCEPT Christ's gifts of faith and salvation by Christ, as expressions of God's love for you.

C – CHRIST'S righteousness is imputed, and we submit to his present reign as king.

E – ETERNAL life as a son of God starts now, with promise of the 1000-year Kingdom to come.

The "Growing Seed" parable in the Gospel of Mark shows that only God's Spirit germinates and gives salvation growth to the kingdom seed sown in the heart (Mark 4:26-29). Salvation is never controlled by a preacher's clever presentation or his persistence within a time frame of a particular Bible course, but only by God's will. His Spirit imperceptibly works underground to produce a harvest in a new believer's life. Our job is to spread the gospel, not to judge the soil of the hearer's hearts (John 12:46-48).

It is important to state that soul winning is not a competition; neither is it to give us the satisfaction of having a big group of members, nor to make us appear successful. It is for the privilege of presenting the fruit of His sacrifice to Him. The life-saving work involves far more than laying out the gospel in clear words, for as Paul remarked to the Thessalonians, "we had a fond affection for you and were delighted to share with you not only the gospel of God, but also our *own lives*, because you had become very dear to us" (1 Thess 2:8). It has been said that people don't care how much you know until they know how much you care. Paul gave both his care and his knowledge to them.

To conclude on the note of preaching the correct message of grace, consider this comment by David Martyn Lloyd-Jones, "If your preaching of the gospel of God's free grace in Jesus Christ does not provoke the charge from some of antinomianism, you're not preaching the gospel of the free grace of God in Jesus Christ".

God did not command the world to go to church. He commanded the church to go to the world. If we never speak out about Christ, could our silence mean we don't see or savour the excellencies of the one who called us out of darkness? Does it mean that we are, deep down, ashamed of Christ? Paul says in Romans 1:15, "I am eager to preach the gospel to you who are in Rome". Have you found a way of introducing the gospel message to others? A question, a tract, an invitation to the Grace Fellowship group, your personal testimony, or a more direct form of public evangelising?

You may not be gifted to preach and teach (see 1 Cor 12:29), but you are *qualified* because Jesus the Teacher lives in you, and His Spirit teaches you all things (2 Cor 3:4-6).

May the good Shepherd stir us to go looking for the lost sheep. May God bless our efforts as we learn to spread the gospel of grace by prayerfully and patiently preaching Christ crucified.

> *"Other men may preach the gospel better than I, but no man can preach a better gospel".*
> *- George Whitefield*

Digging Deeper - How Can We Share the Gospel of Grace?

Scan the QR code for informative links to each of these questions.

1. Can you fill in the rest of this tick-box chart? Please note there will be one or two blank boxes. After establishing a common ground, what was the **gospel preached** by the Paul?

PAUL'S SERMONS	For all nations	Jesus' death, resurrection	Jesus - Lord; Saviour; Judge	Repent	Forgiven
Acts 10:34-43					
Acts 13:23-41					
Acts 17:22-31					
Acts 26:12-23	✓	✓	✓	✓	✓

2. Which comes first, **faith or repentance**?

3. How is the real gospel more than a message of **forgiveness**? (1 Pet 3:18)

4. Is the **preaching work over** because Colossians 1:23 says, "But you must continue to believe this truth and stand firmly in it. Don't drift away from the assurance you received when you heard the Good News. The Good News *has been preached* all over the world, and I, Paul, have been appointed as God's servant to proclaim it"? (NLT)

5. How does the kingdom message preached by **Jehovah's Witnesses** differ from that preached by Christians throughout the centuries?

See Suggested Answers at the end of this book.

Action Point

Meditate on **Romans 9:1-5**, where Paul with deep feeling lists seven positive benefits Israel had received yet had sadly missed Christ. How could you this apply to the JWs who have a Bible Study program, a worldwide brotherhood, and a zeal to preach?

You may wish to glance inside the QR at a leaflet of '20 questions' for additional ideas:

Also in the QR code is a short video of an evangelist as he approaches two JWs.

Additional Information

Please scan the QR code for 21 links, including free **tracts** to help share the gospel and an online **resource** for Practical Personal Evangelism:

Prayer

> Righteous Saviour, as I look out over this city, I see so many who are lost and afraid. And yet in my own strength, I know that there is nothing I can do. I am shy. I am timid. Father, increase my faith. Give me the boldness I need to fill this city with the glorious hope of eternal life in Your Son, Jesus. Amen.

THE TRUTH
You may ask Jesus for anything
in his name - John 14:14

Q22. HOW DO WE GROW IN PRAYER?

If any of you should ask me for an epitome of the Christian religion, I should say it is in that one word – prayer," stated C.H. Spurgeon. Prayer is essential in every believer's walk with God. But how would you define prayer? Many view it as simply talking to God. And yes, it is certainly true that communication is the basis for all human relationships. Imagine if you never spoke to your best friend, would you be remain close friends? Well, our relationship with God is the same. 1 Thessalonians 5:16-18 instructs us to "Rejoice always, *pray without ceasing*, give thanks in all circumstances; for this is the will of God in Christ Jesus for you". However, prayer is far more than just talking to God.

What is prayer[122]?

Through the eyes of grace, we can say prayer is God's quest for us. Based on such scriptures as Genesis 3:8-13 and Romans 8:26-30, it could be said that prayer is Him addressing us. It is His Spirit that prompts us to pray. So, many Christians would likely define prayer as more than merely talking or communicating with God. Rather, they view such precious times of worship as *communion or fellowshipping with their Father*. Prayer, then, becomes the practice of the presence of God. Here are notable quotes from five experienced Christians:

---

[122] **Prayer.** Lawrence Richards writes regarding proseuche (and verb proseuchomai), "In classical Greek was the technical term for calling on a deity. The NT transforms the classical stiffness into the warmth of genuine conversation. Such entreaty in the NT is addressed to God or Jesus and is typically both personal and specific. (Richards, Expository Dictionary of Bible Words: Regency).

Too often, we rush into His presence, blurting out our supplications and requests, instead of approaching His throne of grace with the sense of wonder and reverential fear pictured by the use of the noun proseuche.

The essence of prayer is setting one's focus on God in praise, devotion, and worship. The first priority, when we find ourselves worrying, should be to get alone with God and express our love and adoration to Him, focusing on His glorious and majestic attributes. We are to worry about nothing because we can pray about everything.

Jerry Bridges: "Prayer is not a means of gaining control over God or of manipulating Him to do our bidding, but rather it is a means of putting ourselves in a position to receive His blessing".

Oswald Chambers: "We hear it said that a person's life will suffer if he doesn't pray, but I question that. What will suffer is the life of the Son of God in him, which is nourished not by food, but by prayer. When a person is born again from above, the life of the Son of God is born in him, and he can either starve or nourish that life. Prayer is the way that the life of God in us is nourished. Our common ideas regarding prayer are not found in the New Testament. We look upon prayer simply as a means of getting things for ourselves, but the biblical purpose of prayer is that we may get to know God Himself".

J. I. Packer: "If you want to judge how well a person understands Christianity, find out how much he makes of the thought of being God's child, and having God as his Father. If this is not the thought that prompts and controls his worship and prayers and his whole outlook on life, it means that he does not understand Christianity very well at all."

Mother Teresa: "Prayer is not asking. Prayer is putting oneself in the hands of God, at His disposition, and listening to His voice in the depth of our hearts". She was once asked what she said during her prayers. She replied, "I listen". When further asked, "Well then, what does God say?" Mother Teresa smiled with confidence and answered, "He listens. ... and if you don't understand that," Mother Teresa added, "I can't explain it to you".

Bob Sorge: "The power of prayer is found, not in convincing God of my agenda, but in waiting upon Him to hear His agenda".

Isn't this good news? The realisation that prayer, this intimate conversation, begins with God not you! He, who passionately loves you, initiates prayer; you join in! The desire, the urge, to pray is the result of God's greater desire to talk with you. His Spirit links to your spirit. In this way, prayer is not an action - it is an interaction - and that interaction takes place in and through the Holy Spirit.

Let's turn to the challenges we have all faced regarding prayer at one time or another:

      a. Finding the *time* amid many distractions.
      b. Finding the *words*; avoiding mindlessly repeating phrases.
      c. Finding the *answers* to prayers.

a. Finding time amid many distractions.
There can be structured times to pray. For example, many Christians regularly, first thing every morning, like to run through a passage of scripture and choose a verse or two from it as their day's text. Some find it helpful to write it out, even

memorise it, and pray through the words with God. This practice can help bring our scattered thoughts into focus as we begin to pray.

In his book 'Life in the Presence of God', evangelist and author Ken Boa wrote, "Sure, it's good to give the first – or the last – moments of our day to God. But what about the rest of the day? It's so easy for our hearts and heads to end up somewhere else. ... We [should] take our life with God – and our awareness of his presence – with us everywhere, not just into our quiet times but into our noisy times too, incorporating practices into our lives that help us keep that awareness right in front of us, throughout the day, every day".

Prayer need not be limited to the words uttered between "Our Father ..." and "Amen." Prayer can be a never-ceasing intimate conversation with the One who loves us. Consider these references: "Rejoice always, pray continually, give thanks in all circumstances; for this is God's will for you in Christ Jesus" (1 Thess 5:16-18). "Pray in the Spirit on all occasions with all kinds of prayers and requests" (Eph 6:18). "Walk by the Spirit..." (Gal 5:16). Just as you walk in the Spirit moment by moment, you can continually pray in the Spirit - always rejoicing, always giving thanks in never-ceasing communication with Him - even as you go about your day and other duties. You can live in God's presence and glorify Him when you are commuting to work, while at college, when taking out the garbage, washing the dishes, ironing, or doing any number of menial activities. What ordinary task will you do today – prayerfully in His presence?

Before we move on, here's a personal question: Do you spend more time in front of your mirror and on social media than before your Father's throne?

b. Finding words. Finding the central still place in our spirit is more important than forming the correct word choice. Have our prayers become little more than flares, the sending up of distress signals? How much better if our prayers are a response to what we find in His written Word.

How do we start our prayers? Do we habitually address him as God, Jehovah[123], Yahweh, Creator, or Lord? There is nothing wrong at all in using various forms of address. However, how did Jesus start his prayers? Six times in his John 17 'High Priestly' prayer, Jesus' prayed to "Father"[124]. In the Lord's Prayer, he directs us to

---

[123] **Jehovah.** Scan QR attached to Q9, page 71.

[124] **Father**. We can refer to three expressions which give us the gist of this word in scripture: *Life-giving Father*. In the OT, God is referred to as "father" (אב 'ab) in the sense of being the creator, the One who begot the Israelite nation, or sometimes God used this same relational word to designate his watch care over the Davidic line leading to Messiah (Mal 2:10; Deut 32:6; 2 Sam 7:14).

do the same (Matt 6:6-9). He is like your 'Dad.' No child would repeatedly, if at all, use their parent's name when conversing with them because it would be considered disrespectful. Why should it be different with our creator? The Israelites feared God and did not think they could have a personal relationship with Him. Their focus was on law and works. But our focus is not fear but an intimate relationship of love and friendship. Would you obsess about using exact wording and expressions when talking to your dad or a close friend? Nor should we when approaching our heavenly Father. He loves to hear you and what's bugging you, the messy side of your life. He even knows what you will pray before you speak.

A 17th century Puritan, Thomas Brooks, said, "God looks not at the elegancy of your prayers, to see how neat they are; nor yet at the geometry of your prayers, to see how long they are; nor yet at the arithmetic of your prayers, to see how many they are; nor yet at the music of your prayers, nor yet at the sweetness of your voice, nor yet at the logic of your prayers; but at the sincerity of your prayers, how hearty they are".

Something else we should consider, especially if we find our prayers becoming stale or repetitive, is praying for, and with, others. Sometimes we can find ourselves consumed by the right wording in our personal prayers, whereas it would be better to focus both on God's presence and the other's needs by name. Have you been reminded of someone you know? Take a moment to pray for them. To help in this regard, many Christians keep a prayer journal in which they note down their requests to God, His responses and revelations, and the names of friends and their specific needs. We should keep in mind prayer is not a wish list or running through a checklist. Many Christians thrive and grow in their prayer life when regularly joining in a prayer group.

Love-giving Father: Jesus later came and used the word "Father" over 160 times – it was his favourite term for addressing God – not just in a general or corporate sense but in a warm personal relationship. This familial love is well described in the parable of the prodigal (Luke 15). The exact term Jesus used is still found three times in the NT (Mark 14:36; Rom 8:15-16; Gal 4:6), but the Aramaic term Abba is translated by the Greek pater elsewhere. There is no evidence in pre-Christian Jewish literature that Jews addressed God as "Abba". Abba was a term of a younger one's deep respect and affection for their father.

Legally giving Father: This relationship has a legal basis. Legally Christians have been "adopted" as God's Sons, sworn into the New Covenant, signed in Christ's precious blood, and sealed by Holy Spirit. It's a done deal (John 1:12-13; 1 John 3:1-2; Eph 1:5). Yes, as Sons, we receive God's inheritance, all his promised blessings for eternity! "Consider the incredible love that the Father has shown us in allowing us to be called "children of God"—and that is not just what we are called, but what we are ... Here and now we are God's children" (1 John 3:1-2, Phillips).

c. Finding answers. Be assured our Lord responds to every prayer – but often in ways and with a timing that is unexpected. Be confident that you may ask Jesus[125] for anything in his name. It is understood by many that in the early Christian church, it was common to call on Jesus, yes, prayers to Jesus (John 14:14; Num 20:8; 1 Cor 1:2; 2 Cor 11:31; 12:8-10).

An important lesson to learn is that the purpose of prayer is that we get a hold of God himself, not a hold of an answer. It is not merely a means of getting requests heard and obtained or asking him to rubber-stamp our own ideas. No, it is rather connecting and nourishing the life of God within our spirit. Listen to Him as he speaks through his Word. Take time to savour in silence . We might demand an answer from God instead of seeking God himself, who gives the answer. So, while it is true that 'prayer changes things,' it would likely be more accurate to say that prayer changes *me* and my perspective, and thereby He works through me to enable things to change.

Sometimes hearing "wait" is even harder than hearing "no," because it means we have to develop patience. But we can be thankful God is in control and trust that His timing will be perfect.

God wants the best for your life. He does not want you to suffer needlessly. The sentiment of Jeremiah 29:11 - originally stated towards the Israelites captive in Babylon - could be applied to you today, "For I know the plans I have for you, declares the Lord, plans for welfare and not for evil, to give you a future and a hope". Or in the words of Psalm 46:10, "Surrender your anxiety! Be silent and stop your striving and you will see that I am God" (Passion Translation). We should patiently pray, and when our prayers are answered, or are not answered, remember this: If we knew what the Lord knew, we wouldn't change a thing.

By way of summary, here is the acronym **PRAY**:

P. Person. Do you focus on the right wording, or do you aim for communion with the Person of God? You can be silent in His presence and be loved unconditionally. Cut down on the need to fill the silence with our words.

R. Read, preferably aloud, a passage of scripture before or during prayer. Isolate and ponder over a key verse or phrase before Him. In this way, Bible reading and meditation become an integral part of prayer as worship.

---

[125] **Prayers to Jesus**. Open the QR below and see the link to Maclaren Commentary n Additional Information.

Unit 8: Grow

A. Appointments. As well as specific times and places for prayer, we could adopt Spurgeon's practice, "I always feel it well to put a few words of prayer between everything I do".

Y. Yield. Yield to His will – even if you cannot discern an apparent present answer. Let the Holy Spirit lead you, intercede for you (Rom 8:26-27).

May our Lord continue to pour out His rich blessings of inexhaustible grace upon you as you grow in Christ, in Love, and in Prayer.

> *"Prayer is beyond any question*
> *the highest activity of the human soul.*
> *Man is at his greatest and highest when upon his knees*
> *he comes face to face with God" - Martyn Lloyd-Jones*

Digging Deeper - How do we Grow in Prayer?

Scan the QR code for informative links to each of these questions.

1. How is **Ephesians 6:16-20** perhaps the most comprehensive view of prayer in scripture?

2. Meditate over **Philippians 4:4-8**. How can we keep **calm** in the face of anxiety? (C-A-L-M can be used as an acronym based on this scripture).

3. What can we learn about **answers** to prayers by comparing Daniel 9:21 with 10:12-13?

4. What key point stands out to you in this summary of "The Practice of the presence of God" by **Brother Lawrence** in the 17th century?

5. Select a few of these hundreds of **quotes** on prayer that you find most helpful. Write them down and try to memorise them!

See Suggested Answers at the end of this book.

Action Point
Read through the whole of Psalm 23 on the first day of the week. Pray through one verse of this same Psalm each day thereafter over six days.
What other key chapters would you choose in future prayers?

Prayer
How about a challenge today? Rather than I suggest any prayer sentiments, simply begin a natural, ongoing conversation with God right now! Don't worry if your words falter, sit silently in the embrace of His love, letting your heart fill with praise and thanks and with the desire to bless others.

The God that Jesus revealed is a loving Father who loves us as much as he loves his Son - John 17:23

Q23. HOW DO WE GROW IN LOVE?

"God is love". 1 John 4:8 doesn't say God is *loving*, or God is *lovely*, or that God *has* love. On the contrary, the essence of His being has always been love from eternity past. God's love has never changed or been modified; it can never vary or diminish. To put it another way, the reason for God's existence is love. He does not love to exist: He exists to love.

Love and/or Truth? In today's culture, where 'self-esteem' is nurtured, where egotism is elevated, many applaud the concept of a God who 'indulgently' loves everyone unconditionally, without boundaries. Hence, out of this sense of 'personal freedom,' they feel prompted to be overly lenient about their own unholy leanings and practices and limitlessly tolerant of the beliefs and practices of other people, no matter how extreme. Moral relativism asserts that there's no ultimate authority; nobody can tell you how to behave morally. Misreading God's love can lead to an obfuscation or suppression of His clear commands in scripture. Tolerance is of course, desirable, but should the concepts of truth and authority[126] be suppressed or even rejected?

Some reason that, as long as love predominates, it doesn't matter whether a person:

(a) Professes Christianity (has an "in Christ" relationship with the risen historical Jesus of Nazareth).

(b) Is a follower of a 'Christ-like' (messianic) figure.

(c) Views Christ as being a universal presence (similar to Buddhist thinking).

(d) Is a radical unbeliever.

---

[126] **Authority.** For example, the small letter of Titus refers to "the faith of those chosen of God, and the knowledge of the truth" and "not paying attention to Jewish myths and commandments of men who turn away from the truth". (1:1,14). Then, after describing a grace-filled right living, Titus 2:15 continues, "These things speak and exhort and reprove with all authority. Let no one disregard you". This sounds like an unpopular approach to life, the absolute opposite of the culture in which we live.

Does "love of the truth" matter? (2 Thess 2:10). Love should go hand in hand with truth (Eph 4:15). Truth without love would be harshly judgmental and dogmatic. Love without truth would be blindly sentimental. Truth as found in Jesus is loving, and real love is truthful. You cannot divorce the two.

Inclusive or Exclusive? On the one hand, Christianity can be viewed as _inclusive_ in that it teaches that salvation is freely available to all people, _regardless of their background or circumstances_ (John 3:16). However, there are also passages in the Bible that suggest a more _exclusive_ view of Christianity. "Salvation is found in no one else, for there is no other name under heaven given to mankind by which we must be saved" (Acts 4:12; John 14:6; Mark 16:15-16). These passages suggest an _exclusive_ view of salvation only available through belief in the Son of God, the Jesus Christ who died on the cross, not a vague universal 'Christ.' Our personal experiences, activities and how 'progressive' we feel we are, should not override or dispense with Truth. Yet, at the same time, we recognise that we do not need to have it all 'right'- dotting every theological T. To put this another way, knowing this God of love, basking in His presence, and living in the Spirit as born again children – including manifesting Christian fruits – are all based on knowing the Truth, who is, in essence, Jesus (2 John 2:1-2).

Holy Love. Think too, how does God's love relate to His holiness[127]? God's intrinsic holiness does not flinch from warning of His wrath poured out upon sin and upon unrepentant sinners who sin against the Holy Spirit by rejecting the Lord, thereby rejecting life. God hates sin. At the same time, His love is demonstrated, as Romans 5:8-9 says, "God has shown us how much he loves us— it was while we were still sinners that Christ died for us! By his blood we are now put right with God; how much more, then, will we be saved by him from God's anger!" (GN) In other words, the Bible presents God's love as a _holy love_ - a redeeming love that is demonstrated at the cross. Holiness perfectly permeates all facets of His nature, including His love. God's holiness constrains God's love, like water is constrained by the pipe through which it flows. Of course, that means that God's holiness ultimately serves the purposes of his love, as the pipe does water.

Fallen humans want God's love to be a permissive, indulgent love; yes, accept us as we are, but then _leave us as we are_. Men desire an 'unholy' love which would save them by grace but then pander to their sinful pleasures, not purity. God's way, though, seeks our highest good, our purity. To leave us in filthiness would not be loving. So, Paul refers to God's chosen ones as "_holy people he loves_" (Col 3:12, NLT). It is true that God loves unconditionally, yet, especially Christians,

---

[127] **Holy**. See "God is Holy". - Question 9.

know that they do not always do the things pleasing to Him and therefore need to repent in their thinking and conduct (Rom 12:1-2).

In the New Testament, two verbs are used to describe the manner in which God loves. The first verb, **agapaō**[128], means to be well pleased, fond of, or contented with. It is the *unconditional* love God the Father has for his Son, for the whole world (John 3:16), and for his children. This means, amazingly, that, as you believe in His Son, God loves you the same way he loves Jesus, just as Jesus prayed as recorded in John 17:23,"I am in them and you are in me. May they experience such perfect unity that the world will know that you sent me and that you *love (agapaō) them as much (kathōs*[129]*) as you love (agapaō) me*" (NLT).

The love of God is born from within God, not from what he finds in us. His love is uncaused and spontaneous. How did C. S. Lewis succinctly state this? "He loved us not because we are lovable, but because He is love". The abundance of your love does not increase his. The lack of your love does not diminish his. Your goodness does not enhance his love, nor does your weakness dilute it. What Moses said to Israel is what God says to us: "The LORD did not choose you and

---

[128] **Love - Agapaō**. William Barclay notes that agape indicates an "... unconquerable benevolence, invincible goodwill. ... If we regard a person with agape, it means that no matter what that person does to us, no matter how he treats us, no matter if he insults us or injures us or grieves us, we will never allow any bitterness against him to invade our hearts, but will regard him with that unconquerable benevolence and goodwill which will *seek nothing but his highest good*".... In the case of our nearest and our dearest, we cannot help loving them; we speak of falling in love; it is something which comes to us quite unsought; it is something which is born of the emotions of the heart. But in the case of our enemies, (agape) love is not only something of the heart; it is also something of the will. It is not something which we cannot help; it is something which we have to will ourselves into doing. It is in fact a victory over that which comes instinctively to the natural man. Agape does not mean a feeling of the heart, which we cannot help, and which comes unbidden and unsought; it means a determination of the mind, whereby we achieve this unconquerable goodwill even to those who hurt and injure us. Agape, someone has said, is the power to love those whom we do not like and who may not like us".

Note a few final thoughts on agape: Biblical agapē love, an attitude of selfishness, is a matter of the will and not a matter of feeling or emotion, though deep feelings and emotions almost always accompany love. We have no capacity to generate agape love of ourselves. It is a spontaneous, unmerited, creative love flowing from God to the Christian, and from the Christian to others. It is impossible for the unconverted to manifest this divine love, and in fact, it is impossible even for a believer to demonstrate it in his own strength. It can only be exhibited by the power of the indwelling Holy Spirit. Agape love is beautifully described in 1 Corinthians 13. Also, open the QR link below and see the first note under Additional Information

[129] **Kathōs**. See footnote 48 on page 73.

Unit 8: Grow

lavish his love on you because you were larger or greater than other nations, for you were the smallest of all nations! It was simply because the LORD loves you" (Deut 7:7–8, NLT). The apostle John pithily states: "This is love: not that we loved God, but that he loved us" (1 John 4:10 NIV).

Think about how Jesus reflected this love: he knew the name of every soldier who beat him, every person who mocked him, and every Pharisee who thought he was the devil. Yet he still went to the cross so that they might be reconciled to God. The wonder of the cross reveals this *unconditional* aspect of love for us.

The second verb, **phileō**[130], means to have feelings of fondness and affection. It is the affection that God the Father has for his Son, Jesus, and the disciples. Jesus said to his disciples, "For the Father himself is fond (phileō) of *you* because you have been fond (phileō) of *me* and still are, and have believed that I from the presence of God came and still hold to that belief" (John 16:27, Wuest). So, God looks at you with a feeling of deep contentment, knowing that you are his dearly loved child.

Sadly, man-made religion portrays God as capricious and his love as a variable. "He loves me; he loves me not...". Religion thereby prostitutes the love of God by putting price tags on his affection. They say that you have to earn God's favour or at least impress him with the fervency of your love. But the gospel of grace - grace is what God's love looks like to us humans - declares that God loved you while you were a sinner, and nothing can separate you from his constant, limitless, and shadowless love.

I must reiterate the point: He won't love you any more if you succeed, and he won't love you any less if you fail. If you lead hundreds to Christ or none at all, he will love you just the same. There is nothing you can do to make him love you more and nothing you can do to make him love you less. His love endures forever.

---

[130] **Love - Phileo**. Wuest explains that phileo love is "an unimpassioned love, a friendly love. It is a love that is called out of one's heart as a response to the pleasure one takes in a person or object. It is based upon an inner community between the person loving and the person or object loved. That is, both have things in common with one another. The one loving finds a reflection of his own nature in the person or thing loved. It is a love of liking, an affection for someone or something that is the outgoing of one's heart in delight to that which affords pleasure. The Greeks made much of friendship, and this word was used by them to designate this form of mutual attraction"...".We gather, therefore, that agape is a love of devotion, while phileō is a love of emotion. There is another distinction we must be careful to note, and that is that agape is love that has ethical qualities about it, obligations, responsibilities, where phileō is a non-ethical love, making no ethical demands upon the person loving".

Does he love us because of our goodness? Because of our kindness? Because of our great faith? No, he loves us because of *His* goodness, kindness, and great faithfulness. God loves you simply because he has chosen to do so. He loves you when you don't feel lovely. He loves you when no one else loves you. Others may abandon, shun, divorce, and ignore you, but God will love you. Always. No matter what.

As we read the description of love in action found in 1 Corinthians 13:4-7 notice how Paul found the three dominant races of his time lacking in what really mattered, namely LOVE. "If I speak with the *tongues* of mankind *[the Greeks emphasised their power of oratory]* and of angels, but do not have love, I have become a noisy gong or a clanging cymbal. If I have the gift of *prophecy [the Jews emphasised the power of the prophetic word]* and know all mysteries and all knowledge, and if I have all faith so as to remove mountains, but do not have love, I am nothing. And if I give away all my possessions to charity, and if I surrender *my body* so that I may glory *[the Romans emphasised the power of military might and action]*, but do not have love, it does me no good. Love is patient, love is kind, it is not jealous; love does not brag, it is not arrogant. It does not act disgracefully, it does not seek its own benefit; it is not provoked, does not keep an account of a wrong suffered, it does not rejoice in unrighteousness, but rejoices with the truth; keeps every confidence, it believes all things, hopes all things, endures all things. Love never fails" (NASB).

From this description, an additional three things become apparent:

(1) This divine love is consumed with the **other person**. True love seeks nothing for itself; it is unselfishly other-focused, even to our enemies.

(2) We **cannot match up** to this perfect standard of love.

(3) **Jesus** fits the bill. Agape became flesh in Jesus. John 1:18, "No one has ever seen God; but God's only Son, he who is nearest the Father's heart, he has made him known". Love is the Son's heartbeat. Jesus did not come to chiefly reveal the Father's *arm* of power, nor primarily the Father's *mind*, but crucially the Father's heart – the heartbeat of love. He is always patient, kind, trusting, never arrogant or self-seeking – He never fails! He is love, and has loved you to death. God in Christ loves you with an enduring love that never gives up on you (Rom 8:38-39). Only from this divine love is it possible to love.

What about your love for God? Jesus was once asked, "Teacher, which is the great commandment in the Law?" According to Josephus, a Jewish historian, Israel had more than 3,600 commandments at that time. Which one did Jesus choose to summarise the *Law*? "You shall love the Lord your God with all your heart, and with all your soul, and with all your mind, and with all your strength" (Mark 12:30).

Under the old law-keeping covenant, you were commanded to love the Lord your God with all your heart (Deut 6:5; 10:12). The flow was from you to the Lord. But in the new covenant of grace, we love because he first loved us (1 John 4:19). It is only because we know the love of Christ that we are enabled to grow in our love for Him and walk in his love (Eph 3:19; 5:2).

To love God means to set our whole being – spirit, soul, and body, with heart, mind, and strength – absolutely on Him. Let our entire being be occupied by Him and lost in Him so that He becomes everything to us, and we are with Him practically in our daily life. In this way, we have the closest and most intimate fellowship with God (Ps 73:25; 25:14). As lovers of God, we NOW possess rich blessings. This is the sense of 1 Cor 2:9, "Just as it is written: "Things which eye has not seen and ear has not heard, and which have not entered the human heart, all that God has prepared for those who *love* Him". We are now children of God, possessing Christ's imputed righteousness having eternal life. The world cannot comprehend these present blessings. The human eye has not seen them. No ear has heard them. Man's rationality has not revealed it to them. They cannot be seen. They cannot be tasted. They can only be known as God had revealed them to us.

What about your love for others? Paul in 1 Corinthians 13 doesn't ask: How loving are you on a scale of one to ten? The real question, the priority, is: do you have love – that is, *God's love* through Jesus - downloaded into your heart by the Holy Spirit? (Rom 5:5). If so, his love will overflow from us to others without the need for policing or policies, for example, on neutrality[131], beards and attire[132], or blood[133]. To illustrate, does a man on his wedding day, deeply in love, need to be

---

[135] **Neutrality** in warfare. Note some expressions we encounter in Romans 12 and 13. "As far as it depends on you, be at peace with all men .... Never take revenge .... Overcome evil with good" – then onto chapter 13 – "Be in subjection to the governing authorities .... It is an avenger who brings wrath on the one who practices evil .... Your conscience's sake".- but then concludes - "put on the Lord Jesus Christ". The bottom line is the putting on of our Lord Jesus, first, by accepting Him in being saved, then growing in Him and His grace. Matters related to neutrality and warfare, and many other issues, are largely for the individual saved Christian to work out according to Scripture and the Spirit. Among Christian denominations that generally advocate for nonviolence and discourage participation in war are the Quakers, Mennonites, Jehovah's Witnesses, Brethren, Amish, and Catholic Peace Fellowship. Within these groups, some members may hold personal views that differ from the official stance of their denomination.

As we know, John the Baptist, Jesus, and Peter met military men but never demanded them to quit their job but rather become fair in their dealings with others. How did the early Christians view involvement in warfare? See Additional Information inside the QR below.

Christians may reach different conclusions: a) Limited Non-Resistance, b) Absolute Pacifism, c) Limited Defensive, d) Preventive First Strike. The Christian has a deep antipathy to war even though he recognises its inevitability in a world of sin (James 4:1-2). However, the Christian Church has generally recognised that the Christian may have to fight for his country as a last resort - but only in a just war and must refuse to fight in an unjust war, with the burden of proof being on the Christian more than on the state. Is he prepared for the consequences, either in his participation in the military or in dissenting?

In OT times, Israel was sometimes involved in God-authorised killing (not murder) to secure the land promised in the Abrahamic covenant. If you check these accounts, invariably, God was just with sinners while providing a means of deliverance. The apparent differences in human relations to God from the Old to the New Testament are based on the death of Christ on the Cross. It was not because God learned a new way to deal with people but because of what God in the person of Jesus Christ made possible. In both OT and NT, justice had to be done. That is, wickedness and rebellion had to be punished. And the Lord received our punishment. Today, Christians are primarily in spiritual warfare – Ephesians 6. Jesus (the greater Joshua) is all pieces of the armour – we put Him on. We eagerly say, "Come, Lord Jesus!"

Note: Christian denominations that generally avoid direct involvement in partisan politics: Quakers, the Salvation Army, Amish, Mennonites, and Bruderhof Communities.

[132] **Beards and Attire**. See inside the QR below the link to Additional Information. Several Christian religious denominations have strict codes of dress: Amish, Mennonites, Hutterites, some Pentecostal denominations, and various Brethren groups. The strictness and level of adherence can vary among individual members and congregations within each denomination.

In response to a question about beards, one branch office of JWs replied in 2009 with the comments: "Therefore, it would not determine a person's salvation if he chose to wear a beard, nor would it prevent him from getting baptised, sharing in field ministry, or enrolling in the Theocratic School". But then added the rider, "If a Christian man is "reaching out" for special privileges and yet desires to wear a beard, he might ask himself whether wearing even a neatly trimmed beard could become a matter of disturbance or controversy in the congregation. (1 Timothy 3:1) If most Christian males in a congregation or community have refrained from wearing beards for the Scriptural reasons outlined above, it is reasonable to expect that those taking the lead as ministerial servants or elders would be exemplary in this respect".

In 2016 the official journal of the JWs, the Watchtower, slightly softened its stance by indicating that beards may be acceptable in some cultures. "In some cultures, a neatly trimmed beard may be acceptable and respectable, and it may not detract at all from the Kingdom message. In fact, some appointed brothers have beards. Even so, some brothers might decide not to wear a beard. (1 Cor 8:9, 13; 10:32) In other cultures or localities, beards are not the custom and are not considered acceptable for Christian ministers. In fact, having one may hinder a brother from bringing glory to God by his dress and grooming and his being irreprehensible. —Rom. 15:1-3; 1 Tim. 3:2, 7". [WT 2016 Sept p21].

We should ask in what cultures are beards unacceptable? This vagueness still leaves little room for beards, particularly where local elder bodies are strongly opinionated on the topic. Such policy makers would do well to take to heart the words of Colossians 2:19-23, "He is the Head and we are the body. We can grow up healthy in God only as he nourishes us. So, then, if with Christ you've put all that puffed-up and childish religion behind you, why do you let yourselves be bullied by it? "Don't touch this! Don't taste that! Don't go near this!" Do you think things that are here today and gone tomorrow are worth that kind of attention? Such things sound impressive if said in a deep enough voice. They even give the illusion of being pious and humble and austere. But they're just another way of showing off, making yourselves look important" (Message Bible).

[133] **Blood**. Of the 362 OT uses of the word 'blood', almost all refer to violent death and only in seven cases is the word connected to life. Would letting a person die place more importance upon the symbol than the reality it symbolizes? If a robber threatened you, "Hand over your gold wedding ring, or I shoot your wife!" Would you say, "Take my wife? My ring is worth more!" Christ made clear that the law was made for man, not man for the law (Mark 2:27). Thus, if life was at stake, Israelites were not obliged to hold to Sabbatical rules, even though it was the life of a sheep or bull (Matt 12:11-12). Today, strict Orthodox Jews say blood transfusions are perfectly acceptable because of the Jewish law called "Pikuach Nefesh"-preserving human life overrides virtually any other religious consideration - one must break a commandment if failing to do so might jeopardize life.

Should an organisation assume the wisdom and authority to impose a complicated set of standards based on their interpretation of a few scriptures rather than leave such health matters in the realm of personal conscience? Paul spoke of those "who want to be under law" (Gal 4:21). Today, men can, by a legalistic approach to Christianity, convert it into a law code,

handed a thick manual on marriage, marital breakdown, and parenting? True, the couple may need guidance, even counselling, at some point, but love transcends any laws and penalties.

The same goes for our love for others, inside or outside our family. We love because we cannot help it. Love is the applied edge of faith. As D L Moody put it: "Love is faith in shoes – going out to serve the least, the last and the lost". Love has a divine spontaneity. Christians are such incorrigible lovers!

A missionary tells how on her arrival in China many years ago, she was taken in a rickshaw through the city's crowded streets. As she viewed the people a wave of revulsion swept over her. "O God," she cried, "how can I love these people – they are so revolting. I can't even begin to love them unless You help me". Then, as she sat in the rickshaw, a fresh sense of how much God loved her invaded her being. She was instantly changed – and for the rest of her days, she loved them with God's love.

Another story, this time of a missionary to India, Harold Groves. He travelled from Calcutta to Bombay to visit some friends. The hosts sent their servant to the railway station to meet him, and when he asked how he might recognise the missionary, they said, "Look for a white man helping somebody – that will be him". The servant saw a white man helping an old lady step down from the train, went up to him and said: "Are you Mr Groves?" – and he was. If you want to recognise someone maturing in Christ, look for someone helping someone else. We are as mature as we are mature in sacrificial love.

The question was, 'How do we grow in love?' The starting point is to know that the Father loves you because you believe in and love Jesus, His Son (John 16:27).

> *"Who delivered up Jesus to die?*
> *Not Judas, for money; not Pilate, for fear;*
> *not the Jews, for envy; – but the Father, for love!*
> *- John R.W. Stott,*

---

a burdensome body of rules. How far from grace and freedom in Christ! See the link in Additional Information below.

DIGGING DEEPER - HOW DO WE GROW IN LOVE?

Scan the QR code for informative links to each of these questions.

1. Can you answer the **ten questions** in this quiz about Christian love?

2. How does God's love differ from the **world's definition** of love?

3. How is it possible to love your **enemies**? (Matt 5:44)

4. Meditate over **Ephesians 1:6**, "To the praise of the glory of his grace, by which he made us accepted in the Beloved". Can you answer the following questions?
   a. When opening this link to Eph 1:6, click on the (Strong's) numbers 5485 and 5487 in the top row of the interlinear. What do you notice?
   b. What does the expression "accepted in the Beloved" mean to you?

5. According to **Revelation 2:4**, what was the root of the Ephesian church's problem?

See Suggested Answers at the end of this book.

Action Point

Spend some time meditating on the words of **1 Corinthians 13:13**. "But now faith, hope, love, abide these three; but the greatest of these is love". (See answer document for a few thoughts.) You can view a paraphrased version in the QR code:

Prayer

Lord, how I wonder at Your love for me, in that while I was yet a sinner, that in your grace and mercy, you sent the Lord Jesus Christ to die for my sins, so that in Him I might become your child and be made the righteousness of God. Thank You that you first loved me with such unchanging and unconditional love. Help me more and more to come to a new and deeper understanding of what your love means, so that I may love you, Father. This I ask in the name of Jesus my Saviour. Amen.

THE TRUTH
Grow up into Him - Eph 4:15

Q24. HOW CAN WE GROW IN CHRIST?

A new Christian was reading through the Gospels. After she finished, she told a friend she wanted to read a book on church history. When her friend asked why, the woman replied, "I'm curious. I've been wondering when Christians started to become so unlike Christ". There is a big difference between professing Christianity and being in Christ and growing in Him.

Growing in Christ involves developing a closer relationship with Him and so becoming more like Him. Therefore, our final subject here is growing in Christ. This is so important, especially if we have been influenced by religious elders who equate *spiritual growth to greater loyalty to their group's hierarchy*, along with conformity to their ever-changing views and practices, rather than growing in Christ. Sadly, millions are still conditioned to grow in a climate of men's religious authority – which breeds a fear of displeasing men or an organisation. Instead, we need to assess whether we have Christ and are growing up, or maturing, in him (Col 2:6-7).

An obvious question to ask first is, 'What does it mean to be *in Christ*?'

Being "in Christ"[134] means that we have *identified* with him. We were once "in Adam," outside the family of God. However, when we first responded to the Holy

---

[134] **In Christ**. This phrase is found over 150 times in Paul's letters. We once were "in Adam" by natural birth, but by faith in Christ, we were "born from above" and transferred from the kingdom of darkness "in Adam" and into the kingdom of light of His Son so that our spiritual home address is now "IN CHRIST". Along with all other members of Christ's one body, we have individually and collectively been hidden in the righteousness of Christ as new creations in the new covenant. When God looks at you, He no longer sees your sin because you are clothed in his Son's righteousness (Heb 8:10-12; 2 Cor 5:16-17). Yes, it's true that we daily need to repent (reorient our thinking in line with Christ's) and turn away from sin, but it is not the amount of our confession and repentance that forgives and saves a person - it is only the blood of Christ (Rom 12:2; Eph 1:7-8; Rev 2:5; 3:3).

We should note the reverse wording in the phrase "CHRIST IN". Simultaneously the believer is in Christ, and Christ is in the believer (note the contrast between John 17:21 and 17:23). John 15 illustrates this well. As branches of the true vine, we are "in Christ," but at the

Spirit's drawing by accepting Jesus' sacrifice as payment for our own sin, we were "baptized" into the adopted[135] family of God as sons. Being "in Christ" is not some advanced spiritual state into which some especially holy Christians manage to enter after years of spiritual discipline or by being part of a particular denomination. No - all believers are equally in Christ from the very first moment that in true repentance and faith, they put their trust in the Son, and it is God who by His grace puts them in Christ (1 Cor 1:30; Gal 3:28). Like Noah and his family knew they were in the ark and safe from the flood, so every believer realises that they are saved and secure because they are in Christ.

We can illustrate this IN-NESS by saying that when we enter an aeroplane we can take off and enjoy flying. Unfortunately, certain religions, like the Jehovah's Witnesses, want you to fly the Christian life without entering into a relationship with Christ. No wonder many find themselves constantly flapping their arms, trying to take off and fly, only to find themselves exhausted in their religious quest. Rather, you will find your true identity, the real you, in Christ alone. It is as though we died and came to life! A divine exchange occurs at the foot of the cross: our old sin nature for His perfect one. To be "in Christ" means we abide[136] in him;

---

same time, we need "Christ in us" as the sap of his Spirit flows in and through us. A fish to be alive must be in the water and the water in it.

Paul says, "But when it pleased God to reveal His Son in me". Later in he says, "It is no longer I who live, but Christ lives in me" (Gal 1:15-16; 2:20; 4:19; Col 1:27; 2 Cor 13:5). Here Paul did not say, 'I live in a Christ-like way', or 'I glorify Christ through my behaviour' – although that is the result. No, he said, "Christ...lives in me," clearly telling us that Christian life is not a matter of struggling to behave 'religiously' like Christ but of allowing Christ himself to live in and through us.

Christ dwells in all his people, but sometimes there are areas of our hearts so full of other things that there is no room for Christ in them - we might keep the door to certain compartments shut to him. That is why Paul often prayed the Christians might be strengthened so that Christ may take up residence without any reserve in the home of their hearts (Eph 3:14-21). As Christ dwells evermore fully in our hearts, we find ourselves led ever more deeply into the enjoyment of our union with every other believer; we are perfected into one.

[135] **Adoption**. See footnote 11 on page 166.

[136] **Abide.** To abide in Christ is to rest, dwell, stay in his love from the day you decide to trust in him. Your eternal rest does not begin the day you die, but the day you give your life to Him. Then, because Jesus has done the work, you can rest in him, choosing to be anxious-free. The parable of John 15 shows that we should be united with Christ in a very personal way. This is not a formal attachment by joining a religious organisation or performing external duties; it is a union of the soul with Christ, or in the apostle's words, it is "Christ formed within us" (Gal 4:19). No longer self-reliant, we thrive as a branch in the vine is dependent

that God no longer sees our imperfections - He sees the righteousness of His own Son. Only "in Christ" is our sin debt cancelled, our relationship with God restored, and our eternity secured (Eph 2:13; Heb 8:12).

Or, as Colossians 3:3 says, "For you have *died,* and your *life* is hidden with Christ in God". This exact word, "life" (zoe) – is also used in Ephesians 4:18, where it refers to the Gentiles who were "excluded from the life (zoe) of God". We need to understand that the Bible speaks of three kinds of "life":

a. **Physical life** - Greek, bios (the root for the word 'biology'). It's the life of our body that includes our five senses. This life enables us to contact the material world (Luke 8:14).

b. **Psychological life** - Greek, psyche (note the word 'psychology'). Within our physical body, we also have our distinct personality - our soul with our mind, emotion, and will (Mark 10:45).

c. **Eternal life** - Greek, zoe (from which we derive "zoology'), means not only the animate aspect of life, as opposed to the non-animate, but also life in the absolute and complete sense. The bible's focus is on this deeper life - eternal life, divine life, the life of God and Christ – which we can enjoy now, before our physical death (John 3:15; 2 Pet 1:4).

---

on the vitality flowing through it (John 15:4-5,9; 1 John 4:15). Abiding means we guard our garden from the little foxes that spoil the vineyard when they are in bloom (Song of Sol 2:15). It is so often the little invasions that mess up our fruitfulness. All potential threats to our relationship with Jesus must be removed.

Unit 8: Grow

Baptized Into Christ
Romans 6:3
Galatians 3:27

Outside - *Lost With No Hope*

1) No Spiritual Blessings
2) No Redemption
3) No Forgiveness of Sins
4) Condemnation
5) Old Sinful Creature
6) No Salvation
7) No Eternal Life in Heaven

In Christ

1) Ephesians 1:3 - Every Spiritual Blessing
2) Ephesians 1:7 - Redemption
3) Ephesians 1:7 - Forgiveness of Sins
4) Romans 8:2 - No Condemnation
5) 2 Corinthians 5:17 - New Creation
6) 2 Timothy 2:10 - Salvation
7) 1 John 5:11 - Eternal Life

So much then for being in Christ as life, receiving from him life (zoe) abundantly (John 10:10). Now, how do we grow in Him? Just what is the primary purpose of the 'body of Christ,' the church? Is it to evangelise, to fight error, or to keep things smoothly organised?

Our main scripture today will be taken from the book of Ephesians. In a sentence, Ephesians emphasizes unity, new identity, love, growth, and spiritual armour in Christ. It's all about growing in Christ. Here is **Ephesians 4:11-16**. I will highlight a few keywords:

> "He himself gave some as apostles and some as prophets and some as evangelists and some as pastors and teachers for the **equipping of the saints**, for the work of the ministry, for building up the body of Christ, until we all reach the **unity** of the faith and the knowledge of the Son of God, to a mature man, to a measure of the maturity of the fullness of Christ, so that we may no longer be infants, tossed about by waves and carried about by every wind of teaching, by the **trickery** of people, by craftiness with reference to the **scheming** of deceit. But speaking the **truth in love**, we are to **grow into him** with reference to all things, who is the head, Christ, from whom the whole body, joined together and held together by every supporting ligament, according to the working by measure of each single part, the growth of the body makes for the building up of itself in love" (Lexham).

Before we unpack these verses, we should take a moment to look at a suggested chiastic structure, or pattern, of Ephesians chapter 4.

a) Eph 4:1-6, <u>walk</u> in a manner worthy of the calling.

b) Eph 4:7-12, gifts for growth, to <u>build up the Body.</u>

> **c)** Eph 4:13 [central axis], "Until we all reach the unity of the faith and the knowledge of the Son of God, to a mature man, to a measure of the maturity of the fullness of Christ.

    b) Eph 4:14-16, no longer infants, but grow up into Him, build up the Body in love.

    a) Eph 4:17-24, no longer walk as the Gentiles.

We see that the focus of our life should be primarily growing up in Christ, manifesting his spiritual completeness and exercising our spiritual gifts to build others up.

vs 11-12. What is the purpose of appointed elders[137] in a congregation? It is to **equip all** of us to be involved in some aspect of ministry (see vs 16). Guzik, a theologian, quips, "Some people think of the church as a pyramid, with the pastor at the top. Others think of the church as a bus driven by the pastor, who takes his passive passengers where they should go. God wants us to see the church as a body, where every part does its share". Christianity can become little more than a Sunday-morning spectator sport, much like the definition of football: 22 men down on the field, desperately in need of rest, and 20,000 in the grandstands, desperately in need of exercise! Could you be trained in a new role? Perhaps to visit the sick in hospital or the housebound? Could you volunteer behind the

---

[137] **Elder** (episkopos). A comparison of scriptural passages shows that the terms overseer, bishop, shepherd, pastor, elder, presbyter, and ruler are synonymous and interchangeable. They are simply different words for the same thing. In the earliest churches, their local congregation leaders were simply called "elders". In the Pastoral Epistles, Paul speaks twice regarding their qualifications as experienced exemplary individuals of high integrity who can teach, thereby equipped to help the spiritually weak (1 Tim 3:1-7; Titus 1:5-9). These elders generally served as teams rather than single leaders (Acts 20:17; Php 1:1).

Wayne Grudem after deliberating the matter of appointing elders in a local church, comments, "In the New Testament there are several examples where church officers were apparently chosen by the whole congregation" (Acts 1:15; 6:3; 15:22,25). He continues, "These factors combine to indicate that although scripture does not explicitly command one specific system of choosing church officers, it would seem most wise to have a system whereby the entire church has a significant role in the selection and recognition of the officers of the church - perhaps through a congregational vote, or through some other process whereby congregational recognition is required before the church officers can assume office …. Scripture is silent regarding the actual process; therefore, God has decided to leave the matter to the wisdom of each congregation in its own setting". (Systematic Theology, Intervarsity Press, 2019; p. 920-923)

scenes in the care of individuals living in poverty or those experiencing homelessness? How about handing out some tracts in the street or as you talk informally to a neighbour? Is there a role you could fill in the local church or group on the tech side of things - a webpage, for example? Are you aspiring to the office of an overseer? Remember though, the priority, of course, is to be personally in Christ.

vs 13. What is this unity[138]? We need to know that the overall theme of the Book of Ephesians is unity, that is, **unity in Christ** – faith in the person of Christ - not an organisational unity, but as a living, loving, organism as members of His body. We can illustrate this by how a pianist uses the fingers of both hands to play the many keys on a piano. How boring and annoying if he trained every finger to play only middle C continually! As those in Christ, let us enjoy diversity without discordance.

vs 14. Glancing again at the diagram, or chiasm, we see that our Christian walk, whether as individuals or as a body, should grow from being wobbly infants, easily influenced by false teachings, to that of mature people in Christ. The word '**trickery**' (kubeia, giving us our English "cube," dice) literally refers to professional gamblers who, by sleight of hand, manipulated "loaded" dice to their

---

[138] **Unity.** Eph 4:3,13 (henotes from heís [one] + henós [of one]) speaks of unanimity, a state of oneness or of being in harmony and accord. It does not describe an external, ecclesiastical union or uniformity, but internal, spiritual unity. The Spirit in the Body has created a fundamental unity (wrought by the New Covenant) that nothing can destroy, even though believers can still have differences of opinion regarding some issues.

In commenting on Acts 4:32, Kent Hughes explains, "'All the believers were one in... mind.' They shared the same basic mental focus and thought about many of the same things. This came about as the fundamental, inarticulate unity of their hearts effervesced upward into their souls! They were truly soul brothers and sisters. This was the greatest, most profound, most satisfying unity the world has ever seen! As a result, there was no division. This was astounding because, just a few days before, when 3,000 were converted, they came from everywhere! This does not mean these believers saw everything eye to eye. It is wrong to suppose, as sadly some do, that when believers dwell in unity they will carry the same Bible, read the same books, promote the same styles, educate their children the same way, have the same likes and dislikes—that they will become Christian clones. The fact is, the insistence that others be just like us is one of the most disunifying mind-sets a church can have because it instills a judgmental inflexibility that hurls people away from the church with lethal force. One of the wonders of Christ is that he honors our individuality while bringing us into unity".- (See Acts: The Church Afire)

Therefore, Paul pleads for the saints at Ephesus to "burn" with zeal to guard the unity which Christ bought at Calvary and to live at peace with one another.

advantage, which is a perfect picture of men coming into a congregation and manipulating the Word of God to make it say what they want it to say! And many do! Here's a conundrum, though: the verse states that false teachers use deceitful schemes to trick people. But surely not all such teachers deliberately and cunningly plot to mislead their followers. Here is a suggestion: Paul uses the very same word for 'schemes' (μεθοδεία, giving us the word method) just one other time, and it is found in this same letter at Ephesians 6:11,"Put on the full armour of God, so that you can take your stand against the *devil's schemes*". So, whether the intention of these bad leaders is to mislead deliberately or not, they are used as mere puppets in the Devil's scheming hands.

vs 15-16. What is a good sign that we are growing into Christ individually and collectively? We will learn to speak the "**truth in love**". We can go to two extremes. We can speak the *truth but not in love*, in which case we are being ungracious, even offensive, alienating the people we seek to help. Or we can speak in love and *suppress the truth*, in which case we are being unfaithful. To avoid hurting someone's feelings, we may say nothing and allow a sinful situation to continue. True love, however, will speak at the right time, with the right words, in the right spirit, and using the right approach. This is the route to a fully mature Christian unity.

Let's get practical here. Is there any evidence that a Christian is likely to display as he or she grows in their relationship with Christ? Before you consider this short list below, though, please remember that the work of Christian growth is to think less of ourselves and our performance and more of Jesus and his performance for us. Ironically, when we focus mostly on our need to get better, we actually get worse, becoming self-absorbed. Christian growth, in other words, doesn't happen by first behaving better, but by believing better – believing in Jesus in deepening, widening ways. Focusing on Him and on what he has already secured for sinners. Hence, the following are what a Christian, fixing his attention on Christ by the Spirit, comes to desire in his heart:

- Study: His loves for the Word grows deeper; He likely sets aside time each day to read and study the Bible (Ps 1:2-3). He can't absorb enough about Jesus!

- Prayer: He enjoys lingering in prayer; in communion with the Lord; seeking the Spirit; praying in the Spirit (Luke 11:13; John 7:38-39; Jude 20).

- Fellowship: He desires to be with other believers, both in conversation and worship (Rom 1:11-12; Heb 10:24-25). This may lead him to find a local church, or get involved in a Bible study group.

Unit 8: Grow

- **Serving**: He has the impulse to serve others in the community, church, or workplace; to share the love of Christ with others; to live out his faith through actions and words (1 Pet 4:10-11).

- **Mentor**: He appreciates the company of a trusted friend or mentor who can hold him accountable in his walk with Christ; sharing his struggles and successes with them, and asking for their guidance and support (Prov 27:17).

In 'The Gospel-Driven Life,' Michael Horton makes this helpful comment: "Paul does not say, "Be like Jesus". He says, " You *are* like Jesus," ... It's easy for us to rely on the gospel for forgiveness and justification but then to look elsewhere for our renewal and sanctification. However, Paul says that it's all there: "in Christ," Only after saying this does Paul then issue the imperative to live a life that is consistent with this truth ... Being in Christ is the perpetual source of our becoming like Christ, not vice versa." (Col 1:27; 2:6-12; 3:3)

Evangelist and author Ray Steadman once wrote regarding our growth in Christ, "The proper attitude for a healthy Christian is an eagerness to grow. I once asked a boy how old he was. Quick as a flash, he said, "I'm twelve, going on thirteen, but soon to be fourteen". That's the kind of eagerness for maturity we all should have! We do not need to ask ourselves, "Am I mature? Am I completely like Christ?" Instead, we should ask ourselves, "Am I on the way? Is there progress? Am I growing in the right direction?" Do not be discouraged if you are not experiencing overnight spiritual maturity. Remember that it takes God years to grow an oak tree, but He can grow a squash in three months and a radish plant in a few weeks! Which would you rather be?!"

By God's grace, may we patiently and progressively "grow up in all aspects into Him, who is the head, that is, Christ" (Eph 4:15). He is the TRUTH who we have no wish to obscure!

"I gave up all for Christ, and what have I found?
Everything in Christ".
- John Calvin

Digging Deeper - How Can We Grow in Christ?

Scan the QR code for informative links to each of these questions.

1. All six scriptures below mention one of the three words for '**life**.' Mark which is which: bios, psyche, or zoe? Inside the QR code is a useful online interlinear tool:
   a. John 12:27
   b. John 14:6
   c. Rev 6:9
   d. Luke 21:4
   e. Matt 7:14
   f. 1 John 2:16

2. The apostles, prophets, evangelizers, and pastor teachers – do we have them **today**?

3. Read **Galatian 4:19**. Does this refer to our initial salvation as 'born again' ones, or to maturing afterwards in Christlikeness?

4. What examples of '**windy teachings**,' or perhaps new fads in doctrines, are you aware of? (Jude 12-13)

5. What is the purpose of the **church**? Is it to evangelise, to fight error, or to keep things smoothly organised?

See Suggested Answers at the end of this book.

Action Point
Please read and consider the following article "Are You Growing In Grace?" (4-5 pages) in connection with Acts 2:42.

Prayer
Lord, make me to know You aright, that I may more and more, love, serve, enjoy and possess You. And since in the life below I cannot fully attain this blessedness, let it at least grow in me day by day, until it all be fulfilled in the life to come. Amen. (St Anselm)

CONCLUSION

This completes our Grace series of articles. Thank you for taking the time to dip into some, or all, of the contents. What can we conclude? In agreement with the Apostle John:

"I love all of you in the **truth** [*the truth about the Gospel of Jesus Christ*], and all those who know the truth love you. We love you because of the truth that lives [abides; remains] in us and will be with us forever". (2 John vs 2-3, The Expanded Bible).

How Christ-dishonouring that high-control religions obscure, hide, and can obfuscate the one essential TRUTH that you only need Jesus for your salvation. Rather these groups, though including the name of Jesus in their teaching, devalue or side-line Him. This is evident when they seek to accentuate their particular brand of Christianity or elevate their leaders as the way of salvation. (Please refer to Question 10 for a refresher if you wish.)

Here is a summary of the key points which are to be found in the boxed headings at the beginning of each article. It will be beneficial to draw them together as one - IN CHRIST, because this has been the overarching intention of this manual. Jesus is our lens.

1. Jesus is the door – enter life through Him (John 10:9-10).
2. Jesus is the FACE of Grace (John 1:17).
3. Whatever you do, work heartily, as for the Lord [Jesus] and not for men (Col 3:23).
4. The Bible is the Spirit's biography of our Saviour – King Jesus (Rev 19:10).
5. Jesus is the greatest affirmation of Scripture (John 17:17).
6. By GRACE consider Christ and context (Luke 24:25-27).
7. By Him [Christ] all things were created in all their complexity (Col 1:16-17).
8. "What God was the Word was" (John 1:1, NEB; NET footnote).
9. The Son reveals the Father (Matt 11:27).
10. No-one can say "Jesus is Lord" except by the Holy Spirit" (1 Cor 12:3).
11. Not so much WWJD but WIJD (Gal 2:20).
12. Jesus, the One who brings us to God (1 Peter 3:18).

Suggested Answers

13. Jesus promised another Helper who would glorify the Son (John 16:14).
14. Jesus sends the Spirit to testify about Him (John 15:26).
15. Jesus at the cross disarmed the spirit rulers (Col 2:15).
16. Jesus' blood is the remedy (Eph 1:7).
17. Jesus carried our suffering (Isa 53:4).
18. Jesus is the resurrection and the life (John 11:25).
19. Everyone who believes that Jesus is the Christ has been born of God (1 John 5:1).
20. Whoever believes in the Son has eternal life (John 3:36).
21. Preach Christ crucified (1 Cor 1:23).
22. You may ask Jesus for anything in his name (John 14:14).
23. The Father loves you because you love Jesus (John 16:27).
24. Grow up into Him (Eph 4:15).

From the above we see the TRUTH. Jesus. He reveals the Father, by the Spirit, through the Word. So that, through His death and resurrection we may be saved, justified, and glorified – all to Father's glory. As you considered alternative answers to some often-asked questions, I pray that it has helped you move forward in your Christian grace walk.

Jesus invites us today - in fact, commands us - to repent, turn from all that is wrong in our lives and find forgiveness and new life in Him. Martin Luther, writing nearly 500 years ago, expressed the significance of our response to Jesus' death and his invitation to us: "Either sin is with you, lying on your shoulders, or it is lying on Christ, the Lamb of God. Now if it is lying on your back, you are lost; but if it is resting on Christ, you are free, and you will be saved. Now choose what you want".

Let's remind ourselves of Peter's words in reply to the question, "What should we do?" He responded, "Each of you must repent of your sins and turn to God, and be baptized in the name of Jesus Christ for the forgiveness of your sins. Then you will receive the gift of the Holy Spirit. This promise is to you, to your children, and to those far away - all who have been called by the Lord our God". Then Peter continued preaching for a long time, strongly urging all his listeners, "Save yourselves from this crooked generation!"

Don Walker, a British TV presenter, hit the headlines because of his unwillingness to work on Sundays. He has always loved football, but everything changed for him one day in 1989 when at church he heard someone preach on the importance of knowing Jesus Christ as your personal Saviour. He says: "I was rooted to the spot. For the first time in my life, my mind wasn't wandering ... I felt the depths of my sin. I knew that I was offending God by the life I was living, and the prospect of going to hell terrified me. I wanted to go to heaven - I wanted to be in the presence of God, thanks to the saving love of his Son, the Lord Jesus Christ ... that night, I went to bed a different person. I knew that my sins had been forgiven".

On the flyleaf of this book you may have noticed a quote of the exchange between Jesus and Pilate. Jesus said, "Everyone on the side of truth listens to me". Pilate's response was the question, "What is truth?" (John 18:37-38). The king of heaven revealed his identity and mission as the true signpost by which all lost children find their way home. However, for Pilate, soldiers and armies were the truth, Rome was truth, Caesar was truth, and political power was truth. For many in today's society, there is no true truth about God; there is only my truth and your truth, and one is as good as the other. Then, religion often muddies the waters of truth with half-truths, bent truths, and damnable lies. But Jesus testified to the truth – Himself - because only the truth can set you free (John 8:32). If you have never received Christ personally as your Lord and Saviour, you may wish to look at the prayer suggestion on pages 89-90, or see the heading "Turning to the Lord".

Of course, there are innumerable additional questions we could have entertained:

What about the End Times? The incarnation? Divorce? Speaking in tongues? The list is endless. So, what can you do? Just three basic things will help you.

Open your *Bible with expectation as you pray* to the Lord for Holy Spirit to open up your eyes of understanding. We hope that some tools mentioned during these articles will also be helpful in your personal research. Often in utilising these mostly online tools, you will discover a number of alternative solutions to a Bible question. This is not a cause for worry but for prayer and perhaps open discussion. (see Q6. How do You Study the Bible? – note Question page, q4).

Suggested Answers

Secondly, many find open *discussion with other Christians* to be beneficial. They discover the satisfaction in joining a local face-to-face Christian home group. Some, in time, overcome previous prejudices and visit different churches. Why not engage in a conversation with a local minister - if you feel comfortable with the idea?

Finally, and most importantly, keep your *focus on Christ* himself as grace personified. Avoid becoming so bogged down in detailed academic knowledge of theologians and charismatic figures, along with the plethora of YouTube videos, that you miss Him. It is easy to find ourselves overly impressed by another's knowledge, theology, or 'wise persuasive' words. We have no desire to follow any man as leader, nor an organisation, as essential for salvation (1 Cor 2:1-4; 3:4-11).

Here is a short concluding checklist to help us avoid religion's trap of obscuring the TRUTH. Please be on the alert by asking these questions about any group that you encounter:

a) *Does this group adhere to the Bible?* "Go to God's teaching and His testimony to guide your thoughts and behavior! If any response disagrees with the word of God, then it's muddling and wrong and not the least bit illuminating". (Isa 8:20 Voice; 1 Thess 5:21). Note, we are not asking whether this religion quotes lots of scriptures, even accurately, but clearly exegetes scriptures according to their context and historical background. Is 'eisegetical doublespeak' exploited, for example from the book of Revelation, to misapply passages to fit their own religious group's history? Are Bible words and expressions redefined according to their preconceived ideas? Do they favour their own bias Bible translation?

b) *Is Jesus' true identity and role rightly honoured?* – How does this group view Jesus' 'divinity, mediatorship, and full value of his shed blood?

c) *How about their view of salvation?* Is it clearly stated all is by His grace, not about our graft? (Rom 4:1-4; 11:6; Eph 2:8-10; 2 Tim 1:9; Tit 3:4-7). Is salvation assured? (John 5:24; 1 John 5:13).

d) *Does this religion try to micromanage?* By imposing strict regulations, and demanding absolute obedience, does the religion create a highly regimented religious environment? Do they seek to exert control of their follower's behaviour, information, thinking and emotions (B.I.T.E - Information)? (Matt 23:4,23; Acts 15:10).

e) *What is their fruit?* As a result of their disciplined approach, is the fruitage of the Spirit manifest in their daily lives?

Yes, for over 60 years every aspect of my life was monitored by a highly controlling religious group – Jehovah's Witnesses. Yet, by the grace of God in Christ I was saved. How patient is our Lord. Let Him receive all the praise. You may like to listen to my 23 minutes story on United Christian Broadcasters radio from 2022. If so, you will find the link at the end of the Additional Information in Question 24 above.

Our final words, highlighting God's grace in Christ, are to be found at 2 Peter 1:2; 3:18 (Wuest):

"[Sanctifying] grace to you and [tranquilizing] peace be multiplied in the sphere of and by the experiential knowledge [which the believer has] of God, even Jesus, our Lord".

"But be constantly growing in the sphere of grace and an experiential knowledge of our Lord and Saviour Jesus Christ. To him be glory both now and to the day of eternity".

Yes, may our Lord continue to pour out His rich blessings upon you as you grow in Prayer, in Love, and in Christ. All praise to our Lord of inexhaustible Grace, Amen.

Suggested Answers

Suggested Answers (1)
Is Religion the Way to God?

1. Has God always had an **organisation** on earth?

- The Bible never uses the word "organisation".
- Israel (Yahweh's nation) was organised but turned apostate. "And this people has an apostatizing and rebelling heart. They have turned aside, and they go on". (LSV)
- The early Christians had autonomous congregations meeting in house groups. They were united by God's Word, Spirit, and love – not micro-managed by a central governing body.
- Until the future harvest, genuine Christians remain scattered like wheat amidst weeds.

2. Why do you think that religion often imposes so many **rules**? With what consequences?

Matthew 23:4-11 (Message): "Instead of giving you God's Law as food and drink by which you can banquet on God, they package it in bundles of rules, loading you down like pack animals. They seem to take pleasure in watching you stagger under these loads, and wouldn't think of lifting a finger to help. Their lives are perpetual fashion shows, embroidered prayer shawls one day and flowery prayers the next. They love to sit at the head table at church dinners, basking in the most **prominent positions**, preening in the radiance of public flattery, receiving honorary degrees, and getting called 'Doctor' and 'Reverend.' "Don't let people do that to you, put you on a pedestal like that. You all have a single Teacher, and you are all classmates. Don't set people up as experts over your life, letting them tell you what to do. Save that authority for God; let him tell you what to do". (also, John 12:43)

This religious rule-making leads to, among other things, an unhealthy fear of walking on eggshells before a hard-to-please God, the denigration of Jesus as the Truth, and a prideful judgmentalism of others based on the group's exclusivity.

3. Read **Matthew 12:1-8**. What is the main point?
Jesus never violated God's command to observe the Sabbath but often broke man's legalistic additions to that law. In fact, Sabbath was the busiest working day for the priests at the temple. Jesus loved mercy over sacrifice. He is the Lord, the greater David, the Temple, and Sabbath!

4. How could you explain **Luke 13:24**, "strive to enter through the narrow gate"?
Jesus described the exertion needed when we come to the point of belief in him. At that time we need to offload the proud tendency of self-righteousness in carrying the heavy workload of obedience to religious law in order to enter into salvation - the gate of grace, rest and life - Jesus Christ.

5. Read **Philippians 3:8**. From the context, what was the "rubbish" that Paul threw out?
Paul regarded his past of morality, activity, theology, and ancestry as rubbish compared to his personal relationship with Jesus Christ.

SUGGESTED ANSWERS (2) - WHAT IS GRACE?

1. What is the point of the **railway track** illustration? (2 Tim 1:9)
All are in a broken condition under sin's condemnation. No one can climb the legalistic law ladder, trying to love God perfectly. Jesus has invited us to enter on the Grace train – the price is paid, the journey empowered by the Holy Spirit. Rest!

2. In its broad meaning, how does the word GRACE include more than "undeserved kindness"? What is your **definition of grace**?
   It is **F**ree, **A**ccepts, is **C**hrist, and **E**mpowers.
   Grace is all of God's blessings wrapped up in Christ.
"What actually took place is this: I tried keeping rules and working my head off to please God, and it didn't work. So I quit being a "law man" so

that I could be God's man. Christ's life showed me how, and enabled me to do it. I identified myself completely with him. Indeed, I have been crucified with Christ. My ego is no longer central. It is no longer important that I appear righteous before you or have your good opinion, and I am no longer driven to impress God. Christ lives in me. The life you see me living is not "mine," but it is lived by faith in the Son of God, who loved me and gave himself for me. I am not going to go back on that. Is it not clear to you that to go back to that old rule-keeping, peer-pleasing religion would be an abandonment of everything personal and free in my relationship with God? I refuse to do that, to repudiate God's grace. If a living relationship with God could come by rule-keeping, then Christ died unnecessarily" (Gal 2:19-21 Message).

3. Why can we say grace is a **person**?
John 1:17 says, "The law was given [passed on] through Moses, grace and truth came [in person]through Jesus Christ". You cannot separate truth from grace and grace from truth as they are both embodied in the person of Jesus Christ.

4. What is the **purpose** of grace?
"All this is why we are constantly praying for you, so God will make you worthy of the great calling you have received from Him and will **give you the power** to accomplish every good intention and work of faith. Then the great name of our Lord **Jesus will be glorified** through your lives, and **you will be glorified** in Him according to the grace of our God and the Lord Jesus, the Anointed One, our Liberating King" (2 Thess 1:11-12 The Voice).

5. How is our God of grace the greatest **heart surgeon**?
God gives to the undeserving sinner a new heart. Jesus lives in me. He is now our heartbeat. He is my life, not part of it.

SUGGESTED ANSWERS (3)
WHAT IS THE PURPOSE OF LIFE?

1. What should be our primary **purpose** in life?
"Everyone who is called by My name, and whom I have created **for My glory**, whom I have formed, even whom I have made" (Isaiah 43:7). We were created by God to enjoy Him as his children, and to radiate and glorify Him. As we enjoy Him, He unconditionally loves us and enjoys fellowship.

2. How is **grace** involved in glorifying God? (Eph 1:6)
One way to express this is that God is only glorified by His grace to you, not your behavior towards Him, which is merely *His grace fruiting*. God's grace is His glory fully realized within us.

3. What does seeking first His **kingdom and righteousness** involve?
When you repent and yield to Jesus' authority as Lord, and when He is in control of your life, through a new birth - that is the kingdom of God. It is not rules and regulations, but "righteousness and peace and joy in the Holy Spirit" (Rom 14:17). The gospel of the kingdom is the gospel of Christ, which is the gospel of God, which is the gospel of grace. They are different labels for the same gospel message. The Jews were familiar with the righteousness that came by the law, which never made anyone righteous (Rom 9:31), but Jesus introduced them to another kind of righteousness that came from God (Matt 5:20,48; Rom 5:17; 10:1-5; 2 Cor 5:21, Php 3:9).

4. Seven days from **John 17:20-26**. How would you answer the following?
Day 1- v20 How can you be involved in this verse today?
 Jesus was confident in the work of God through the disciples. Could I share the gospel today?
Day 2 - v:21 Is being "one" based on organisational unity?
Christ's body is organic (not organisational) enjoying oneness with Father, Son, and each other.
Day 3 - v22 Name 3 gifts from Jesus (vs 2, 14, 22)
 His eternal life, His Word, and His glory!

Day 4 - **v23** What does "even as You have loved me" mean to you?
God loves you tenderly the same way he loves Jesus. The words to Jesus,
He says to you, "This is my beloved Son, in whom I am well-pleased" (1
John 4:17; 3:7).

Day 5 - **v24** What is Jesus' deep desire? (Song of Solomon 6:5)
Jesus is enthralled by us! He wants his bride to be alongside him forever.

Day 6 - **v25** How does Jesus refer to God six times?
Jesus always addressed his prayers to Father (not to Jehovah), including
at the cross, crying out, "O righteous Father!" You can talk intimately to
Father as a child to his daddy.

Day 7 - **v26** What does the "name" mean? Why does Jesus make the name
known?
He revealed the nature of Father to the disciples, that they would be filled
with the love of the Father, and know the indwelling presence of Jesus
Himself.

SUGGESTED ANSWERS (4)
WHAT IS THE BIBLE ALL ABOUT?

1. Try this ten-question **quiz** 'How the Bible Came To Be.'
Here a few more facts worth reviewing: Information (1–2-page article)

2. How many parts comprised the original **Hebrew Bible** (OT)?
The original OT was written on 22 scrolls. The Jewish Tanakh is a
collection of Hebrew scriptures from a period of about 1,200 years. It
consists of the three parts Torah (law, directive), Nevi'im (prophets) and
Ketuvim (writings, also called "other books" or "psalms" since they first
appear in the group). The initial letters "TNK" gave the Hebrew Bible the
name TaNaKh.

3. Summarize the Bible 's message in one sentence? (1 John 5:11-12)
Some key word to include could be grace, cross, redemption, sons,
kingdom, new creation, eternal life.

4. What are the main differences between various popular **Bible
translations**?

Some are "word for word" translations, while others are "thought for thought". Word for word Bibles translate as precisely as possible from the original languages (Hebrew, Aramaic, and Greek). "Thought for thought" versions convey the central idea, and are easier to read, but not as accurate.

5. Read **Ephesians 1:6-11.** What stands out to you in this "Look at the Book"?
It is God's good pleasure to make Jesus the sum total of all things in all periods of time. He is at the centre of God's household management.

SUGGESTED ANSWERS (5) - IS THE BIBLE TRUE?

1. In addition to the **Pilate** stone, what other evidence proves his existence?
Numerous ancient texts provide information about him, including Philo, Josephus, and Tacitus. In 1968-69 an artifact, a copper ring with Pilate's name on it came to light. A bronze prutah coin, minted by him, dated to the 17th year of Tiberius (30/31 AD) has been unearthed.

2. Which one of these nine **archaeological** finds confirms the Bible's accuracy most to you?
If you find Biblical archaeology interesting, you may like to check out other sites under Additional Information for more recent discoveries.

3. Answer the following apparent **contradictions**:
  a. **Gen 4:17 -** where did Cain get his wife?
     Cain married his sister (or possibly a niece). Later those kinds of marriages were restricted in the Law of Moses (Lev. 20:19).
  b. **John 20:22** - was the Holy Spirit received by the disciples before Pentecost?
     Some scholars believe that "receive" is intended to denote the future "you will receive". If so, then there is no conflict, because they did receive at Pentecost. If they, however, did receive the Spirit in John 20:22 it was in the sense of being able to affirm forgiveness (vs 23), not to provide power to be his witnesses.

c. **1 Cor 15:29** - does 'baptism for the dead' contradict that people must believe individually?
The Bible is emphatic that baptism does not save, but only by grace through faith in His blood. Some believe Paul is referring to a cultic practice among the Corinthians. Paul would be saying, "If you don't believe in the resurrection, then why engage in the practice of baptizing people for the dead. You are inconsistent with your own (false) beliefs". Others suggest that Paul is referring to the fact that baptism symbolizes the believer's death with Christ (Rom. 6:3–5). The Greek word "for" (eis) can mean "with a view to". In this sense. saying, "Why are you baptized with a view to your death and resurrection with Christ, if you do not believe in the resurrection?"

d. **James 2:21** – does James contradict Paul, by saying we are justified by works?
Paul looks at what goes on internally (before God – Rom 3:20; 4:2-5; Gal 3:11) through faith alone; James talks about the external results (before men – James 2:18, 22) evidencing faith by works. Simply stated, Paul says, "We're saved by faith". James says, "This is what saving faith looks like".

4. How does one theologian reason on the Bible's authenticity of the **Old Testament** stories?
Since Jesus of Nazareth endorses the Old Testament, we simply have to find out who Jesus was and decide if we believe his claims.

5. This video clip estimates the chances of **Messianic prophecies** being fulfilled. What fact or two could help you reason with others?
Josh and Sean McDowell quote Stoner in their book, Evidence That Demands a Verdict: "We find that the chance that any man might have lived down to the present time and fulfilled all eight prophecies is 1 in 10^{17} (1 in 100,000,000,000,000,000)".

Suggested Answers (6)
How do You Study the Bible?

1. What is the **goal** of Bible Study?

The main purpose for getting into the Word of God – knowing and enjoying Jesus. No, not knowing about Jesus - actually knowing Him, the Person.

2. Explain the differences between formal equivalence, functional equivalence, and paraphrase Bibles. Which **Bible versions** do you prefer?

- Formal equivalence (complete equivalence) is a more word-for-word translation.
- Functional equivalence (dynamic equivalence) utilises a phrase-for-phrase or thought-for-thought manner.
- Paraphrase (free translation) is more of a commentary than a translation.

3a. What is the **OIA** Inductive Bible Study?

OIA – Observation, Interpretation, Application.

3b. What is the **GRACE** Bible Study Method?

GRACE - God, Read, Analyse, Christ, Engage.

4. Which **Bible tools** would you recommend?

Also see list of Bible tools from Logos

Information (29 Bible Study Tools for Reading the Bible More Effectively)

5. How are these scriptures often taken out of **context**?

This link may prove helpful:

Information (5 examples on relevantmagazine.com)

e.g. 1. "For where two or three are gathered in my name, there am I among them". – Matt 18:20

It is true that the size of a Christian gathering is irrelevant to our Lord. But this verse falls specifically within the context of church discipline and dealing with wayward believers. The "two or three" are the authorized leadership of the church, who have witnessed a sinner cause offense to another member of the community and fail to turn from it. It is an encouragement to these elders that God would be present as they try to correct and restore a fallen brother.

e.g. 2. "Judge not, that you be not judged" – Matt 7:1.

This verse is not a warning against speaking out against certain actions or behaviours. In fact, in other places of Scripture, we're told "we'll know them by their fruit". We must be prepared to distinguish between a true brother, who may have sinned (Matt 7:1-5, 7-12), and a pig-dog, or false brother (Matt 7:6, 13-23). If we are aware of reciprocity, that we will be treated the same way as we treat others, we may avoid the tendency to jump all over everything others do that hurt us. We will likely examine our own attitudes and behaviour first (Matt 7:3-5). There is a clear difference between being a censorious critic and making a balanced perceptive evaluation or critique.

Suggested Answers (7) - Does God Exist?

1. Where does the **Bible** attempt to prove that God exists?
Nowhere in the Bible is there a case made out to prove that God exists. The writers of Scripture state that His existence is obvious to all.

2. What facts impress you about the **bacterial flagellum?**
If a bacterial flagellum came into existence out of a random unintelligent event, does that make a man-made 3 phase induction motor the same? Did it assemble itself? Did it wind its own copper around the stator core? Or, do you reason that one is inanimate, the other animate?

3. What is there about structure of the **DNA** that convinces you that we have a designer? It is the densest information storage mechanism known in the universe.

4. If evolution doesn't explain the origin of life itself, does **abiogenesis**?
Abiogenesis is the idea of life originating from non-living material (non-life). There is presently no theory sufficient to explain how life could have come about by purely natural causes.

5. When someone **questions the existence** of God, what should we try and ascertain?
The possible reasons underlying their unbelief.

- Human suffering?
- Hypocrisy in religion?
- Advance of atheism?
- Freedom of accountability to God's laws?

Suggested Answers (8)- One or Many?

1. Can you find the names of at least five 'Christian' **denominations** that do NOT believe the Trinity?
Scientologists, Jehovah's Witnesses, Church of Jesus Christ of LDS, Iglesia Ni Cristo, Christadelphians, Christian Scientists, Dawn Bible Students, Oneness Pentecostals, Unification Church (of Sun Myung Moon), Unitarians.

2a. How would **you define the trinity**? Does it mean that the Father, Son, and Holy Spirit are parts of God?
The trinity is an attempt to state the truth that the Father, Son, and Spirit are one in essence (one being) but exists in three persons. There are not three Gods, nor are they parts of God. The illustrations of LDS Bishopric or JW Service Committee may be helpful to a point but do not accord with the definition of the trinity.

2b. What is **modalism**?
Modalism falsely teaches that God is a single person who has eternally existed and yet He has revealed himself in three modes or forms. The trinitarian belief is that God exists at all times as three distinct persons - Father, Son, and Holy Spirit – not that God is one person made known in three modes or roles.

3. What would you say to the objection, "The trinity teaching is both illogical and **incomprehensible**"?

From our limited three-dimensional human view, the trinity concept of three persons as one being, may well appear to be largely incomprehensible and illogical.

4. Would you say that the trinity is taught in the **New Testament or by the early church fathers?**
Among the scripture references mentioned in the video are: Matthew 9:2-6 (Jesus forgives sin); Mark 14:61-64 (He is the "son of man" – Dan 7:13-14); John 8:58 (The "I Am"); and John 14:17,21,23 (all three dwell in the believer). Most of the early church fathers indicated quite clearly a belief in the divinity of Christ, less clearly a belief in the distinct personality of the Holy Spirit.

5a. What is **henotheism**?
Webster's: "Henotheism: the worship of one god without denying the existence of other gods". The New Bible Dictionary: "Henotheism: devotion to one God (or god) in a polytheistic setting".

5b. But isn't **Satan** called the "god of this world" in 2 Corinthians 4:4?
Yes, Satan is called the "god of this world" - yet are not wooden idols are also called "gods" many times. These no more exist as gods than the devil does as a god. It is figurative language. We could, for example compare Philippians 3:19 where it calls the human stomach a god! The suggestion is that the word "god" is used in a metaphorical sense to refer to the ruler or prince of this world, not as a reference to a deity. The use of the term "god" in this context does not imply that Satan is considered a deity.

SUGGESTED ANSWERS (9)- WHAT IS HIS NAME AND NATURE?

1. What is the **Name** which we hallow or sanctify in the Lord's Prayer?
God's name speaks of His identity, His character, and His actions, which must be set apart as holy in this world. One of the ways in which we hallow God's name is to recognise Jesus as Lord and live our lives to honor God (1 Pet 3:15).

2. Is the regular use of the name **Jehovah** a mark of true Christians?
The Gospels and the other apostolic writings in the New Testament did
not use the name YHWH (as evident from the thousands of Greek NT
manuscripts that are extant, not one of which ever uses the name
YHWH). Jesus and the apostles did not think it important to use the name
YHWH in religious communication.

3. What does "**a people for his Name**" mean in Acts 15:14 (17)?
Gill's Commentary: "To take out of them a people for his name; for
himself, for his own glory, to call upon his name, and to be called by his
name, to bear his name, and support his Gospel, cause and interest ... to
separate them from the rest by his powerful and efficacious grace, and
form them into a church-state, that they might show forth his praise and
glorify him". – Cf. Exod 19:5; 2 Chron 6:6. Jesus stated regarding his name,
"Everyone who has left houses or brothers or sisters or father or mother
or children or lands, for my name's sake, will receive a hundredfold and
will inherit eternal life".

4. Is there any **manuscript evidence** that indicates that the Hebrew name
of God was used in the New Testament?
a. How about the Greek Septuagint (LXX)?
Mogens Müller says that, while no clearly Jewish manuscript of the LXX
has been found with Κύριος representing the Tetragrammaton, other
Jewish writings of the time show that Jews did use the term Κύριος for
God, and it was because Christians found it in the LXX that they were able
to apply it to Christ.

b. What is the scroll from Nahal Hever?
Nahal Hever is a Greek manuscript of a revision of the LXX dated to the 1st
century CE. New fragments have been found in 2021 and are being
studied for the textual reconstruction of the manuscript. In this
manuscript the tetragrammaton in Old Hebrew script appears in Jonah
3:3; 4:2; Mic 1:1-3; 4:4-7; 5:4; Hab 2:14-20; 3:9; Zep 1:3, 14; 2:10; Zec 1:3-4; 3:5-
7; 8:20; 9:1, 4.

5. A few questions about two of God's **communicable** attributes:

a. God is **Holy** – what does holiness mean? How can we share in His holiness?

God is set apart as utterly unique. Holiness for us, is not ultimately about living up to a moral standard, it's about living in Christ and living out of our vital union with him.

b. God is **Love.** Should we say that God's love is unconditional? This clip expresses the view that, yes, in a general sense God demonstrates love to the world of mankind – a love shown by sending His Son. Yet, he also has an electing love. What's your take?

SUGGESTED ANSWERS (10) - WHO IS JESUS?

1. How do certain **prepositions** focus on our relationship with Jesus?
- What do we receive **THROUGH** Christ?
  We enjoy justification, peace with God, hope, and joy in Christ.
- How do you abide **IN** Jesus?
  To abide in Christ is to rest in his love (John 15:9) with complete dependence, realizing that apart from him we can do nothing.
- What results when we come **UNDER** his authority?
  We are not independent of Christ's body, his church. As a body we rest under his kind authority.
- What happens to us first before we can live **FOR** Christ?
  We died to our former self-centred life, and have been raised to a new life to bear fruit to God's glory (Rom 6:4,22).
- Are we **WITH** Jesus now or in the future?
  The believer has been crucified with him, buried with him, raised with him in order to live with him and reign with him. By His grace we are alive to God and now have eternal life in Christ Jesus.

2. Is Jesus the archangel **Michael**?
- Hebrews 1:5-6? Hebrews chapter 1 differentiates between Jesus and the angels. If some believe that Jesus is Michael the archangel, and pray to Jehovah through Jesus, then are they praying through an angel? Why don't they conclude their prayers, "in Michael the archangel's name, amen"?

- Daniel 10:13? Jesus the "King of kings" is never called a "chief prince" (or in the Greek LXX text "one of the commanders of the first order") as Michael is here.
- 1 Thess 4:16? Suppose a man introduced himself with a very loud voice – I might say that "his voice was that of a lion," – would you think that the man literally was a lion, or such a statement was a metaphor? Also, if being accompanied by an archangel's voice makes him an archangel, by the same logic could we say that his coming with the sound of God's trumpet means that Jesus is God?

3. Who did the **earliest Christian** writers say Jesus was?
From Polycarp to Origen, they asserted that Jesus was God.

4. What can we say to the explanation that Jesus is just a **representative** of God?
The idea that Jesus is just a representative of God is a belief held by some religious groups and is based on their interpretation of scripture and tradition. According to this perspective, Jesus is seen as a messenger or prophet of God, but not as God himself.
From Hebrew chapter 1 we can glean that:
- Jesus is outside of time ("the ages") implying he is eternal – vs 2.
- He shows us exactly what God is like, not a mere copy; "The Son reflects [or radiates; shines forth] the glory of God [John 1:14] and shows exactly what God is like [is the exact representation/imprint/stamp of his being/essence/nature]". Expanded Bible, vs 3.
- Jesus upholds, or sustains, all creation – vs 3; cf. Psalm 33:9.
- He is worshipped by the angels – vs 6.
- God calls Jesus, "God" and "Lord" – vs 8,10.

5. What is a simple way to understand **John 1:1** and the absence of the definite article "the" in the final clause?
- Dr. William Barclay: "John 1:1 translated, "the Word was a god,' a translation which is grammatically impossible. It is abundantly clear that a sect which can translate the New Testament like that is intellectually dishonest".

- If the NWT followed this principle in the rest of John 1, verse 4 would read "by means of him was *a* life"; verse 6 would read "There came a man sent from *a* God whose name was *a* John".
- There are not two Gods in John 1:1. John, a strict Jew, a monotheist, would never say there was more than one God in existence. Idols and angels, Satan, and demons – may be falsely viewed as being gods, but Jehovah remains the only God: "See now that I – I am he, and there are no gods apart from me" (Deut 6:4; 32:16,17,21,39; Isa 43:10).
- In the beginning the Word already "*was*," that is, already there, present, therefore he did not have a beginning.

SUGGESTED ANSWERS (11) -
WHAT DO YOU LOVE ABOUT JESUS?

1. Water into wine (John 2:1-12)
- He enjoyed social occasions; he was no austere killjoy.
- His compassion in action to save a couple of newlyweds from humiliation.
- An estimated 180 gallons of the best wine; his super abundant grace.
- Without Jesus life is dull, flat, but when Jesus enters our life, it becomes vivid, exciting.

2. The Loaves: one, five and seven (Mark 8:16-21)
"This is Mark's signal to the reader to review the narrative, as Jesus reiterates the symbolic number clues (8:19f). The five loaves and the twelve baskets left over in the first wilderness feeding represent the *Jewish* world (the books of Moses, the tribes of Israel). The seven loaves and baskets left over in the second feeding symbolize the inclusion of the *gentile* world (in Jewish numerology seven was a symbol of completion). To make this clear Mark even uses different terms for "basket"; the first feeding story uses a Jewish term and the second uses a Greek term. 'Do you not yet understand?' (8:21). It is as if Mark is warning us not to proceed with the rest of the story until we have correctly comprehended the 'meaning of the loaves.' The social, economic, and political implications of

Jesus' Jubilee practice have been spelled out further in the double cycle of Mark 4-8. There is only *'one loaf'* around which the Church is called to gather, and it symbolizes enough for everyone". ("Say to This Mountain" – C Myers , 1991 – p89)

3. The Samaritan woman at the well (John 4:1-42)
Jesus made a three-day detour to meet her. He broke through the barriers of sex, race, religion, and morality to engage in a conversation that broke social convention. She was the first person He told directly that he is the Messiah. He took a foreign woman of five failed marriages and made her the first evangelist. She was seeking satisfaction in her relationships with men. Jesus should be her life's satisfaction – her man! Make Jesus our true love.

4. Jesus Heals The Leper (Matt 8:1-3)
Leprosy was a common incurable disease, a progressive death. Jews kept six-feet social distancing from lepers. Who would want to touch a repulsive "scaly" disfigured man, with staring eyes, rasping voice and vile odour, anyway? Imagine the man's emotions when this rabbi touched him, let alone healed him! You may have experienced shunning, ostracization, because of your stand on Christian issues. On a deeper level, leprosy denotes the working of sin, just as described at Leviticus chapter 13: deeper than the skin (vs 3); spreading (vs 7); isolating (vs 45-49); fit for the fire (vs 52, 54). See also Isaiah 1:5-6. Under LAW: clean is contaminated by unclean. Under GRACE: clean Jesus "infects" the unclean with His wholeness (Matt 9:20-22).

5. Jesus and the children (Matt 18:1-6)
When we welcome a child (or a Christian believer), we welcome Christ (vs 5). The Father cares for them and the angels watch over them (vs 10). In these days of child neglect and abuse, we need to take Christ's warning seriously (vs 6).

Suggested Answers (12)
What do Jesus' Death, Resurrection, and Kingdom mean to you?

1. Was Jesus **raised bodily** from the dead?

All Christian religions accept the bodily resurrection of Jesus as foundational to Christianity.

Whereas the JWs, the Unitarian Universalists, and a few other minor sects - do not. Archaeologists have at times persuasively asserted that they have found the family tomb of Jesus, and possibly some evidence of Jesus' body. This to many though sounds like dogmatic speculation. Jesus predicted that he would raise his body (John 2:19). The tomb was found empty; the women being the earliest witnesses. He became identifiable to those seeing him post-resurrection in his glorified body (Luke 24:16,37-39; 1 Cor 15:4-6; Phil 3:21). The overriding and centrepiece of Christian teaching is that we need to individually accept Jesus as our personal raised Lord and Saviour, as our substitutional sacrifice, righteousness, and as now living in us!

2. Read Titus 2:14. How does Jesus being the redeemer relate to **works**?

The love *from* God, and resulting love *of* God, creates an intolerance for sin. Grace engenders the power of new affections, a holy heartburn. We are not saved *by* works but *for* works (Eph 2:8-10; Tit 3:5-8). Good works are evidence of grace.

3. Using cross references from 2 Corinthians 4:5 can you find other verses which encourage us to **preach Christ**?

1 Cor 1:23; 2 Cor 4:4-6; Phil 1:18; Acts 10:42; Luke 24:45-48.

4. Is the **Kingdom** present or future?

The answer is that it is partly present and partly future. Many of its blessings are here to be enjoyed now; but many of them are not yet here. Some of its power is available now but not all of it (Matt 12:28 cf. Luke 19:11-12; Heb 2:8).

5. What is the connection between the **cross and the Kingdom**? Col 1:13-14 and Rev 1:5-6

The cross is the crowning achievement of Christ's kingdom mission. The cross is central (the climactic mid-point of the story) and the kingdom is telic (the end-goal of the story). The kingdom is the ultimate goal of the cross, and the cross is the means by which the kingdom comes. The kingdom comes in power, but the power of the gospel is Christ crucified. It is a Cross-Shaped Kingdom.

SUGGESTED ANSWERS (13)
IS THE HOLY SPIRIT A PERSON?

1. When John chapters 14 to 16 calls the Holy Spirit "he," is it using **personification**, similar to wisdom (Luke 7:35) and sin (Rom 5:21)? Personification is an example of poetic license: saying something that *ordinary logic tells us is impossible*. For example, a martyr's blood does not literally cry out from the ground (Gen 4:10). Tongues do not literally strut or parade (Ps 73:9). If this ordinary signal is absent, it stands to reason that the passage is not using personification. However, there is nothing in the descriptions of the Holy Spirit in the NT that cannot be true of an actual spiritual (ie nonphysical) being. For example: "If I do not go away, the Helper will not come to you. But if I go, I will send him to you" (John16:7); "The Spirit himself intercedes for us" (Rom.8:26); "The Spirit searches everything, even the depths of God" (1 Cor.2:10).

Now, turning to the Gospel of John, John 15:26-27 for example, "But when the Helper comes, whom I will send to you from the Father, the Spirit of truth, who proceeds from the Father, he will bear witness about me. And you also will bear witness". Note that Jesus says the Spirit will bear witness just as the disciples will bear witness ("you also..."). Jesus regards the Spirit (the Helper) as being just as much a person as each of the disciples and speaks of them in the same terms. Beyond that, the actions He attributes to the Spirit - coming, being sent, proceeding, bearing witness - do not fit a mere personification of some aspect of God.

2. Why does the Holy Spirit lack a **name** if it is a person?

Holy Spirit is identified by His chief characteristic: holiness. If the Holy Spirit can't be a person because we don't know His personal name, then all the angels and demons in the Bible who are unnamed can't be persons either.

The Holy Spirit's lack of a specific name may be due to the idea that the Spirit is a mysterious and elusive aspect of the divine, as well as the biblical focus on describing the Spirit in terms of its actions and attributes rather than a name.

3a. What does the Holy Spirit do for **unbelievers**?
Convicts of sin and points to Christ (John 16:7-11; Acts 10:44-45).

3b. What does the Holy Spirit do for **believers**?
Knowing the indwelling Spirit as a personal friend who participates in our feelings gives us a sense of security and hope.

Helper	... giving peace and joy
Teacher	... giving understanding and wisdom
Indweller	... giving new birth, salvation, and sealing
Giver	... fruitage of Spirit and Gifts of Spirit

4. Can you list some **gifts** of the Holy Spirit? How does Paul describe their purpose? (1 Cor 12:4-31; Eph 4:12)
Knowledge, wisdom, prophecy, faith, healing, miracles, discernment, tongues, interpretation of tongues. Their purpose was to build up the faith of the whole church so that they serve others.

5. Can you summarise different viewpoints of **speaking in tongues**?
Some believe that God uses tongues to speak in an unknown heavenly language, whereas others think that the Spirit prompts speaking the gospel in a language of another nation.
1 Corinthians 14:27-28 counsels that there must be an interpreter of tongues present if the whole congregation is to be edified.
Cessationists believe that speaking in tongues was a gift for an allotted period of church history, that is, for Apostolic times, and is no longer given. However, it is important to avoid putting God in a box and saying what He can or cannot do. God is fully capable of allowing the Holy Spirit

to give someone the gift of speaking of tongues if He saw a purpose for it. After all, God changes not.

SUGGESTED ANSWERS (14)
DOES THE SPIRIT AFFECT YOU?

1. Name at least three **roles** of the Holy Spirit in our lives?
Convicts unbelievers (John 16:8-11)
Guides into all the truth (John 16:13-15)
Gift-giver (1 Cor 12:4-11)
Fruit-producer (Gal 5:22-26)

2. Is being **in** the Spirit the same as walking **by** the Spirit?
We were IN Adam (in the flesh) but now we are IN Christ (in the Spirit; in the kingdom of light). We may be tempted to WALK in the old ways by responding to old habitual thinking. Be who we are now. You are located permanently IN Christ, so WALK in the Spirit.

3. If the Spirit indwells us, why and how do we need to "**be filled with the Holy Spirit**" - Eph 5:18?
At conversion we are filled with the Spirit. The spirit indwelling us and seals us (Eph 1:13-14; 4:30). As we comprehend the love of the Father for us, we are "being filled" inside – like a shaken bottle of cola bubbling and building up pressure.

4. What lessons can we learn from the account in **Acts 16:6-10**?
Keep walking forward, actively listening for the Spirit's direction.

5. What is the unpardonable sin of **blasphemy** against the Holy Spirit? (Mark 3:22-30)
One perspective is that this condemnation only applied to the Pharisees who saw the miracles of Christ and attributed them to Satan's work - accusing Jesus of being demon-possessed instead of Spirit-filled. Another view is that the unpardonable sin today is the state of persistent unbelief. The Spirit currently convicts the unsaved world of sin,

righteousness, and judgment (John 16:8). To resist that conviction and willfully remain unrepentant is to "blaspheme" the Spirit.

Suggested Answers (15)
What are the Angels and Demons up to?

1. How many angels are there? (Deut 33:2; Heb 12:22; Rev 5:11)
While the Bible leaves the precise number of angels unspecified, some believe there could be as many angels in existence as the total number of humans in all of history. Psalm 68:17 says the angels of God number "tens of thousands, thousands and thousands" (CSB). Clearly, the writer has trouble even coming close to estimating the number of angels in existence.

2. What contrasting views do Christians, Muslims, and Hindus have regarding **guardian angels?**
Catholics and many Protestants believe in each person having a lifetime guardian angel, based on Psalm 91:11-12; Matthew 18:10; Acts 12:15. Some Protestants, and indeed Jews, believe that an angel may be selected according to a person's need. In Islam, believers say that God assigns two guardian angels to accompany each person throughout his or her life on earth. One sits on the right shoulders recording their good choices while the angel who sits on their left shoulders records their bad decisions. Hinduism asserts that every living thing has a guardian spirit.

3. Should we **pray to, or worship,** angels? (Matt 4:10; Col 2:18; Rev 22:8-9)
Both prayer and worship should be offered to God alone because only He is worthy of prayer and worship. Luke 4:8," You shall worship the Lord your God and serve Him only".
Colossians 2:18 warns us, "Let no one keep defrauding you of your prize by delighting in self-abasement and the worship of the angels, taking his stand on visions he has seen, inflated without cause by his fleshly mind" (Rev 22:8-9).

4. Can angels or demons **read our mind**? (Dan 2:27-28; Luke 6:8; 11:17)

God knows people's thoughts (Gen 6:5, Ps 139). Also, Jesus knew people's thoughts (Matt 9:4; 12:25; Mark 2:8; Luke 6:8; 11:17). But nowhere are we told Satan or demons know people's thoughts. On the other hand, 2 Corinthians 10 and other passages show demons can influence our thinking. They can deduce what's on our minds since they can see us from the outside. They know what we're reading, watching, talking about, and can observe our physical responses.

5. Where does Satan attack – what is his **battlefield**?
Most spiritual warfare takes place in the battlefield of your mind - 2 Cor 10:3-5. Not every thought that comes into your mind is good. Some thoughts come from the world. Others come from the demonic realm. When a dark thought or lie enters your mind, grab it by the scruff of the neck and make it bow down to King Jesus.

Suggested Answers (16) - How do we Defeat Sin?

1. I'm a **nice person**, I don't sin as badly as terrorists or drug pushers, in fact, I give to charity".
Rom 3:11, 23 shows that all are sinners (Ps 14:3; 1 Pet. 2:25).
James 2:10 is clear that a person who breaks even one commandment is as guilty as a person who has broken all of God's laws.

2. How would you help someone **overwhelmed with guilt**?
A certain level of temporary guilt is normal in our fight against sin. Listen compassionately to any confessions of past sins, and when it is fitting to do so, urge repentance in prayer, trusting God to forgive. Consider one or two reassuring verses (Rom 5:17-21; 6:14-15; 7:17-25; 1 John 1:7-9; 3:19-22). Satan is "the accuser" of believers (Rev. 12:10), we don't need to accuse ourselves over sins that Christ's blood paid for. What practical steps can they suggest so that the sin does not become an ingrained practice? Pray with them and for them. Check in on them soon.

3. Is grace a **license to sin**?
Paul was asked the same question when he preached the full grace gospel (Rom 6:1,15). People sin abundantly without any licence! Contrariwise,

Titus 2:11-12 shows that grace empowers us to avoid sin, as was the case in the story of the adulterous woman of John 8. She was told that Christ did not condemn her, so therefore, as a result of this divine grace she was enabled to sin no more.

4. What does 1 John 3:9 mean when it says, "No one who is born of God practices sin, because His seed abides in him; and **he cannot sin**, because he is born of God".?

John is not saying believers will never sin (1 John 2:1). He is saying it is no longer in our nature to sin because we have been given a new nature. We were naturally born into Adam's family, but are now born from above and placed in Christ, a partaker of His divine nature with new desires (2 Pet 1:4). This is not talking about sinless perfection but simply saying that the old habit of sinning is contrary to our new nature, our new identity, that when we sin, we are acting at odds with who we are in Christ.

5. Will God whip me into shape if I sin? Doesn't Hebrews 12:6 say we are "**scourged**" by God?

In Hebrews 12:6 the word mastigoō is used which appears in the NT seven times. In every case it is associated with unjust punishment inflicted by the unjust upon the just – either upon Jesus (four times), his disciples (twice), or Paul (once). Hence, some reason that when Paul mentioned "scourging" he was talking about the endurance of persecution from the Judaizers and other opposers. Note the context: Hebrews 11:32-40 records how the prophets of old suffered for righteousness, then 12:1-3 continues that Jesus "endured the cross". Such persecution could have been avoided if, instead of enduring faithfully, they renounced their faith. The endurance of the "scourging" of persecution, including shunning, is evidence of God's sonship and accomplishes a training so that those in Christ can experience a harvest of righteousness and peace (1 Pet 4:16).

Suggested Answers (17) - Why do we Suffer?

1. What key **factors**, do you think, will help in understanding the matter of evil and suffering?
The loving gift of free agency. the comparison to eternity, and moral outrage, implies a God of standards. Moreover, God is sovereign and He intervenes with judgement whenever He feels is proper to do so. He also intervenes with mercy whenever He thinks is proper (Jer. 18:7-10). He abandons sinners to the consequences of their choices whenever He thinks is proper to do so (Rom. 1:24-32; 11:8; Ps 81:12: Isa. 29:10; Hos 4:17).

2. Read **Ps 139:17**. Is this verse describing David's amazement at the extent of God's thinking processes in general, or at the incomprehensible knowledge of God for him personally?
When we check out the context, for example verses 1-6, and the cross references, like Job 7:17; Ps 8:4; 144:3, we can understand that David is trying to grasp God's vast knowledge of him personally. This should produce in us a sense of pardon, peace, and praise.

3. Why does God allow **Satan** to live?
> God's glory shines more brightly as we withstand the devil's temptations, in that we experience evidence of God's wisdom, mercy, and sustaining grace, than if God just quickly destroyed him.

4. Read Job 4:8 and Gal 6:7. Is reaping what you sow just **karma**?
Karma condemns us, we get what we deserve; Christ saves us, we receive by grace what we don't deserve.

5. Can you begin a list of seven **promises** in scripture that give you hope? Now, how about considering one each day in prayer over the next week? For example, Ps 33:18-22; Jer 29:11-13; Rom 5:5; 15:13; 2 Cor 4:7-10,17-18; Eph 1:18; Phil 1:6; 1 Pet 5:10.

Suggested Answers (18)
What Happens at Death?

1. How do many Christians explain the **three-part** (trichotomy) nature of man?

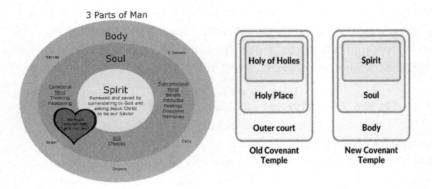

2a. What is the **soul**? Is it the same as the spirit?

While the two words are often used interchangeably, the primary distinction between soul and spirit in man is that the soul is the animate life, or the seat of the senses, desires, affections, and appetites. The spirit is that part of us that connects, or refuses to connect, to God.

2b. What happens to the **spirit** at death?

Psalm 31:5 "Into your hand I commit my spirit; you have redeemed me, O Lord, faithful God".

Luke 23:46 "Then Jesus, calling out with a loud voice, said, "Father, into your hands I commit my spirit!" And having said this he breathed his last".

Acts 7:59 "And as they were stoning Stephen, he called out, "Lord Jesus, receive my spirit".

Ps 146:3-4 and Eccl 3:21; 12:7. Also see Heb 12:23 but this is mistranslated in the NWT Bible.

3a. How Can you overcome **fear of death**? Heb 2:14-15.

If we are born once (physically) we will die twice (physically and spiritually).

If we are born twice (physically and spiritually) we need die only once (physically).

Three Kinds of Death

Physical death – separation of the spirit and soul from the body
Spiritual death – separation of the human spirit from God
Second death – separation from God for eternity

3b. How can I overcome **fear of dying?**
Psalm 23 likens death to a shadow. Jesus took the reality head on for us and conquered death for us. We can face death either with fear, or faith in Jesus who holds the keys of death (Luke 16:22).

4. Does the Bible point to a **resurrection of the body**?
We are alive spiritually in Christ now, controlled by the Holy Spirit. Paul discusses in 1 Cor 15 the mystery of continuing alive after death as we will put on a glorified spiritual body – apparently still possessing a physicality.

5. Are our loved ones **looking down** on us from heaven?
When David's child passes away, David makes this statement: "But, now that he is dead, why should I go on fasting? Can I bring him back again? I will go to him, but he will not return to me" (2 Sam 12:23). The "great cloud of witnesses" in Hebrews 12:1 are the faithful saints of the previous chapter who lived victorious lives by trusting God. Those saints are witnesses in that they speak to us by their example; not passive witnesses who watch us with their eyes.

> Furthermore, there will be no tears in heaven which would occur if these spirits of the dead were presently witnessing our tragedies on earth. Revelation 21:4, we read that in Heaven "there will be no more death or tears or crying or pain". If our loved ones can look down on this tragedy-filled world and watch us struggle through it, how can they be without tears?

Suggested Answers (19)
What does it mean to be Born Again?

1. Enjoy watching this 3-mins clip based on **John 3** then consider the following questions:

a. What did Jesus mean by the wind blowing?
Jesus is talking about the mystery of new birth. The Spirit breathes where he wills, and no one can tell where he comes from or where he is going. The gospel is preached all over the world and some receive it while others do not.

b. Why did Jesus refer to the serpent on the pole in the wilderness?
Just as the Israelites needed to look in hopeful faith to God's provision for their physical deliverance in the wilderness, so we need to simply look in hopeful faith to God's provision for our spiritual deliverance in the form of Jesus' death on the cross.

c. What decision faced Nicodemus and us today too?
He was a religious man who most likely tried to live as God would have him to, but he had to come to God in repentance and allow the Holy Spirit to take up residence in his heart! This wasn't something that he could do for himself by human effort.

2. Do our **morality and good works** contribute to our being born again? Can you locate a scripture which supports your answer?
John 6:18,19,47; Acts 22:10; Eph 2:8-10; Tit 2:11-12.

3. Must **all Christians** be born again?
The Bible makes it clear that there is no other way to be forgiven of sin and eternally reconciled to God as one of His children, except by being born again - John 1:12-13; 3:3-5; Acts 2:38-39; Rom 8:8-9; 1 John 5:1,12.

4. What comes first, putting on the **new personality,** or being born again? (John 15:4-5; 2 Cor 5:17; 1 John 5:18)
Justification precedes sanctification. False religions reverse this to become a constant works-based striving to attain initial salvation. Ephesians 4:22-24, "You have *put off* once for all with reference to your

former manner of life the old self who is being corrupted according to the passionate desires of deceit; moreover, that you *are being constantly renewed* with reference to the spirit of your mind; and that you have *put on* once for all the new self who after God was created in righteousness and holiness of truth. Wherefore, having *put off* the lie once for all, be speaking truth each one with his neighbor because, we are members belonging to one another". (Wuest – An Expanded Translation)

Some have observed that "put off" and "put on" (vs 22, 24) are aorists, suggesting once-for-all-time, whereas verse 23, sandwiched in-between, is in the present, hence translated above as "are being constantly". This agrees with Romans 12:2, "And do not be conformed to this world [any longer with its superficial values and customs], but be [a]*transformed and progressively changed* [as you mature spiritually] by the renewing of your mind [focusing on godly values and ethical attitudes], so that you may prove [for yourselves] what the will of God is, that which is good and acceptable and perfect [in His plan and purpose for you]" (Amplified).

5. Can you list some of the **blessings** received at regeneration?
>   New covenant; forgiveness (Jer 31:31; Heb 10:17-18)
>   New anointing; sealing (Eph 4:30; 1 John 2:27)
>   New indwelling Spirit; new heart (Ezek 11:19;1 Cor 6:19)
>   New inheritance (Titus 3:5-6)
>   New creation (2 Cor 5:17)
>   New self (Eph 4:24)

Suggested Answers (20) - Is our Salvation Secure?

1. Philippians 2:12, "So then, my beloved, just as you have always obeyed, not as in my presence only, but now much more in my absence, **work out your salvation** with fear and trembling".

In Philippians 2:12-13, Paul is instructing us to work out (not work for!) our salvation because God has already worked something beautiful in - Christ. In short, Paul is saying, "Work out what God has worked in". When a musician has a fine composition placed before her, that music is not the musician's masterpiece; it is the composer's gift to the musician. But it becomes the task of the musician to work it out, to give it sound and expression and beauty as she applies her skills. When she does, the composition reaches its completed purpose and thrills the hearts of her listeners.

2. Hebrews 3:14, "For we have become partakers of Christ, **if we hold fast** the beginning of our assurance firm until the end". (NASB)

In the Greek, it does not say we "become" but "have become" (perfect tense – a completed action with lasting results - 1 Cor 4:13) partakers of Christ. The fact that we are enabled to endure gives evidence to others that we have already been genuinely saved; just as the fruitage of the Spirit is external evidence to onlookers of having been internally changed in heart by Christ's Spirit dwelling in us. We have been made partakers of Christ – it's done – but we won't experience the life of Christ unless we hold firmly to the confidence we had when we began. Perseverance in believing on Christ is evidence of union to him.

3. John 15:1-2, "I am the true vine, and my Father is the gardener. He **cuts off** every branch in me that bears no fruit". (NIV)

One suggestion is that "He cuts off," is a poor translation; a better one is "He lifts up". The word in question is 'airo' which means to lift, pick, or raise up and this is how the word is translated in many other places (eg. Mark 16:18, Luke 5:24, 17:13, John 11:41, Acts 4:24, Rev. 10:5). Unfruitful branches are lifted out of the dirt and re-dressed so they can be nourished by the sun.

4. John 14:15, "If you love Me, you will keep My commandments".
When you know how much Jesus loves you, he is easy to trust and obey.
His great love inspires us to trust him. This is the essence of faith.
Keeping His commands is a by-product of love of God and neighbour.

5. James 2:26, "For just as the body without the spirit is dead, so also **faith without works is dead**".
Martin Luther is recorded as stating, "Works are necessary for salvation, but they do not cause salvation; for faith alone gives life". John Murray supported this view, "Faith alone justifies but a justified person with faith alone would be a monstrosity which never exists in the kingdom of grace. Faith works itself out through love (Gal 5:6). And Faith without works is dead (James 2:17-20). Genuine life-saving faith is revealed by doing the only work that counts – believing in Jesus (John 6:29).

Suggested Answers (21)
How Can We Share the Gospel of Grace?

1. What was the **gospel preached** by Paul? Please note that the resurrection of Jesus was central to the apostles' message (Acts 4:33; 2 Tim 1:10; 2:8).

PAUL'S SERMONS	For all nations	Jesus' death, resurrection	Jesus - Lord; Saviour; Judge	Repent	Forgiven
Acts 10:34-43	✓	✓	✓		✓
Acts 13:23-41		✓	✓	✓	✓
Acts 17:22-31	✓	✓	✓	✓	
Acts 26:12-23	✓	✓	✓	✓	✓

2. Which comes first, **faith or repentance**?
"Whether a whole precedes one of its parts, or is preceded by it, since no man can give a sound definition of evangelical repentance which will not include faith, it is altogether wrong to perplex the minds of serious

Christians with useless questions of this sort. Let the schoolmen discuss such matters to their heart's content, but let the humble Christian rest in the plain and obvious meaning of the words in Scripture. The effect of divine truth on the heart is produced by general views, and not by nice and metaphysical distinctions". - Archibald Alexander on whether faith precedes repentance or repentance precedes faith.

3. How is the real gospel more than a message of **Forgiveness**? (1 Pet 3:18)
1 Peter 3:18 shows the purpose of the good news is that Christ may bring us to God. A Christian is a person "in Christ".

4. Is the preaching work over according to **Colossians 1:23?**
Notice that earlier in Colossians chapter 1, the gospel message of God's grace in Christ is said to continue to spread and to bear fruit, see verses 4-6. Later letters of the NT describe the work of preaching Christ being continued (1 Tim 2:6; 2 Tim 1:7-9; 4:1-5; 1 Pet 3:15). In our present day we have the words in Matt 28:18-20; Mark 16:15; Acts 1:8; Rom 10:14; 2 Cor 4:13-15; Rev 14:6-7; 22:17.

5. How does the kingdom message preached by **JWs** differ from that preached by Christians throughout the centuries?
Rather than Christ being preached, their message emphasises faith in the Kingdom of 1914 and baptism into their organisation.
"Let the honest-hearted person compare the kind of preaching of the gospel done by the religious systems of Christendom during all the centuries with that done by Jehovah's Witnesses since the end of World War I in 1918. They are not one and the same kind. That of Jehovah's Witnesses is really "gospel" or "good news," as of God's heavenly kingdom that was established by the enthronement of his Son Jesus Christ at the end of the Gentile Times in 1914". (Watchtower, May 1, 1981, p. 17)
Please note the JW's two baptism questions – especially the second one:
1. Have you repented of your sins, dedicated yourself to Jehovah, and accepted his way of salvation through Jesus Christ?
2. Do you understand that your baptism identifies you as one of Jehovah's Witnesses in association with *Jehovah's organisation?*
Contrast their baptism questions with: Matt 28:19; Acts 2:38-39; 10:48; 19:5.

The gospel of the King and Him crucified and risen includes the hope of His kingdom (Phil 3:20-21; Col 3:4; 1 John 3:1-2). But the proclamation of the kingdom and its ways is not itself the gospel. You can only see the kingdom of God through the cross of Christ. The hope of a changed world given to unchanged people is not what Jesus preached. The call to repentance was preparatory for the cross and all that it would open. The coming of the kingdom of God is only good news for those who are born again, reconciled to God, and in the new covenant (Matt 26:27-28; John 3:3-5; 2 Cor 5:17-21). Remember the acronym C.P.R as you present the real gospel.

SUGGESTED ANSWERS (22)
HOW DO WE GROW IN PRAYER?

1. How is **Ephesians 6:16-20** perhaps the most comprehensive view of prayer in scripture?

>Prayer is for ALL situations.
>Prayer is for ALL seasons.
>Prayer is ALL in the Spirit.
>Prayer is in ALL steadfastness.
>Prayer is for ALL the saints.

2. How can we keep **calm** in the face of anxiety? **Philippians 4:4-8**

C – Closeness of God – Php 4:4-5 "Rejoice in the Lord always". Paul, while chained to Roman soldiers and facing possible execution, urged us to lift our eyes to our Lord who loves us beyond words. He "is near" (vs 5). Celebrate His presence.

A – Ask God for Help – Php 4:6 "Be saturated in prayer throughout each day". Don't delay an instant. Immediately after a fear triggers an anxiety, present that specific problem to our Father. Find a promise in His Word that fits your problem and pray over it.

L – Leave your Concerns with Him – Php 4:7 "Peace of God will guard your heart". This is not living by the 'I will sort everything out' approach. But just as you leave a broken item at the expert's repair shop and go home, we leave all in God's hands.

M – Meditate on Good Things – Php 4:8 "Dwell on these things" – eight positive things are listed. Pick on one to ponder over. Think intentionally.

3. What can we learn about **answers** to prayers by comparing Daniel 9:21 with 10:12-13?

Both prayers were answered instantly but the manifestation of one prayer took maybe three minutes, while the other took three weeks. What was the variable? Not God! There was demonic resistance to the second prayer.

4. What key point stands out to you in "The Practice of the presence of God" by **Brother Lawrence**?

"It consists in taking delight in and becoming accustomed to his divine company, speaking humbly and conversing lovingly with him all the time, at every moment, without rule or measures; especially in times of temptation, suffering, aridity, weariness, even infidelity and sin".

5. Select a few of these hundreds of **quotes** on prayer that you find most helpful to you?

E.g. "Is prayer your steering wheel or your spare tire?" - Corrie Ten Boom.

SUGGESTED ANSWERS (23)
HOW DO WE GROW IN LOVE?

1. How many of these **ten questions** about Christian love did you answer correctly?

Review any that you answered incorrectly. Were there any answers which surprised you?

2. How does God's love differ from the **world's definition** of love?

God's love is all-encompassing, not according to race, power, or wealth. God's love is sacrificial, whereas worldly love is often selfish, self-serving. God's love is sure, not fickle.

3. How is it possible to love your **enemies**? (Matt 5:44)

Jesus in the Sermon on the Mount was ramping up the Law, which was already impossible to measure up to. Why? So that the Jewish audience would see their need of God's grace through the Saviour at the cross. So, in this sense fully loving one's enemy is impossible for imperfect people. Yet, if we have already experienced the unconditional love of God through the cross, while once being an enemy, we will be moved in a similar fashion, by the Spirit, to love others. This gives evidence that you are a child of God looking forward to an eternal reward. We are prepared to leave any pay-back in the hands of our perfectly just God (Rom 12:17-21).

4. Meditate over **Ephesians 1:6**

(a) A literal translation could be, "to the praise of His glorious grace, with which he has graced us in his loved One" Out of the riches of the Father's grace, God has graced you, through Jesus alone. The verb, charitoó, is the same one the angel uses when he says to Mary, "You are highly favored" (Luke 1:28).

(b) God accepted you into his family not because of anything you have done but on account of his grace. Your Father's acceptance is not something you ever need strive for; you already have it on account of his Son. If you want to know how acceptable you are to God, you only have to look at his Beloved Son. What God thinks of Jesus is what he thinks of you. When Jesus was baptized, a voice from heaven said, "This is my beloved Son, in whom I am well-pleased" (Matt. 3:17). When God looks at you, he says the same thing. "You are my dearly loved child, and I am well pleased with you".

5. According to **Revelation 2:4**, what was the root of the Ephesian church's problem?

One suggested explanation: In the same way a wife may leave her loving husband, the Ephesians had left the loving Lord Jesus. Or, we could say, like the prodigal son, they had walked away from their Father's love. It wasn't so much their love for Him as the revelation of His deep love for them. He loves us unconditionally through Christ first. "This is love: not that we loved God, but that he loved us and sent his Son as an atoning sacrifice for our sins" (1 John 4:10, 19). These Ephesian brothers had reversed the divine order regarding salvation: (a) first receive love from the Father which (b) results in a desire in us to display love in action by the indwelling Spirit (Rom 5:5; Php 2:13; Heb 13:20-21). Years earlier, in his letter to the Ephesians, Paul encouraged them to know more fully the multi-dimensional love that Christ had for them (Eph 3:18-19). Now, Jesus knowing their weakening relationship with him, told them in Revelation 2:4 to remember the height from which they had fallen. Remember God's love for you, then you will desire to love.

Thoughts on the Action Point

Faith, hope, love. Faith stems from hope (Heb 11:1) which comes from love. The greatest of these is love because without the love of God there would be no hope and no reason for faith. Some reason that, the objects of faith and hope will be fulfilled and perfectly realised in heaven, but love, is everlasting. It is not necessarily that love outlasts faith and hope but that it outranks them as the essence of Christianity, because love alone is divine, belonging to His essence. After all, God does not believe, nor hope, but he loves.

SUGGESTED ANSWERS (24)
HOW CAN WE GROW IN CHRIST?

1. All six scriptures below mention one of the three words for '**LIFE**.' Mark which is which: bios, psyche, or zoe?

a.	John 12:27	psyche
b.	John 14:6	zoe
c.	Rev 6:9	psyche
d.	Luke 21:4	bios
e.	Matt 7:14	zoe
f.	1 John 2:16	bios

2. The apostles, prophets, evangelizers, and pastor teachers – do we have them **today**?

The foundational early church enjoyed appointed ones in all these roles. The prophets were of lesser authority than the apostles. Many opine that the first two roles gradually faded out as the church was established and that today we have the services of evangelizers along with pastors who are teachers. Others feel that the gift of prophecy is still being used today. See Biblehub link in Additional Information.

3. Read **Galatians 4:19**. Does this refer to our initial salvation as 'born again' ones or to maturing afterwards in Christlikeness?

It appears that such ones had Christ born into them but not yet maturely formed in them.

Ellicott comments on the above verse: "Just as the formless embryo by degrees takes the shape of man, so the unformed Christian by degrees takes the likeness of Christ. As he grows in grace that likeness becomes more and more defined, till at last the Christian reaches the "stature of the fulness of Christ" (Eph 4:13). We grow in grace as we become more dependent upon the Holy Spirit.

Howard Hendricks once said that, "The Bible was not written to satisfy your curiosity, but to make you conform to Christ's image. Not to make you a smarter sinner, but to make you like the Saviour. Not to fill your head with a collection of biblical facts, but to transform your life".

4. What examples of **'windy teachings'**, or perhaps new fads in doctrines, are you aware of?

We may immediately bring to mind the errors of groups or cults with which we were formerly associated. However, the weedy tentacles of corrupt teachings have taken hold in most, if not all, religious systems, like weeds in the wheatfield. May the Holy Spirit help us, through scripture, to identify falsehoods of those who " did not welcome the love of the truth [of the gospel] so as to be saved [they were spiritually blind, and *rejected the truth* that would have saved them]" (2 Thess 2:10, Amplified), but rather seek out association with those "who *love our Lord Jesus Christ* with incorruptible love" (Eph 6:24).

Christian author, William MacDonald wrote: "Most serious of all is the danger of deception. Those who are babes are unskilful in the word of righteousness, their senses are not exercised to discern between good and evil (Heb 5:13-14). They inevitably meet some false cultist who impresses them by his zeal and apparent sincerity. Because he uses religious words, they think he must be a true Christian. If they had studied the Bible for themselves, they would be able to see through his deceitful juggling of words. But now they are carried about by his wind of doctrine and led by unprincipled cunning into a form of systematized error". (Believer's Bible Commentary, 1995)

5. What is the **purpose of the church**?

Ray Stedman puts it this way – "It is important to realize that, according to this passage in Ephesians, the supreme purpose of the church is not the evangelization of the world. The Great Commission is often held up to us as the supreme aim and purpose of the church, and it is certainly a crucial and essential task. Jesus has clearly sent us out to preach the Gospel to every creature. But the Great Commission is not God's supreme and ultimate goal. Romans 8:29 tells us that God's ultimate plan for us is that we be "conformed to the image of his Son". Evangelization is a means of bringing people into a relationship with God, so that God's ultimate goal for them – Christlikeness - can be achieved in their lives...God's overarching goal is to produce men and women who demonstrate the character qualities of Jesus Christ. God does not want a church filled with white robed saints. He does not want a church filled with theological authorities or cultured clergyman. He wants a church filled with ordinary men and women who exemplify the extraordinary integrity, temperament, wholeness, compassion, individuality, boldness, righteousness, earnestness, love, forgiveness, selflessness, and faithfulness of Jesus Christ!"

PICTURE CREDITS

This QR code contains the links listed below:

Cover
https://pixabay.com/photos/ripped-paper-paper-copy-space-3343947/

Q. 1   **Religion in England & Wales**
https://www.bbc.co.uk/news/uk-wales-63792911

Q. 1   **Narrow Gate**
https://i.ytimg.com/vi/hlrJ8s5TF-c/maxresdefault.jpg

Q.3   **Father and son wash the car**:
https://farm1.static.flickr.com/15/21335535_57a2a15a8a_m.jpg

Q.11   **Jesus' Journeys across Galilee**
https://www.thebiblejourney.org/

Q.14   **The Fruit of the Spirit**
https://i.pinimg.com/736x/fc/e2/08/fce208cd1da832a4933124273d0e5dac.jpg

Q.16   **He Bore our Sins**
https://clipart-library.com/search1/?q=our%20sins#gsc.tab=1&gsc.q=our%20sins&gsc.page=1

Q.18   **The Threefold Nature of Man**
https://3.bp.blogspot.com/_tWhSj5H4CZE/TLzDGPfKE0I/AAAAAAAABqE/cHn3d4NDcTM/s1600/body+soul+spirit.gif

Q.24   **In Christ**
https://www.lockportchurch.com/images/stories/chart.gif

Suggested Answer 18 Three Parts of Man
https://i.pinimg.com/originals/b7/c6/99/b7c6998401d9224ad47b9ebe6eb6563f.png

INDEXES

Footnotes

Abba 125

Abide 211

Abiogenesis 69

Anecdotal accounts 128

Angelic intercession 129

Apocrypha 45

Aramaic 45

Armageddon 111

Arminianism 172

As much as 90

Atonement 104

Audio recordings 61

Authority 200

Automatic learned responses
.... 73

Background 99

Baptism 169

Basic doctrine 79

Beards and Attire 206

Beloved Son 90, 257

Bible Reading plans 61

Bible translations 61

Blood 207

Calvinism 173

Canonicity 45

Co-crucified 138

Condemnation 175

Conscience 125

Cross 26, 148

Cult 22

Day of Atonement 141

Deity of Christ 78

Devil 75

Eisegesis 62

Elder 214

Eternal life 137, 175

Eternal Life 123

Evolution 69

Faith 164

Father 195

Fine-tuning 68

Flesh 135, 146

Forgiven 26, 136

Forgiveness 162

Free Will 146

Governing Body 183

Grace 21, 177

Hell 111

Higher Education 39

Holy 201

In Christ 126, 175, 210

Inspired by God 51

Intelligent design 68

Irreducible complexity 68

Jehovah 195

Justification 40, 105, 184

Kalam 67

Kathōs 202

Key words 61

Kingdom 183

LDS 154, 182

Legalism 30

Lesser gods 75

Love 176

Love - Agapaō 202

Love - Phileo 203

Memorial 163

Micah 5:2 55

Michael 128

Moral Argument 70

Mortalism 154

Name 82

Names of God 82

Natural disasters....................147
Neutrality.................................206
New Age channelling............130
New Heavens and New Earth
....184
Obedient........................ 59, 168
Passover..................................112
Prayer.......................................193
Prayers to Jesus......................197
Ransom............................106, 149
Reconciliation........................... 111
Related to Jesus Christ........... 90
Repent................................. 34, 164
Repentance....................110, 136
Resurrection...................109, 159
Resurrection of Christ.........149
Righteousness.................26, 106
Salvation............................ 39, 162
Sanctification...........................184
Seals.. 110
Second Coming......................184
Sect... 22
Self-righteous........................... 23
Shunning................................... 26
Sin...134
Sinners.......................................139
Soul.. 157
Symmetry..................................99
Tactful..186
Tanakh..45
Teleology....................................68
Ten Commandments............134
Thermodynamics....................66
Tiberium..................................... 53
Tritheism...................................115
Truth..19
Unity...214
Walking by the Spirit............ 122
Witness.......................................124
Works-salvation.....................104
Writers.. 52

YHWH.. 82

Old Testament Scriptures
Gen 4:7..134
Gen 4:17..57
Gen 6:8.. 31
Gen 16:7-11...................................77
Gen 18:1-5.....................................77
Gen 32:24-30................................77
Exod 3:14-15................................. 82
Exod 4:16.......................................75
Exod 7:1...75
Exod 21:6.......................................75
Exod 22:8-9...................................75
Exod 34:6...................................... 31
Lev 5:10; 23:28.......................... 105
Lev 16... 141
Lev 23:5....................................... 112
Num 9:2-6.................................. 112
Num 20:8....................................197
Deut 4:28.......................................75
Deut 6:4..75
Deut 6:5.......................................205
Deut 7:7–8.................................. 203
Deut 10:12...................................205
Deut 10:17.................................... 92
Deut 19:21................................... 107
Deut 21:18-21............................... 26
Deut 32:4...................................... 92
Deut 32:6.................................... 195
Deut 33:2.................................... 133
Josh 11:11.....................................157
Jg 6:11-15.......................................77
Jg 13:20-22....................................77
Ruth 2:13...................................... 83
2 Sam 7:14................................... 195
1 Kings 11:33.................................75
1 Kings 13:18.............................. 130
1 Kings 17:21................................157
1 Kings 18:24,37.......................... 93
2 Kings 6:17 128

Job 4:8.................................153
Job 11:7-9............................73
Job 26:14........................73, 144
Job 36:26.............................73
Job 37:23.............................73
Job 42:1-5..........................151
Job 42:1-6..........................147
Job 42:2.............................136
Ps 1:1.................................58
Ps 8:6.................................75
Ps 16:11..............................162
Ps 22:16..............................55
Ps 25:14.............................205
Ps 29:2................................41
Ps 45:6-7.............................91
Ps 50:21..............................83
Ps 66:16..............................40
Ps 73:25.............................205
Ps 82:5................................75
Ps 82:7................................75
Ps 96:4-5.............................76
Ps 102:25-27..........................91
Ps 103:20,...........................129
Ps 107:23-32.........................101
Ps 119:18.........................60, 96
Ps 139:17............................153
Ps 146:3-4...........................161
Ps 147:3-4...........................152
Ps 147:5.............................152
Prov 14:12...........................147
Prov 22: 3...........................147
Eccl 3:19-21.........................156
Eccl 3:21............................161
Eccl 4:2-3...........................156
Eccl 9:1.............................147
Eccl 9:2-3...........................156
Eccl 9:5-6, 10.......................155
Eccl 9:11............................148
Eccl 12:7........................156, 161
Eccl 12:13-14........................156
Isa 8:13-14...........................92

Isa 9:6...............................91
Isa 14:12-15..........................75
Isa 40:3-4............................91
Isa 43:10-11..........................83
Isa 43:11.............................92
Isa 44:3.............................166
Isa 44:6..............................92
Isa 44:24.............................91
Isa 53...............................149
Isa 53:4.............................144
Isa 53:4-6...........................106
Isa 53:7..............................55
Isa 53:9..............................55
Isa 53:10–12.........................149
Isa 55:8-9...........................147
Isa 55:8–9...........................144
Isa 64:6.............................135
Isa 65:17............................184
Jer 5:3..............................151
Jer 33:3.........................60, 96
Ezek. 36:24–27.......................165
Ezek 11:19-20........................122
Ezek 18:4............................156
Ezek 36:24-27........................166
Ezek 36:26.......................36, 185
Dan 2:27-28..........................133
Dan 10:13.............................94
Hos 1:9...............................83
Jonah...............................100
Jonah 1:17...........................100
Jonah 2:10...........................100
Jonah 3:4-5..........................101
Jonah 4:1,4..........................100
Jonah 4:5............................101
Jonah 4:6............................101
Mic 7:18-19...........................92
Zech 1:12............................129
Zech 9:9..............................55
Zech 11:12............................55
Zech 11:13............................55
Zech 13:6.............................55

Mal 2:10 195
Mal 3:6.. 86

New Testament Scriptures
Matt 1:21 .... 82, 162
Matt 2:20.. 157
Matt 3:13... 169
Matt 4:1-11 55
Matt 4:10 133
Matt 5:15 55
Matt 5:16... 39
Matt 5:17-18 134
Matt 5:21-22.................................. 135
Matt 5:27-28................................... 135
Matt 5:43-44 135
Matt 5:44... 209
Matt 6:33.............................. 38, 39
Matt 7:1... 65
Matt 7:13-14.................................... 24
Matt 7:17-18 40
Matt 7:21-23..................................... 23
Matt 7:23 175
Matt 8:1-3 103
Matt 8:25-17 147
Matt 8:28-34 101
Matt 10:22.. 178
Matt 10:28....................................... 157
Matt 11:27 .... 82, 86
Matt 11:27-30 27
Matt 11:28 101
Matt 11:29-30.................................. 30
Matt 12:1-8 29
Matt 12:11-12 207
Matt 12:18-21.................................. 187
Matt 16:17... 90
Matt 18:1-6 103
Matt 18:20.. 65
Matt 20:28..107
Matt 23:4... 22
Matt 23:14... 25
Matt 24:13.. 178

Matt 24:14 183
Matt 24:30 184
Matt 25:11.. 23
Matt 25:34-46 175
Matt 28:9 93
Matt 28:19 169
Mark 1:12.. 126
Mark 1:14-15.................................. 168
Mark 2:5-7,10 92
Mark 2:27.......................................207
Mark 3:22-30 127
Mark 4:26-29 189
Mark 4:35-41 97
Mark 5:20 40
Mark 5:41... 117
Mark 6:31.. 101
Mark 10:45....................... 149, 212
Mark 12:30 204
Mark 13:13.. 178
Mark 14:36 196
Mark 16:15-16 201
Luke 1:71.. 162
Luke 2:11 92
Luke 2:30... 162
Luke 2:40.. 31
Luke 3:1-2...52
Luke 4:18 123
Luke 6:8 133
Luke 6:46... 23
Luke 8:14 212
Luke 10:22...90
Luke 11:17.. 133
Luke 12:22 157
Luke 12:50....................................... 169
Luke 13:1-5.......................................147
Luke 13:3... 168
Luke 13:24 29
Luke 15 196
Luke 15:5.. 168
Luke 17:30 185
Luke 18:31 55

Luke 19:12 110
Luke 20:38 158
Luke 21:8 185
Luke 21:19 178
Luke 24:25-27 58
Luke 24:45 62
Luke 24:46-48 40
Luke 24:47 168
John 1:1 ....73, 75
John 1:12-13 ..... 146, 164, 167, 171, 196
John 1:17 .... 30, 32
John 1:18 204
John 2:1-12 103
John 3:1-21 .... 103, 238
John 3:3-5 .... 163, 171
John 3:15 212
John 3:16 ....44, 167, 201
John 3:17 183
John 3:18,36 164
John 3:35-36............................... 90
John 3:36 ....172, 179
John 4:1-42 103
John 4:24 .... 84, 117
John 4:39 40
John 5:17-47 90
John 5:22-25 187
John 5:23 90
John 5:24 123
John 5:26 85
John 5:39 58
John 5:39-40 .... 49, 62
John 6:27 110
John 6:28-29 24
John 6:37 172
John 6:37,44................................173
John 6:47 123
John 8:58......................................83
John 9:2-2 147
John 10:33-35 75
John 10:9 ....25, 162

John 10:9-10.................................19
John 10:10.......................... 167, 212
John 10:14,26.............................. 173
John 10:26 175
John 10:35.................................... 55
John 11:11, 25-26 158
John 11:25....................................154
John 12:47-48 183
John 12:49....................................116
John 13:8-10 125
John 14:1-3 159
John 14:6 ....25, 167, 201
John 14:9 84
John 14:14 .... 93, 193, 197
John 14:15....................................180
John 14:16 117
John 14:17.............................. 19, 117
John 14:26....................................117
John 15:1-2...................................180
John 15:1-8 .... 94, 168
John 15:4-5............................ 40, 171
John 15:4-5,9.............................. 211
John 15:16....................................146
John 15:26 .... 122, 125
John 16:2 26
John 16:13 .... 116, 126
John 16:14 115
John 16:27..............200, 203, 208
John 17:6, 26 84
John 17:6,9................................. 173
John 17:17 ....51, 55
John 17:20-26 43
John 17:21,23 210
John 17:23 202
John 17:26 82
John 20:22 57
John 20:28........................... 76, 77
John 20:31 164
Acts 1:4-8 40
Acts 1:6-8 185
Acts 1:8 ....38, 111, 124

Acts 1:11.................................184
Acts 2:27.................................157
Acts 2:38 ....126, 168
Acts 2:41.................................169
Acts 2:42 218
Acts 3:16.................................164
Acts 3:19.................................168
Acts 3:26 185
Acts 4:12 ....25, 201
Acts 4:32 215
Acts 5:31...................................34
Acts 5:42.................................185
Acts 7:59...........................93, 158
Acts 8:12,35............................185
Acts 8:13.................................169
Acts 8:35 40
Acts 8:36.................................169
Acts 10:19-20..........................120
Acts 10:25-26............................93
Acts 10:34-43..........................191
Acts 10:42-43 ....40, 185
Acts 11:16................................169
Acts 11:18..........................34, 168
Acts 13:2 ....76, 120
Acts 13:23-41..........................191
Acts 15:11................................162
Acts 15:14 88
Acts 16:6-10.......................76, 127
Acts 16:14–15..........................169
Acts 17:22-31..........................191
Acts 17:24-25 85
Acts 17:25, 28 26
Acts 17:30 162
Acts 17:30-31..........................168
Acts 18:8.................................169
Acts 19:3-5 169
Acts 19:4–5 169
Acts 20:10 157
Acts 20:17 214
Acts 20:21 ....34, 168
Acts 20:24 36

Acts 23:8..................................128
Acts 26:12-23..........................191
Acts 26:20 34
Acts 28:30-31..........................185
Rom 1:5....................................168
Rom 1:20............................78, 188
Rom 3:10..................................106
Rom 3:10-12.....................135, 173
Rom 3:13-14.............................135
Rom 3:15-17,............................135
Rom 3:18..................................135
Rom 3:21-26........................79, 91
Rom 3:22-24...............................31
Rom 3:23 ....135, 136, 167, 187
Rom 3:24 136
Rom 3:27-28.............................179
Rom 3:28 106
Rom 4:1-8.................................187
Rom 4:7-8 137
Rom 5: 15 107
Rom 5:1....................................139
Rom 5:1-2 184
Rom 5:1-2,11 94
Rom 5:5 ....111, 171, 205
Rom 5:8....................................167
Rom 5:8-9 201
Rom 5:10 107
Rom 5:10-11..............................111
Rom 5:17.........................106, 107
Rom 5:18-19.............................106
Rom 5:20-21.............................. 33
Rom 6:4....................................169
Rom 6:7....................................138
Rom 6:11...................................138
Rom 6:14-15 30
Rom 6:14–15 134
Rom 6:23 167
Rom 7:6 ....30, 134
Rom 7:8–9 30
Rom 7:12..................................106
Rom 7:15..................................140

Rom 7:20 140
Rom 8:1 187
Rom 8:1-3 107
Rom 8:4 .... 30, 134
Rom 8:6 135
Rom 8:7–8 146
Rom 8:8-9 171
Rom 8:9 .... 135, 175
Rom 8:11 122
Rom 8:15 .... 35, 126
Rom 8:15-16 196
Rom 8:20-21 147
Rom 8:26 118
Rom 8:26-27 198
Rom 8:27 118
Rom 8:28 .... 132, 147
Rom 8:29-30 .... 172, 178
Rom 8:30-31 173
Rom 9:1 125
Rom 9:1-3 186
Rom 9:1-5 192
Rom 9:11,15-16 173
Rom 9:16 172
Rom 9:20-21 145
Rom 10: 17 164
Rom 10:1-4 .... 23, 24, 106
Rom 10:9 .... 24, 162, 167, 186
Rom 10:13 83
Rom 11:33–34 144
Rom 12:2 .... 34, 125, 210
Rom 13:1-7 206
Rom 14:17 110
Rom 16:17-18 79
1 Cor.1:30 138
1 Cor 1:2 .... 93, 197
1 Cor 1:7 185
1 Cor 1:8-9 178
1 Cor 1:17 169
1 Cor 1:23 182
1 Cor 1:30 211
1 Cor 2:1-4 222

1 Cor 2:9 205
1 Cor 2:10 119
1 Cor 2:11 118
1 Cor 2:14 .... 60, 146
1 Cor 3:4-11 222
1 Cor 6:11 106
1 Cor 6:19 171
1 Cor 6:19-20 107
1 Cor 8:1-2 58
1 Cor 8:9, 13 207
1 Cor 10:4 92
1 Cor 12:3 .... 89, 90, 93
1 Cor 12:4-31 120
1 Cor 12:11 118
1 Cor 12:13 .... 169, 171
1 Cor 13:4-7 204
1 Cor 15:1-8 79
1 Cor 15:14 159
1 Cor 15:14, 17 109
1 Cor 15:22-24 147
1 Cor 15:29 .... 54, 57, 154, 169
1 Cor 15:35-58 159
1 Cor 15:51-52 147
1 Cor 15:53-58 149
1 Cor 15:54-55 105
1 Cor 15:57 31
1 Cor 16:3 31
2 Cor. 1:22 93
2 Cor 1:17 135
2 Cor 3:7-11 134
2 Cor 3:17-18 119
2 Cor 3:18 .... 41, 124
2 Cor 4:3-6 184
2 Cor 4:4 81
2 Cor 4:4-5 111
2 Cor 4:4-6 .... 40, 168
2 Cor 4:5 113
2 Cor 4:5,13,15 42
2 Cor 4:7-12 153
2 Cor 4:13 164
2 Cor 4:16-18 153

2 Cor 4:17-18 147	Eph 1:6 .... 43, 209
2 Cor 5:1-8 158	Eph 1:6-11 50
2 Cor 5:14-15 ....94, 167	Eph 1:7 134
2 Cor 5:16 135	Eph 1:7-8 ....34, 210
2 Cor 5:16-17 210	Eph 1:13 146
2 Cor 5:17 ....165, 171	Eph 1:13-14 159
2 Cor 5:19 137	Eph 1:19-23 94
2 Cor 5:19-21 185	Eph 2:1 136
2 Cor 5:21 ....106, 131	Eph 2:1-10 ....29, 187
2 Cor 9:8 33	Eph 2:1-3 163
2 Cor 10:5 131	Eph 2:4-6 94
2 Cor 11:14 130	Eph 2:5 162
2 Cor 11:31 ....93, 197	Eph 2:8 .... 164, 167, 169
2 Cor 12:8 93	Eph 2:8-10 .... 27, 29, 40, 79, 104,
2 Cor 12:8-10 197	164
2 Cor 13:5 211	Eph 2:13 212
2 Cor 13:11 119	Eph 2:18 25
2 Cor 13:14 93	Eph 3:19 205
Gal 1:4 162	Eph 4:11-12 214
Gal 1:8 130	Eph 4:11-16 213
Gal 1:15-16 211	Eph 4:12 120
Gal 2:20 .... 96, 138, 139, 211	Eph 4:13 ....139, 213, 214
Gal 2:20-21 186	Eph 4:14 215
Gal 3:1-3 23	Eph 4:15 .... 201, 210
Gal 3:28 211	Eph 4:15-16 216
Gal 4:5 35	Eph 4:18 .... 163, 212
Gal 4:6 .... 126, 196	Eph 4:30 .... 118, 171
Gal 4:6–7 88	Eph 5:2 205
Gal 4:19 .... 211, 218	Eph 5:18 127
Gal 4:21 207	Eph 5:26 166
Gal 5:16,25 122	Eph 6:16 131
Gal 5:18 .... 30, 134	Eph 6:18 ....120, 199, 255
Gal 5:22 164	Php 1:1 214
Gal 5:22-23 107	Php 1:22,24 135
Gal 5:22-25 124	Php 1:23 158
Gal 5:22-26 170	Php 1:28 162
Gal 6:7 153	Php 1:29 164
Eph 1:4 139	Php 2:12 180
Eph 1:4-5 173	Php 3:1-11 29
Eph 1:4-6 42	Php 3:4 135
Eph 1:5 .... 35, 196	Php 4:4-8 199

Col 1:10 27
Col 1:13 110
Col 1:13-14 113
Col 1:16 91
Col 1:16-17 .... 66, 71
Col 1:20 105
Col 1:23 191
Col 1:27 211
Col 2:6 167
Col 2:6-7 210
Col 2:9 .... 77, 78, 91
Col 2:11-12 185
Col 2:12 169
Col 2:13 173
Col 2:15 .... 128, 132
Col 2:18 133
Col 2:21-23 168
Col 3:3 212
Col 3:12 201
Col 3:23 .... 37, 42
Col 4:6 36
1 Thess 1:9-10 162
1 Thess 2:8 189
1 Thess 2:13 59
1 Thess 4:16 147
1 Thess 4:17 185
1 Thess 5:16-18 193
1 Thess 5:23 131
1 Thess 5:23-24 172
2 Thess 1:7 185
2 Thess 2:10 201
1 Tim 1:15-16 139
1 Tim 2:3-4 91
1 Tim 2:6 107
1 Tim 3:1 207
1 Tim 3:1-7 214
1 Tim 4:1 116
1 Tim 4:1-2 130
2 Tim 1:9 .... 36, 173
2 Tim 2:14 73
2 Tim 2:19 110

2 Tim 2:25 34
2 Tim 3:7 59
2 Tim 3:15-17 54
2 Tim 3:16-17 52
2 Tim 4:6 158
Titus 1:5-9 214
Titus 2:11-12 .... 33, 106, 141
Titus 2:13 92
Titus 2:14 113
Titus 2:15 200
Titus 3:4-5 39
Titus 3:4-6 92
Titus 3:5 162
Titus 3:5,6 171
Titus 3:5-7 165
Titus 3:5-8 79
Phil 1.18 19
Phil 2:23 27
Heb 1:3 78
Heb 1:5-6 94
Heb 1:6 129
Heb 1:8-9 91
Heb 1:10-12 92
Heb 1:14 129
Heb 2:14-15 .... 105, 161
Heb 2:16 129
Heb 3:14 180
Heb 4:12 63
Heb 5:12 79
Heb 6:1 .... 79, 164
Heb 7:25 173
Heb 7:26-28 141
Heb 8:10-12 210
Heb 8:12 212
Heb 9:11-12 141
Heb 9:12 105
Heb 9:22 141
Heb 10:17 138
Heb 11:1 164
Heb 11:3 .... 67, 69
Heb 11:7 162

Heb 12:6.................................143
Heb 12:22 133
James 2:10 164
James 2:21............................. 57
James 2:26........................... 180
James 4:1-2 206
James 4:8..............................146
1 Pet 4:13.............................185
1 Pet 5:1...............................185
1 Pet 1:2............................... 172
1 Pet 1:3...............................165
1 Pet 1:5-7............................185
1 Pet 1:6-7............................151
1 Pet 1:13.............................185
1 Pet 1:23.............................166
1 Pet 2:2.................................58
1 Pet 2:7-8............................ 92
1 Pet 2:24 149
1 Pet 3:18....................104, 191
1 Pet 4:1-2............................135
1 Pet 5.....................................61
2 Pet 1:1...............................164
2 Pet 1:2............................... 223
2 Pet 1:4.......................137, 212
2 Pet 1:20-21.......................... 52
2 Pet 3:9............................... 147
2 Pet 3:10, 12.......................184
2 Pet 3:13 184
2 Pet 3:18.......................64, 223
1 John 1:5...............................84
1 John 2:19.....................172, 173
1 John 2:27.............................171
1 John 3:1-2...........................196
1 John 3:3............................. 125
1 John 3:5..............................106
1 John 3:9.......................131, 143
1 John 3:23 162
1 John 4:10 203
1 John 4:15.............................211

1 John 4:17............................ 139
1 John 4:19 205
1 John 5:1......................162, 168
1 John 5:1,12........................ 171
1 John 5:1-4 165
1 John 5:9-12.......................... 43
1 John 5:10-13 187
1 John 5:11-12......................... 50
1 John 5:18 .... 130, 165, 171
1 John 5:20 .... 19, 96
3 John 7................................... 82
Jude 12-13............................. 218
Jude 20 120
Jude 24...................................178
Rev 1:4-6................................ 46
Rev 1:5-6................................ 113
Rev 1:9....................................40
Rev 1:17 92
Rev 2:4 209
Rev 2:5 ....34, 210
Rev 3:3 ....34, 210
Rev 5:8,12-14......................... 93
Rev 5:9,12............................. 102
Rev 5:11 133
Rev 6:9...................................110
Rev 6:9-11............................. 158
Rev 8:3-4............................... 129
Rev 8:9...................................157
Rev 12:7-8............................. 128
Rev 12:11 ....40, 157
Rev 17:14............................... 92
Rev 19:1................................. 162
Rev 19:10 ....44, 55, 59, 62, 93
Rev 19:14 185
Rev 20:4-6 147
Rev 21:1-4 186
Rev 21:1-5 147
Rev 22:8-9............................. 133
Rev 22:17 120

Printed in Great Britain
by Amazon

35014630R00150